NATURE CONSERVATION AND COUNTRYSIDE LAW

NATURE CONSERVATION AND COUNTRYSIDE LAW

edited by

CHRISTOPHER P. RODGERS

UNIVERSITY OF WALES PRESS
CARDIFF
1996

© The Contributors, 1996

Published by the University of Wales Press in collaboration with the
Centre for Law in Rural Areas, University of Wales, Aberystwyth.

British Library Cataloguing-in-Publication Data.
A catalogue record for this book is available from
the British Library.

ISBN 0-7083-1303-5

Jacket design by Design Principle, Cardiff
Typeset by The Midlands Book Typesetting Co., Loughborough
Printed in Great Britain by Bookcraft, Midsomer Norton, Avon

Contents

Preface

The Centre for Law in Rural Areas was established in the Aberystwyth Law School in 1989 with the aim of co-ordinating the study of the law relating to distinctively 'rural' problems. The ambit of 'rural' law is deliberately perceived to be wide – it encompasses any field of legal inquiry where the application of the law to rural issues generates special or distinct problems. Clearly, much of the Centre's work concerns environmental law and conservation, and issues of rural land use. The Centre has also been active, however, in sponsoring research into other issues with a distinctively rural dimension – for instance, special problems of rural crime, rural housing and access to justice in rural areas. Many well-established fields of legal study, such as criminal law and property law, have unacknowledged but distinctly rural dimensions, and raise distinct problems when studied in a rural context. The Centre's work, therefore, is aimed at raising the profile of 'rural' law in this widest sense.

This is the third collection of essays to be published by the Centre since its inception. The first – *Agriculture, Conservation and Land Use* (ed. Howarth and Rodgers) – was published in 1992, and addressed a wide variety of legal issues surrounding agricultural land use and conservation. The second – *Legal Provision in the Rural Environment* (ed. Harding and Williams) – was published in 1994. Reflecting the broad scope of 'rural' legal studies within the Centre, the latter examined a wide variety of issues connected with policing, access to justice and penal policy specific to rural areas. This third collection returns to the area of land use law, but has a more focused attention to issues of nature conservation and the rural environment than its predecessor, *Agriculture, Conservation and Land Use*. The essays collected here address differing aspects of the law relating to nature conservation and land use in the countryside. The importance of nature conservation and 'sustainability' in development and land-use policies is receiving much greater public awareness (1995 was, for example, European Year of Nature Conservation). This collection seeks to focus attention on the *legal* issues of nature conservation. If, in some modest way, it stimulates further study and discussion of the issues addressed it will have achieved its purpose. The contributors have endeavoured to state the law as of 1 September 1995.

Christopher P. Rodgers
Centre for Law in Rural Areas
September 1995

The Editor and Contributors

Christopher P. Rodgers, LLM, LLB, FRSA, is Professor of Law and the Director of the Centre for Law in Rural Areas at the University of Wales, Aberystwyth. He is a solicitor and a member of both the UK Environmental Law Association and the Agricultural Law Association. He is also a *délégué général adjoint* of the European Council for Rural Law. He has written widely in the area of environmental and property law. Previous publications include *Agricultural Law* (1991), *Housing — the New Law: A Guide to the Housing Act 1988* (1989), *Private Sector Housing Law* (1995) and (with William Howarth, co-editor) *Agriculture, Conservation and Land Use: Law and Policy Issues for Rural Areas* (1992). He also edits sections on conservation and land use, and on planning law, in *Agricultural Law, Tax and Finance* (ed. Lennon and Mackay) (Longman looseleaf 1990, updated twice yearly).

John E. Alder, LLB, BCL, FRSA, is Professor of Law and Head of the Department of Law at Keele University. He is a member of the United Kingdom Environmental Law Association. His publications include *Constitutional and Administrative Law* (2nd edn, 1994), *Housing Association Law* (2nd edn, 1992), *Development Control* (2nd edn, 1989) and numerous articles on planning law, environmental law and public law. He is a committee member of several housing associations.

Simon Ball, BA, BCL, is Senior Lecturer in Law at the University of Sheffield, where he has taught for fifteen years, specializing more recently in environmental law, planning law and heritage and conservation law. He is the co-author of Ball and Bell, *Environmental Law* (2nd edn, 1994), being responsible for the chapter on nature conservation. He is also editor of *Water Law* and wrote the chapter on wildlife in *Tolley's Environmental Handbook: A Management Guide* (1994). He has a general interest in environmental issues and has lectured widely to public bodies, voluntary groups and industry on the law relating to nature conservation.

Michael Cardwell, MA, qualified as a solicitor with Burges Salmon, Bristol, in 1985 and for the next four years specialized in the law relating to agricultural holdings and the Common Agricultural Policy. In 1990 he took up a post at the Faculty of Law, the University of Leeds, where he has pursued research into agricultural tenancy reform and milk quotas.

William Howarth, BA, LLM, FRSA, FIWEM, is Cripps Harris Hall/SAUR Professor of Environmental Law at the University of Kent at Canterbury. He is Honorary Legal Adviser to the Institute of Fisheries Management; a member of the International Association for Water Law; a member of the United Kingdom Environmental Law Assocation; a member of the Advisory Council to the Environmental Law Foundation; a member of the Environmental Advisory Board to Shanks and McEwan Ltd; and a member of the Agricultural Law Association. His previous publications include authorship of, or contribution to, twelve books and over a hundred academic articles and reports on environmental, water and fishery law.

Donald McGillivray, LLB, Dip. LP, MA, is Lecturer in Environmental Law at the University of Kent at Canterbury where he specializes in planning and conservation law. With William Howarth he has worked on a number of projects reviewing aspects of water resource legislation and practice both in the UK and overseas. He has a particular interest in public law and policy in relation to the environment and he is a member of the United Kingdom Environmental Law Association and the Marine Forum for Environmental Issues.

Colin T. Reid, MA, LLB, is Professor of Law in the Department of Law at the University of Dundee, where his teaching includes environmental law and administrative law. He is an editor of *Scottish Planning and Environmental Law*, devised and edited *Green's Guide to Environmental Law in Scotland* (1992) and is the author of a book on *Nature Conservation Law* (1994). He has been active in the UK Environmental Law Association since its foundation and served on its Council for several years.

Jeremy Rowan-Robinson, MA, LLM, is Professor of Planning and Environmental Law at the University of Aberdeen and a Director of the University's Centre for Environmental Law and Policy. He is author or co-author of seven books on planning law and related topics and has recently undertaken research for Scottish Natural Heritage on public access to the Scottish countryside.

Angela Sydenham, MA, LLB, solicitor, was latterly Chief Legal Adviser to the Country Landowners' Association and is now a solicitor with Birketts of Ipswich. She was formerly a consultant to the Law Commission on commonhold and a lecturer on real property, trusts and conveyancing at the University of Surrey. She is co-author of *Essential Law for Landowners*, and of *Agricultural Tenancies Act 1995*: *Farm Business Tenancies* (Jordans, 1995), and author of *Trust Nutshell*. She is also a contributor to *Halsbury's Laws of England* on allotments, smallholdings, and on commons; and to the *Encyclopaedia of Forms and Precedents* on allotments, smallholdings and commons.

Lynda M. Warren, B.Sc., LLB, M.Sc., Ph.D., is Professor of Environmental Law at the University of Wales, Aberystwyth, where she specializes in environmental law and policy. She is particularly interested in marine and coastal conservation and is a member of the Countryside Council for Wales. She has published widely in marine biology and environmental law and is co-editor of the *International Journal of Biosciences and the Law*.

Introduction

Conservation Law in Context

CHRISTOPHER P. RODGERS

The 1990s have witnessed an increasing focus on nature conservation, and on the legal means by which sensitive habitats and countryside features can be protected. This is due in part to greater public awareness of the need for conservation, and in part to continuing legislative activity, particularly at European Union (EU) level, witnessed by a number of important new initiatives seeking to give greater protection to important wildlife sites. The EU's Habitats Directive of 1992, in seeking to establish and protect a representative cross-section of European ecosystems by the year 2000 (the 'Natura 2000' programme), has focused attention on the problems of conferring adequate legal protection on protected sites and the means for doing so. At the same time, the countryside is subject to ever greater pressures – demands for greater public access and recreational use, for intensive agriculture to produce food as cheaply as possible, and for diversification into non-agricultural activities to bolster agricultural incomes. The *law* of nature conservation cannot be studied in a vacuum. Land use in the countryside, whether damaging to natural habitats or not, is conditioned by economic pressures, and especially by agricultural policy on, for example, price support and subsidies for production. The fundamental reform of the European Common Agricultural Policy (CAP) in 1992, which included the adoption of the 'Agri-environment' regulation in the accompanying measures, gave a new opportunity for the promotion of nature conservation initiatives and a move towards 'environmentally friendly' practices in European farming. The mid-1990s is therefore a period of change and uncertainty for those living and working in the British countryside. For nature conservation it is also a period of opportunity and challenge.

The essays collected in this volume cover a wide range of issues. Some address, from divergent standpoints, the role of the law in promoting and enhancing the protection of the countryside, and in protecting wildlife. Some address the role of the law in regulating land uses, such as public access and recreation, which are potentially threatening to conservation of the countryside (see, for example, the contributions by Angela Sydenham in chapter 8 and Jeremy Rowan-Robinson in chapter 7). Others consider the manner in which European environmental policy, and also CAP reform, have been implemented in the United Kingdom (see for instance Simon Ball in chapter 4 and Christopher Rodgers in chapter 5).

Two broad issues emerge from the essays collected here which will, it is hoped, prove thought-provoking and stimulate further study. Firstly, what is the role of the law (and of lawyers) in nature conservation? Secondly, what do we mean by 'conservation law' as a subject? Is it now possible, in the mid-1990s, to see conservation law as an emerging discrete body of law, with its own identity, objectives and legal values?

Nature Conservation – the Role of the Law

The role of the scientist, the land manager, and statutory agencies like English Nature in nature conservation work is readily defined. Less obvious, perhaps, is the role of the legal system in fostering nature conservation and countryside protection. The law has, it is suggested, a number of tasks to perform. Its central role is to provide a framework of rules and of regulation within which the work of nature conservation can be carried out effectively – whether by scientists, land managers or others. Within this framework, legal rules should exist to encourage positive management of land and habitats, and so to foster more effective conservation of flora and fauna in the countryside. Within this broad objective, several specific roles can be identified for law and the legal system.

Differing techniques of regulation

There is no single body of rules which can be termed 'conservation law'. Nature conservation policy is implemented in the UK using a number of differing legal techniques – for example management contracts (voluntary obligation), development control law and planning consent (regulatory legislation), and codes of practice of differing legal status (some advisory, some of indirect legal effect), e.g. the Codes of Good Agricultural Practice for the Protection of Water, Soil and Air Quality, produced by the Ministry of Agriculture, Fisheries and Food (MAFF). Legal analysis is important because not all of the existing legal mechanisms may be appropriate to deliver the environmental benefit sought in a particular situation, e.g. planning law is unable to deliver *positive* land management for conservation, partly because agricultural land use is largely outside the scope of planning control, and also because of its regulatory nature. This is, therefore, an area where contractual measures have an important role to play (e.g. statutory management agreements under the Countryside Act 1968 s.15). In some cases environmental problems may not be subject to adequate legal control *at all* because of gaps in the legal regime. So, for example, damage to Sites of Special Scientific Interest (SSSIs) caused by neglect and desuetude may be problematic. Management contracts under the 1968 Act may be inappropriate to enforce positive management obligations where neglect occurs in SSSIs, and planning control law has no role to play, there being no 'development' on which the law can bite. These issues are explored more fully in Simon Ball's essay (chapter 4) in relation to SSSIs and implementation of the European Habitats Directive. The problems of devising a suitable legal framework for managing *marine* habits, which are somewhat different, are discussed by Lynda Warren (chapter 3). Similar issues arising from the environmental impact of forestry are considered by Colin Reid (chapter 6). A central task for legal science, therefore, is to devise appropriate *new* legal techniques to carry out environmental policy, to identify areas where modification of the *existing* law would facilitate the more efficient implementation of policy, and thus to facilitate the better protection of habitats and sensitive landscapes.

Dispute resolution

Competing claims on the countryside are not always reconcilable, and considerable scope exists for disputes where nature conservation requirements conflict with the rights or interests of other countryside users. There is potential for conflict between, for example, private property rights and the conservation interest in land; between demands for public access and recreation on the one hand and conservation on the other; and, conversely, between demands for greater public access and private property rights. Land use disputes are currently resolved in a number of different forums and by differing legal mechanisms. These include planning consent procedures (conservation and private property conflicts), the civil courts (e.g. access issues and appeals on a variety of matters), arbitration (terms and compensation under SSSI management agreements), and management contracts, the negotiation of which can be seen as a mechanism for resolving disputes between private property rights and the conservation interest. The current law largely uses pre-existing legal forums for dispute resolution, many of which have a long tradition developed outside the realm of environmental law. Many of the principles governing contractual compensation were, for example, developed by the courts in the nineteenth century when private property rights were seen as sacrosanct, and prior to the 'nationalization' of development rights by the planning legislation. The framework of legal ethics applied by the *courts* to a variety of environmental issues clearly reflects this, as shown in John Alder's contribution (chapter 1). A further function of conservation law, therefore, lies in identifying appropriate forums for resolving countryside conflicts, and in analysing the framework of legal rules and ethics used for decision-making in environmental disputes. The latter may, or may not, make adequate provision for the conservation interest, depending on the forum and the nature of the dispute.

Integration of environmental policy and the law

Land use and recreation in the countryside are regulated by a large corpus of existing legislation, and in some cases by the common (i.e. judge-made) law, some of which is of considerable antiquity. Much legislation affecting land use creates legal rights and duties which reflect those policy concerns/issues which were prevalent at the time of its implementation – often long ago – and does not reflect current concern for environmental protection. A good example is the law governing public access to the countryside. There has been great demand in recent years for increased rights of access to private land for recreation and the 'right to roam'. The creation and variation of rights of way over private land, or other recreational rights, is governed by a disparate mixture of statutes (e.g. the Highways Act 1959) and of common law concepts, including the law of easements and profits *à prendre*. Most of the relevant law was developed long ago without reference to environmental considerations, and is concerned primarily with balancing the property rights of landowners with legitimate user rights acquired by the public – the latter usually acquired by showing an accrued 'right' of user from long usage (for instance under the common-law doctrines of prescription or lost modern grant, in the case of easements). Rights of access are themselves usually classified at common law as a species of private property right attaching to the land of the landowner benefiting (e.g. easements), and not as *public* rights of access unless acquired under statute (e.g. under the Highways Act 1959). Environmental considerations nowhere enter into the rules governing the establishment and variation of footpaths and access rights. To allow entry of the conservation interest into the administration of the existing law would require the amendment of a large number of existing measures, and (probably) statutory revision of a number of common law rules. To introduce rules preventing the diversion of footpaths where this would be environmentally harmful – or to compel diversion if this were necessary on environmental grounds – would for instance require amendments *inter alia* to the Highways Act 1959. These issues are explored in relation to public access in Scotland and England (respectively) in the contributions by Jeremy Rowan-Robinson (chapter 7) and Angela Sydenham (chapter 8).

Another area where integration of environmental policy into the law is lacking is that of landlord and tenant. The rights of most farm tenants are governed by the Agricultural Holdings Act 1986, a consolidating measure which re-enacts security of tenure provisions dating from 1948. The legislation is a product of the post-war era, with its attendant emphasis on increasing agricultural production and, thereby, the food supply of a nation still living with food rationing. Consequently the security of most farm tenants is theoretically dependent on adherence to the 'rules of good husbandry', set out in s.11 of the Agriculture Act 1947, which require an optimum level of efficiency and agricultural output to be maintained. This is flatly at variance with the modern emphasis, highlighted by the 1992 agricultural reforms, on reducing overproduction and encouraging conservation measures which reduce intensive production. As Michael Cardwell shows (chapter 9), the failure to integrate modern environmental policy into the legislation creates unnecessary problems for the tenant farmer and his adviser, and may inhibit the adoption of appropriate conservation measures in some cases. The adoption of more flexible tenure arrangements under the Agricultural Tenancies Act 1995 should eradicate some of these problems for the future – but not all of them, as Cardwell shows.

Perhaps the most important area where a failure to integrate the conservation interest prejudices environmental protection is in development control law. Even when a wildlife habitat has been designated a Site of Special Scientific Interest under the Wildlife and Countryside Act 1981, this does not guarantee it against development which may damage or destroy the conservation value of the site. A grant of planning permission for development gives a defence to any proceedings under the 1981 Act, and provides a gateway through the land use restrictions imposed by an SSSI designation. Where planning permission is required, therefore, the crucial decisions are taken at the planning consent stage, and not within the framework provided by the 1981 Act. There is no presumption against development in an SSSI, however, and the conservation value of the site is merely one factor to be balanced against the other material factors influencing the planning decision, e.g. economic factors such as employment in the locality. This makes it very difficult to challenge a decision to grant planning permission which will lead to the destruction of the site's conservation value, even if the decision ignores advice from English Nature or the Countryside Council for Wales (who are statutory consultees on all applications in SSSIs). The weakness of development control law in protecting conservation sites has been illustrated by several recent cases, where planning permission has been granted in the face of strong conservation objections. In *R* v. *Poole BC ex parte Beebee* (1991) JPL 643, for example, the Council granted itself permission to build houses on an SSSI in Dorset which sustained several rare breeds of snake and lizard, including the smooth snake. Judicial review proceedings to overturn the decision failed, as the planning authority (i.e. the council itself) had considered the ecological case but felt it was outweighed by the local economic factors put before it. The depressing consequence of this approach, of course, is that a large proportion of those SSSIs damaged each year are damaged quite *lawfully*. The degree to which the SSSI system fails adequately to protect the ecological value of sites is illustrated further in Simon Ball's contribution (chapter 4). The implementation of the EU Habitats Directive will require more stringent controls protecting 'European' sites, all of which will in any event be existing SSSIs. The new Planning Policy Guidance Note 9 on Nature Conservation (October 1994) effectively raises a presumption against development in the proposed 'European' SSSIs, but even this is subject to exceptions which raise issues as to the proper implementation of the directive. Until conservation issues are integrated more effectively into the planning process for development in *all* protected sites, it is difficult to see how they can be adequately protected from degradation and loss.

Access problems, land tenure law and planning procedures merely provide three illustrations of a more widespread problem – the need to integrate environmental considerations more fully into our existing legislation, and into the common law. William Howarth and Donald McGillivray (chapter 2), for example, address the need for integration of environmental policy more fully into the law protecting aquatic ecosystems in rivers and tidal waterways. The list of environmental problem areas requiring analysis is a long one. Identifying *where* this needs to be done, and *how* it might be achieved are, therefore, important tasks for conservation law.

Application of the law

Finally, not all environmental legislation delivers the goals it sets out to achieve. The Wildlife and Countryside Act 1981, for instance, has failed to prevent ongoing degradation and destruction of wildlife sites designated as SSSIs – estimated to have affected over 20 per cent of all sites between 1987 and 1993 (National Audit Office, *Protecting and Managing SSSI's*, 1994). If the legislation is failing to meet its intended objectives, *why* is it doing so? To what extent *is* the law on nature conservation failing to deliver environmental gains? There may be a multiplicity of reasons for environmental legislation falling short in delivering tangible advances in nature conservation. The law itself may be defective – witness the loopholes in the 1981 Act exposed by subsequent litigation in the courts (see e.g. *Southern Water plc* v. *Nature Conservancy Council* [1992] 3 All ER 481 HL). Or there may be resource implications in properly 'policing' environmental measures which have not been fully addressed, and inadequate funding of environmental projects – witness the new 'environmental set-aside' arrangements for farmland (see Rodgers, chapter 5). Or other legal issues connected with land tenure and ownership may be complicating the application of environmental measures (see Cardwell, chapter 9). A very important task for nature conservation law, therefore, is to study the practical *application* of the law, and evaluate its effectiveness (or otherwise) in delivering environmental gains.

Conservation Law – A Problem of Definition

There is no single body of rules which can readily be identified with 'conservation law' as a discrete subject. The legal system uses differing legal techniques (as we have seen) to pursue objectives which involve 'conservation'. But conservation of what? The differing Acts of Parliament and subordinate legislation fall into two groups – those concerned with the protection of individual species of animals, birds and/or plants, and those concerned with the protection of habitats. To this may be added laws aimed at protecting the natural beauty of landscapes and sensitive landscape features, e.g. the law governing development in National Parks and Areas of Outstanding Natural Beauty. Conservation law, as a subject, covers a wide field of legal regulation, the parameters of which are difficult to define with precision. It also suffers from an image problem. The very word 'conservation' carries negative connotations, implying that the subject is concerned merely with *preservation*, i.e. preventing development in the countryside, preventing agricultural innovation, protecting wildlife simply for the sake of it. This contributes to the poor view of conservation ideals – and indeed conservationists – often held by the public, who tend to see the latter as modern luddites, opposed at all costs to change and progress in the countryside. In fact 'conservation law' is about much more than simply preserving rare wildlife, rare habitats and sensitive landscapes. It is a dynamic subject with a positive contribution to make in *improving* the diversity of habitats and wildlife in our countryside – not just for their own sake, but also to improve the amenity of the countryside for the wider public who wish to enjoy it.

The most meaningful definition which can be offered of 'conservation law' as a discrete subject is a *purposive* one. The task of conservation law is not just the protection of existing habitats, species, or important landscape features – it has a positive role to play in devising suitable legal mechanisms for the integration of environmental policy into the wide range of laws which currently govern the use and exploitation of land and the countryside. If the current emphasis on nature conservation and protection of the countryside is to bear fruit we need appropriate legal mechanisms for resolving conflicts of interest in the countryside, and an adequate legal framework of rights and duties to be applied to resolving disputes, one which takes adequate account of the conservation interest in protecting the countryside. This is a long way off. The very concept of 'sustainable' development, which underlies the modern system of planning control, assumes that development can be reconciled with conservation – yet the planning process clearly fails to provide a framework for a true balancing of the interests involved. The pressure for change in countryside land use is therefore unlikely to slacken, and the need for suitable means to resolve conflicts of right and interest will remain for the foreseeable future. Perhaps the most important contribution 'conservation law' could make for the future lies in devising dispute resolution techniques to replace the outmoded and fragmentary system of legal regulation which currently prevails in matters of landscape and habitat protection. Ultimately, however, the pursuit of conservation objectives must be a matter for co-operation and partnership between those who live and work in the countryside, the owners and managers of land, the statutory agencies, natural conservationists and the wider public (see *This Common Inheritance* (1990) Cm. 1200, para. 7.81). The task of conservation law is to provide a legal framework within which this partnership can work smoothly to produce positive improvements in the rural environment.

1

Legal Values and Environmental Values: Towards a Regulatory Framework

JOHN E. ALDER

God in his wisdom made the fly and then forgot to tell us why.
— Ogden Nash

Introduction

In *Cambridge Water Company Ltd* v. *Eastern Counties Leather plc* Lord Goff said,

> The protection and preservation of the environment is now perceived as being of crucial importance to the future of mankind; and public bodies both national and international are taking significant steps towards the establishment of legislation which will promote the protection of the environment . . . But it does not follow from these developments that a common law principle . . . should be developed or rendered more strict . . . On the contrary, given that so much well informed and well structured legislation is being put in place for this purpose, there is less need for the courts to develop a common law principle to achieve the same end, and indeed it may well be undesirable that they should do so.[1]

This suggests that the common law and statute law run in separate channels. Alternatively common law and statute could be seen as a single interdependent system complementing, and to an extent checking each

[1] [1994] 1 All ER 53 at 76.

other. The bulk of environmental law is statutory and because in the English tradition statute law is directed to detailed solutions to specific problems, environmental law appears to lack an overall cohesive framework of values and concepts.

In some countries such a framework is provided by the constitution. In the USA for example the federal courts have been instrumental in raising the political significance of environmental issues by recognizing the importance of non-economic environmental values and giving access to pressure groups.[2] In this way environmental values can acquire privileged status in the general law to which the legislature must respond. Although courts are not directly democratic they have a strong democratic element in that they are open institutions where decisions are publicly explained and to which (leaving aside the question of cost) the public have direct access.

In English law, the common law (including for this purpose equity) provides a source of general legal ideas. These must give way to clear statutory language but interact with statutory environmental law in five main ways. Firstly, the common law provides a set of values against which statute law must be interpreted. These values are capable of giving environmental rights a privileged status in the same way that values such as freedom of expression are given special weight. This influences the development of the law and also requires Parliament to express itself in very clear language should it wish to prefer other values.[3] Secondly, the exercise of discretionary powers by public authorities is regulated by common-law principles of fairness and rationality. The courts would be in a position, if they so wished, to ensure that decision-makers pay attention to environmental concerns. Thirdly, the common law is capable of absorbing the general environmental principles radiating from Europe. Under article 5 of the Treaty of Rome all public decision-makers have a duty to give effect to the objectives of the Community. The basic principles of Community environmental policy are these:

the preventive principles;
pollution should be rectified at source;
the polluter pays;
the precautionary principle;
sustainability.[4]

Underlining these is the principle that there should be a 'high level of

---

[2] See below note 8.

[3] See e.g. *Anisminic* v. *Foreign Compensation Commission* [1969] 2 AC 147, *AG* v *Wilts United Dairies* (1921) 39 TLR 781. See Wade, *Administrative Law*, 7th edn (1994), 876–8.

[4] See Com (92) 23 FINAL (5th Action Programme, *Towards Sustainability*).

protection', thus indicating that environmental values are superior to ordinary legal values even if they are not fundamental in the strict sense.[5]

This interpretative role of the common law is especially important in the context of rural conservation and preservation. Statutory law confers few specific enforceable powers. It concentrates upon conferring discretionary powers to designate areas worthy of special protection and to give advice and assistance. Decision-makers must take into account the environmental concerns of these areas but are not usually required to prefer environmental concerns.[6] However, European Community directives confine the scope of some discretionary powers. Much therefore depends upon the law's willingness to absorb European principles. For example, the English courts seem to have accepted the principle established by the European Court of Justice in connection with the Wild Birds Directive that, once designated, a special-protection area can be altered only exceptionally, and not for economic reasons.[7]

Fourthly, Parliament may be inactive, leaving it to the general law to develop principles of liability. It was perhaps for this reason that the US courts were prompted to apply constitutional principles to environmental concerns.[8]

Fifthly, the matrix of values within which individual judges view the world is part of the relationship between statute and the general law. To an environmentalist for example, Lord Goff's words could be read as anthropocentric, atomistic and ecologically insensitive. A plausible case can be made that Lord Denning, possibly the most influential judge of the post-war years, had a romantic pastoral vision embracing the idea of a legal order which included nature's rhythms and the beauty of natural things, interdependence between man and nature and the stability of rural communities. Thus in *New Windsor Corporation* v. *Mellor*[9] Lord Denning spoke of ancient turf, grazing animals and the continuity of local traditions, and upheld the customary right of villagers to indulge in pastoral recreation. Denning regards the law itself as close to nature and inseparable from religion and morality, a matter of atmosphere rather than strict

[5] See Case 240/83, *Procureur de la république* v. *Association de défense des brûleurs d'huiles usagées* [1985] ECR at 542. EC Treaty, articles 100, 100A, 130R, 130S, 130T, 235. See S. Ball and S. Bell, *Environmental Law*, 2nd edn (1994), ch.4.

[6] See *Southern Water Authority* v. *Nature Conservancy Council* [1992] 3 All ER 481 at 484–5, but see the Environment Act 1985 s.62(1).

[7] *R* v. *Secretary of State for the Environment ex parte RSPB* 8 July 1994 CO/464/94. See below p. 28.

[8] E.g. *Scenic Hudson Preservation Conference* v. *Federal Power Commission* 354 F2d 608 (1965). *Sierra Club* v. *Morton 405* US 727 (1972). See Cohen 1970 UTAH LR 388. Sax 1970 68 MICH LR 473.

[9] [1975] Ch.380 at 386. See also *Hinz* v. *Berry* [1970] 2QB 40 − 'bluebell time in Kent'. See also *Corpus Christi College* v. *Gloucester CC* [1983] 1 QB 360 at 363, ancient meadowlands. *Suffolk CC* v. *Mason* [1978] 1 WLR 716 at 717 old reedbeds.

rationality.[10] The general tenor of this is congenial to ecocentric environmental ethics, which place stress upon spiritual values and interdependent relationships based upon community culture. On the other hand Lord Denning's approach is firmly anthropocentric. He values the environment not for its own sake but as a setting for his favoured human life-style. His perspective on heritage reveals the dark side of environmental ethics. Denning appears to prefer a hierarchical feudal society to a market-based society. Environmental benefits can be preserved only by denying access.[11] Developers, particularly outsiders, must be resisted.[12]

The purpose of this chapter is to make a preliminary foray into the common law to see how far it is capable of absorbing environmental values. A mixed outcome can be anticipated. It cannot seriously be supposed that the common law has developed with environmental concerns uppermost in mind. The common law claims to be the product of 'practical reason'[13] generated by the short-term needs of the community mediated by general notions of ethics and policy shared by the legal profession. Its dominant tradition is pragmatic and conservative.[14] Nevertheless, if environmental values are rational and widely accepted, then the common law, claiming as it does to reflect the changing values of society, should be capable of adapting to them, even if in a hesitant and gradual fashion due to its dependence upon the adversarial culture of litigation and upon reasoning by analogy.

There are two basic issues. Firstly, is there a rational environmental ethic capable of pushing the law towards expressing coherent environmental principles and able to command widespread support? Secondly, which common law concepts are sufficiently 'green' or at least sufficiently flexible to be capable of absorbing them?

Environmental Values

There is no single cohesive theory as to why we should protect the environment and in whose interests. Environmental ethics has developed out of political and moral philosophy, and displays the full range of overlapping, contradictory and confused ideas generated by these disciplines. When it comes to practical issues, different kinds of environmentalists might be as much at loggerheads with each other as with developers. For

[10] See Klinck [1994] OJLS 25, to which I am indebted for these examples.

[11] *Fawcett Properties* v. *Bucks CC* [1961] AC 636 at 680. *BRB* v. *Glass* [1965] ch.538 at 551.

[12] *Myers* v. *Milton Keynes Development Corporation* [1974] 2 All ER 1096. *Hoveringham Sand and Gravels* v. *Secretary of State* [1975] 1 QB 754 at 760. *Re Brocklehurst's Estate* [1978] 1 ch.14. *Re Johnson's Trust* [1974] 1 QB 24.

[13] See Lawson, *The Rational Strength of English Law* (1951) (Hamlyn Lectures).

[14] See Loughlin, *Public Law and Political Theory* (1992).

example, from a conservationist perspective – concerned with saving resources for future use – culling deer might be necessary. From a preservationist perspective the position is less clear. Those who consider that environmentalism is about intrinsic rights would fight to protect animal life, trusting in nature's mechanisms to keep the balance. Another preservationist philosophy would allow culling in order to preserve the species for the greatest good of the greatest number.[15] Basic notions such as sustainability reflect different philosophical starting points. One view requires us to hand on to our successors a greater capital resource than that which we inherited, but is not concerned about the form which that resource should take. Thus one form of environmental destruction can be compensated by environmental or other benefits elsewhere. A rights-based approach by contrast requires resources to be used either not at all or only where absolutely necessary unless they are replaced. These different perspectives also influence our choice of methodology. A conservation-based approach, for example, is likely to favour utilitarianism, and hence economic analysis. Economic analysis is more difficult to fit to preservationist arguments. At their most conservative, these appeal to utilitarianism widened to include the aesthetic, but broaden into extending moral rights to non-human entities on the basis of mystical values.

Any method of establishing a consensus upon which the law can draw is therefore problematic. It might be possible, however, to discover common ground in the sense of areas where differing philosophies point the same way. One task of the law is to ensure that all relevant opinions are taken into account by official decision-makers. How far, for example, should standing be given to deep ecologists who discount human interests in favour of abstract notions of the ecosystem? This kind of environmental philosophy requires a major change in our ideas about the nature of the world and man's place in it, and is subversive of widely held political and social beliefs about individualism and liberal democracy. What are the boundaries of the environmental debate?

A loose classification of environmental ethics is possible by distinguishing broadly between anthropocentric approaches (orientated towards human welfare) and biocentric approaches.[16] The latter can be split into ecocentric and individualistic approaches. Particular concerns, conservation, preservation, sustainability, apply differently to each. There is some common ground. The preventive principle, the polluter-pays principle, rectification at source seem equally relevant to both camps. Sustainability on the other hand would apply differently. What distinguishes them is

---

[15] See Passmore, *Man's Responsibility for Nature* (1974), ch.4. Des Jardins, *Environmental Ethics* (1992), ch.3.

[16] For a useful overview see D. W. Pearce and R. K. Turner, *Economics and Natural Resources* (1990), ch.15.

essentially whether they see man as separate from and master of nature in the sense that nature is a resource for the use of man, or whether they regard man merely as part of nature, not necessarily to be valued more than any other element of the biotic community.

There are conflicts within the biocentric camp between those who regard individual life as sacred and those who regard ecosystems as the focus of protection. For the latter, individuals or even species might be killed off for the greater good.[17] Moreover our knowledge of ecology is such that it may be difficult to evaluate claims that nature is self-correcting, a proposition that paradoxically would allow man, as part of nature, freely to despoil the environment.

Environmental ethics have evolved in three phases. These have produced three main groups of ethical values: anthropocentric values, non-human individualistic values and ecocentric values. These labels, as with most ethical discourse, mark a wide variety of competing values, the state of environmental ethics being a continuum of overlapping arguments. Nevertheless for my present purpose the threefold distinction relates conveniently to legal thinking.

Anthropocentric thinking attempts to apply traditional ethical theories to the new problems caused by environmental degradation. The main concepts are firstly utilitarianism with its search for the greatest good of the greatest number, secondly deontological theories which attempt to identify basic rights, and thirdly natural-law traditions based upon the assumption that what is natural must be right. This third principle makes sense only as part of religious belief and relates most closely to the non-anthropocentric beliefs which I shall discuss later.

Neither utilitarianism nor rights theories have proved capable of doing the job. Utilitarianism depends upon concrete human preferences and cannot cope with the preferences of hypothetical and unknowable future generations. Utilitarianism also has difficulty when it has to compare quantifiable economic preferences with the aesthetic and spiritual values associated with the environment. For example in *Boomer* v. *Atlantic Cement Company*[18] the value of a home environment polluted by a factory was equated with the rent receivable if the occupiers were to let the premises. Utilitarianism looks to consequences in terms of their overall benefits. It therefore has no time for the notion that a landscape or an animal may have intrinsic value.

Rights theory recognizes intrinsic value but provides little help in solving practical problems. Rights have to be weighed against other rights or

---

[17] See Aldo Leopold, 'The Land Ethic', in *A Sand Country Almanack* (1949). It is unclear whether Leopold's approach is essentially anthropocentric, but he discusses the moral dilemma. See Des Jardins, op. cit., ch.9.

[18] 257 NE 2d 870 (1970). See also Carr (1992), 12 *Legal Studies* 92.

more general social concerns. There is the problem of how unborn generations can have rights. How far into the future beyond the two or three
directly knowable generations do such rights extend? What is the content
of the right of our descendants to sustainable development? Is it to a
given value of capital resource irrespective of its nature or is it limited to
specific environmental benefits? Anyway why should the enjoyment of
present rights be sacrificed to future claims? How can we be sure that
what we save will be needed or that it might not do more harm than
good? Who represents the future?[19]

The first attempt to develop anthropocentric concepts falls within the
mainstream values of western Europe. Man is inherently separate from
the rest of nature, and nature is a resource for man's benefit, even though
each generation might be only a steward of the resource. Conservation
can readily be accommodated as an example of good stewardship. Preservation on the other hand is not primarily concerned with nature as a resource
but regards nature as worth keeping for its own sake. Anthropocentric
values would justify preservation in terms of the spiritual and aesthetic
benefits that nature brings to mankind. Other anthropocentric arguments
for preservation include the scientific value of diversity, abhorrence of
cruelty, and, given that ecological science is undeveloped, the risk of
unnecessary destruction. Thus conservationists and preservationist arguments often overlap.

In the context of countryside preservation, anthropocentric arguments
raise conflicts with social justice. The aesthetic and spiritual values of
the countryside can be preserved only by confining enjoyment to a privileged
few. Either private-law property mechanisms, including price, or public-
law regulation could do the job. However private law would ignore social
justice since the common law is concerned only with protecting and transmit-
ting existing rights. In the case of public law, a set of values must be
identified capable of being applied to the competing interests that demand
to be heard by decision-makers.

The second kind of environmental ethic raises problems that differ
perhaps in degree of complexity rather than kind. Individualistic biocentric theorists extend ethical concerns to non-human entities. They argue
that animals, plants, inanimate objects and even habitats should have
'rights'. While not anthropocentric, they are sometimes anthropomorphic.
They suggest that animals etc. are sufficiently like human beings to be
capable of having rights. They disagree among themselves as to how far
into the non-human world 'moral considerability' should extend, and whether
the mechanism of rights is the best way of protecting non-humans. There
is a shift of perspective in that man is no longer treated as above nature

---

[19] See Passmore, loc. cit.

but as part of nature, although where rights conflict man's own interests might still be superior, albeit for no clear ethical reason.[20]

As a matter purely of legal mechanics, anything – animal, plant, building or stone – could be regarded as the focus of a legal right. The bearer of a right does not have to know of its right or indeed of the existence of law. Just as a permanently unconscious person has a claim to legal protection – in that sense a right[21] – so does a tree, although in both cases a human agent is needed to implement the law on behalf of the rightholder.

This extension of human rights theory is not especially radical. The law is well used to balancing competing claims. Extending rights to non-humans makes the balancing exercise more complex but is feasible as a matter of legal mechanics. Furthermore labelling an interest as a right is an important political symbol that special importance is attached to the interest in question, that it is not negotiable in the political market. Passmore correctly states that the law can protect an interest without making it a right, simply by prohibiting defined anti-social behaviour.[22] However this does not address the merits of the issue. Whether we should call something a right depends on what we wish to achieve. Passmore thinks that the concept of right should be confined to human beings, but seems to base this on the present state of the law rather than upon any particular insight as to the nature of a right. A right is an enforceable claim vested in a particular entity to which the law attaches special respect. That entity can be anything, a person, a stone or a habitat. Its 'interest' can again be anything the law wishes to protect. In the case of a stone the interest is presumably in its integrity. The remedy is to restore as far as possible the previous integrity of the protected object, for example by restocking a river or replanting a tree. Financial compensation for irretrievable loss can be paid to be used for providing a compensating environmental asset.

This extension of human rights to the non-human sphere raises formidable problems, and creates fundamental conflicts. For example the need to conserve a species may justify killing individual animals or a habitat, a practice which individualistic animal-rights proponents would reject.

Secondly, the problems of balancing human against animal rights, and animal rights against each other, have no obvious solution. When should horticultural interests justify interfering with an animal's habitat? Should we protect predators or their prey? Are pets more important than farm animals? Animal-rights theorists differ among themselves as to whether

---

[20] See Des Jardins, op. cit., ch.9.

[21] See Fienberg in Blackstone (ed.), *Philosophy and Environmental Crisis* (1974). See Stone below note 76.

[22] Op. cit., 115–16.

all animals or only the higher animals are worthy of moral consideration.[23] Attempts to rank the animal kingdom have been extrapolated from the human model and therefore carry no independent moral force.

Thirdly, individualistic ethics may be contrary to other environmental priorities. For example causing suffering to an animal by experimentation may advance species or habitat preservation. Conversely it may be preferable to let the last two elephants die naturally than to harm one of millions of cows. Fourthly, in the present state of ecological science it is not always clear how far disputes involve genuine value conflicts or merely factual uncertainty. What is clear is that the conceptual basis for extending rights beyond the human model is disputed, just as in anthropocentric territory there is no convincing reason for giving future generations any particular moral weighting.

The common law appears, unsurprisingly, to be firmly anthropocentric. This is illustrated by charity law. Charitable status has among other advantages the capacity to create a perpetual trust for the benefit of public purposes, whereas non-charitable property arrangements must benefit individuals and are subject to the rules against perpetuities and accumulations. These rules ensure that land remains marketable.

Charitable status requires public benefit so that the preservation of a wilderness for its own sake or of animals against human interference is unlikely to qualify. Originally a trust for animals could be charitable only if the animals in question were 'useful to man'.[24] However, in *Re Wedgwood*[25] a trust for animal welfare was held to be charitable by virtue of the moral qualities thereby encouraged in mankind. This decision is of limited importance because the trust was for the purpose of preventing inhumane slaughtering. In *Re Grove-Grady*[26] by contrast, a trust for an animal refuge from man was held not to be charitable because the public would obtain no tangible benefits from it. The spiritual satisfaction of knowing that such a refuge existed was not enough. It seems that the law will oppose cruelty to animals, protect animals from suffering, favour preservation for education, cultural or scientific reasons[27] but will not extend beyond these direct human concerns. A trust for the preservation of natural beauty or historic interest can be charitable, but again only

---

[23] Compare Regan, *The Case for Animal Rights* (1983) – higher animals only – with Taylor, *Respect for Nature* (1986) – inherent worth of all life but conflicting claims can be balanced on the basis of e.g. self-defence, proportionality and equitable distributions of burden and benefit. See Des Jardins, op. cit., 152–62. See also Singer, *Animal Liberation*, 2nd edn (1990) – utilitarian approach based on avoiding suffering.

[24] *London University* v. *Yarrow* (1857) 1 De G and J 72.

[25] [1915] 1 Ch.113.

[26] [1929] 1 Ch.557.

[27] *Re Lopes* [1931] 2 Ch.130 at 136.

because of direct educational or aesthetic benefit to the human community.[28]

These cases reveal confusion. Why should man's morality be furthered by discouraging cruelty but not by protecting animals in their habitat? One is drawn to infer that the courts are pandering to popular sentiment. The law could therefore be nudged by public opinion, fed by the arguments of moral philosophers into a broader approach to the nature of environmental values.

It is noteworthy that in *Re Grove-Grady* (above) Lord Hansworth MR did not think there was any public interest in leaving nature alone so as to respect the natural balance. He appeared to believe that leaving animals to prey on each other does not deserve the law's support, thus reflecting the traditional notion of man as master of nature.

The Australian case of *AG for New South Wales* v. *Sawtell* [29] is sometimes regarded as a breakthrough in that a trust for the preservation of natural wildlife was upheld as a charitable trust. The court explained that the boundaries of charity can shift with changing public opinion and pointed to the changes in public knowledge and opinion in relation to environmental matters that has taken place over the last fifty years. Nevertheless the court's reasoning remained firmly anthropocentric and indeed utilitarian. The trust was upheld on the familiar grounds of scientific value, the benefits to agriculture of a diverse gene pool, education and health and recreation. The public interest in recreation raises problems because of the inherent clash between the concerns of preservation and those of access. Moreover the court placed stress upon the fact that the purpose of the trust was to preserve *native* species appearing to link this with nationalistic values. As in *Grove-Grady* the idea that a sanctuary should leave nature 'red in tooth and claw' to fend for itself was disparaged.

The third kind of environmental ethic, ecocentrism, is more radical. It is a response to the problems posed by individualism. It adopts a holistic perspective regarding individuals, whether human, animal or vegetable, as of value only as part of an ecological system. Again there are many variations, shading at one extreme into animal-rights theory by regarding the biosystem as a value primarily as life support for individuals, and at the other extreme, including mystical 'Gaian' theorists who regard the planet earth as a purposive organic entity in its own right.[30] From our perspective what they have in common is that they regard natural ecosystems as having intrinsic value even if human beings did not exist. A system is seen as a community and could be a habitat, a mountain range and ultimately

---

[28] *Re Verrell* [1916] Ch.100. See Charity Commissioners, Annual Reports (1973), para.40; (1979), paras.61–5.
[29] [1978] 2 NSWLR 200.
[30] Lovelock, *Gaia: A New Look at Life on Earth* (1974).

the planet itself. This kind of deep ecology does not necessarily rule out human intervention in nature, but it does require that human intervention be strongly justified if there is a risk of upsetting the balance of the system. In particular, material values are of little importance, and all human members of the system have a responsibility to participate in preserving its well-being.

This reordering of our moral world is far removed from the conceptual framework of English law. Indeed it has been described as fascist in that it does not value the interests or even the life of the individual except as a contributor to the system.[31]

Ecocentrism raises problems for the law in that the law is predicated upon a desire to civilize – to protect man against the evils of nature. If an ecosystem has value for its own sake, then the killing of individuals or the destruction of species can be justified for the greater good. There seems to be no reason to exempt humanity from this. The balance of nature might best be preserved by destroying man the polluter, or conversely by leaving man free to destroy the environment, whereby either he will destroy himself or nature will correct his abuses in some other way. If nature is self-correcting then this may be the best way of preserving the environment. In other words non-anthropocentric theories, certainly ecocentric ones, give us no reason for acting. Ecosystems depend upon predator and prey.

Some deep environmentalists have a mission to revolutionize man's relationship with nature. The gap between their perspective and the assumptions of the law means that they are, from their internal point of view, entitled to resort to extra-legal – even violent – action ranging from 'ethical shoplifting' to bombing. Even where they peacefully promote their views, deep ecologists are vulnerable not only to prosecutions under public order legislation but to the ancient common-law offence of sedition which protects the state against violent or potentially violent attacks on the established order. Sedition does not extend to attacks upon particular government policies but could include a challenge to basic assumptions that underpin the status quo.[32] The common law rarely obstructs new ideas but does not provide a fertile environment for them.

This brief review of the main varieties of environmental ethic suggests unsurprisingly that the common law is individualistic and anthropocentric, and that environmental values are as yet insufficiently coherent to be clothed with full legal recognition. The main issue as regards non-anthropocentric perspectives is whether the common law is willing to

---

[31] Des Jardins, op. cit., 201–8.
[32] See Feldman, *Civil Liberties and Human Rights in England and Wales* (1993), 675ff. Public Order Act 1986 s.5. Criminal Justice Act 1994.

recognize them at least to the extent of giving them standing to argue their case.

The three approaches to environmental ethics share much common ground. Specific items on the deep ecology agenda would readily be accepted by anthropocentric environmentalists. These include the value of diversity, the dangers of technology, participation and the importance of spiritual values. Overpopulation raises more sinister issues and is a source of conflict between the three philosophies, but fortunately this lies beyond our present concerns. Similarly the main precepts of European environmental law are consistent with all three philosophies.

Within this common ground we can now examine some basic legal principles.

The Common Law – Property Rights

There is, unsurprisingly, no discernible biocentric element in the common law. The charitable trust is our only vehicle for pursuing environmental values unrelated to the benefit of particular individuals, and even this must be related to human interests.[33] Moreover, because biocentric ethics challenge the legal status quo, a trust for biocentric purposes might be a political trust and as such denied charitable status.

There is an inbuilt conflict within trusts law between furthering the ethical objects of a trust and the trustee's fiduciary duty to maximize the financial return on investment consistently with prudence. In *Harris* v. *Church Commissioners*[34] the court drew attention to the limits upon a trustee's right to take ethical considerations into account when making investment decisions. A trustee must not act inconsistently with the purposes of the trust nor hamper the work of the trust by alienating its supporters. Where a potential investment is clearly undesirable on ethical grounds, the trustee can reject it even if this means severe financial loss. But where the matter is controversial, the trustee can act on ethical grounds only where there is no significant financial loss to the trust, and even then must not use his position to advance a moral crusade. We have seen that many environmental issues are likely to fall within this contentious area because there are no clear answers to basic questions as to why we should preserve or conserve. However the terms of the instrument which creates the trust are overriding and could give specific authority to the trustee to override financial considerations.

The ownership of property is the most comprehensive method of environmental protection. For example, interest groups such as the League Against Cruel Sports have pursued their objectives by purchasing tracts

[33] Above p. 17.
[34] [1993] 2 All ER 300.

of land and protecting them through the law of trespass. The National Trust is one of the United Kingdom's largest landowners. On the other hand, English property law leans in favour of facilitating the circulation of land in the market, so that the National Trust requires statutory support to protect its interests.[35]

Apart from charitable trusts, the law gives little protection to the commons of wild animals, air, water and landscapes. The law regards the commons as a resource ripe for exploitation.

Possession is the root of title to property. In other words the law encourages the exploitation of natural resources in the interests of wealth creation. Those who conquer resources are favoured over

> those who move lightly through [the land] living with the land and its creatures as members of the same family rather than as strangers who visited only to conquer the objects of nature . . . The common law gives preference to those who convince the world that they have caught the fish and hold it first.[36]

There are many examples of this. Airspace can be owned only for the purpose of ordinary use and enjoyment.[37] Wild animals, other than those too young to escape, cannot be owned while free but can be killed or captured by anyone, subject to the first claim of the landowner on whose land they happen to be.[38] Water is not seen as part of a system or cycle with an integrity of its own, but allocated on the basis of practical convenience between economic claims. A distinction, ludicrous in ecological terms, is made between percolating water and water in defined channels. Percolating water cannot be owned, and a landowner has an absolute right at common law to abstract the entire supply from on or under his land irrespective of the consequences, whether physical or financial, to his neighbour, even if his motives are wholly malicious.[39] It is unfortunate that the doctrine of 'abuse of rights' is undeveloped in English law.[40] Under abuse-of-rights doctrine the exercise of property rights in a way that unjustifiably harms the legitimate interests of others can be unlawful. This would have considerable potential for absorbing environmental

---

[35] National Trust Act 1907 s.21. National Trust Act 1937 s.8.

[36] See Carol M. Rose, *Possession as the Origin of Property*, 52 U. Chi. L. Rev., 73. Haar and Liebman, *Property and Law* (1977), ch.1, particularly at 15.

[37] *Bernstein* v. *Skyviews* [1978] QB 479.

[38] *Pierson* v. *Pist* 3 Caines, 175 (N.Y.S. Ct 1805) – no rights prior to the kill. Case of Swans (1592) 7 Co. Rep. 156. *Blade* v. *Higgs* (1865) 11 HL Cas. 621.

[39] *Ballard* v. *Tomlinson* (1885) LR 29 Ch. D 115. *Chasemore* v. *Richards* (1859) 7 HL Case 349. *Rugby Joint Water Board* v. *Walters* [1967] Ch.397. *Bradford Corporation* v. *Pickles* [1895] AC 587.

[40] See *Hubbard* v. *Pitt* [1976] QB 142. *Thorne* v. *Bunting* [1972] Ch.470. *The Kostas Melas* [1981] 1 Lloyds Rep. 18. *Air Canada* v. *Secretary of State* [1981] 3 All ER 336 at 342–3. Cf. *Bayliss (Inspector of Taxes)* v. *Gregory* [1986] 1 All ER 286.

values, for example if the operation of the ecosystem were interfered with.

In the case of water in a defined channel, there is a weak kind of sustainability principle. A landowner can consume an unlimited quantity for 'ordinary' domestic and agricultural purposes, but otherwise must return the water unaltered in quantity or quality to the stream. He has no right at all to take water for purposes unconnected with the riparian land.[41] However the duty is owed only to other riparian owners. Presumably the owner nearest the mouth of the stream could exhaust the supply. Nor do fish enjoy protection. There is a public right to fish in tidal waters, but in non-tidal waters the riparian owner has fishing rights which are transferable in the ordinary way. Fish are regarded as profits of the land and, as such, consumable income.[42] Although fishing rights could be supported on conservation grounds, because they are proprietary they seem to outweigh the public interest in combating pollution.[43]

English property law has little provision for inter-generational equity. The rules against perpetuities and accumulations prevent land being tied up for more than about two generations. However, charitable trusts are not subject to these rules and can be used for preservationist purposes provided that there is direct human benefit. There is no authority where purely contingent future benefit suffices. The Settled Land Act 1925 contains measures to ensure that the capital resources of the land held on trust for future generations are not dissipated by the present tenants at the expense of future beneficiaries. For example, there are restrictions on the granting of forestry and mining leases.[44] These rules ensure that while the capital remains as land it retains its value. They do not prevent the land from being sold. The basic assumption of the law is that property represents disposable value. The Act goes to great lengths to ensure that the tenant for life is free to sell the land for development whenever he wishes, converting the interests of the beneficiaries into interests in the proceeds of sale.[45]

On the other hand, it is not clear what sustainability requires of us. Arguably it suffices that we hand on an enhanced capital asset to the next generation leaving the more remote generations to decide for themselves whether to continue the process. The interests of future generations seem

---

[41] See *Rugby Joint Water Board* v. *Walters* (above note 6). *Attwood* v. *Llay Main Collieries* [1926] Ch.444. An abstraction licence under the Water Resources Act 1991 does not confer immunity from civil liability (see s.70).

[42] *Attorney General for British Columbia* v. *Attorney General for Canada* [1914] AC 53 at 167. *Blount* v. *Layard* [1891] 2 Ch.681.

[43] See *Pride of Derby Angling Association* v. *Derby Corporation* [1953] Ch.149.

[44] Settled Land Act 1925 ss.41, 45, 48 – although a statutory intervention this relates closely to general equitable concerns. See e.g. *Howe* v. *Dartmouth* (1802) 7 Vis 137.

[45] Ibid., ss.38, 39, 104(1).

necessarily to be discounted against those of the present, but to what extent? Why should we sacrifice our own generation so that non-renewable resources can be eked out a little longer? Moral philosophers may provide different and conflicting answers but there seems to be no firm basis for an acceptable legal theory. There is not only moral uncertainty but also inadequate scientific knowledge.[46]

In the USA there has been much interest in the concept of the Public Trust under which the state holds non-renewable natural resources on trust for present and future generations.[47] This concept has been extrapolated from the English doctrine that the Crown owns the foreshore and the bed of tidal waters. The analogy is misleading. Historically the Crown's owner-ship was not based upon any concept of public trust but was ordinary beneficial ownership capable of being granted away.[48] The soil below tidal waters is regarded as 'waste' for the Crown to dispose of as it wishes. Perhaps confusion arose because the Crown's rights are subject to the public right of navigation and fishing. The United Kingdom constitution is distorted by the historical dual nature of the Crown. On the one hand the Crown is the government. On the other hand the Crown is a person with the capacities of an adult human being, capable of acting for selfish purposes. The feudal principles from which the common law developed owe nothing to modern ideas of statehood and citizenship, but presup-pose a trade-off of rights and obligations between possessors of land in the feudal hierarchy among whom the Crown was pre-eminent.

Property law regards land as an exploitable resource and its dynamics tend towards maximizing its short-term productive use. For example, a squatter can acquire title even if the paper owner has future plans for development with which the squatter's occupation is compatible, provided that the squatter shows an aggressive intention to exploit the land now. The paper owner's loss of title against an adverse possessor punishes the neglectful and encourages commercial certainty.[49]

The Lockean defence of property rights based upon the idea that a person has a moral right to exclude others from land to which he has added his labour has influenced legal thinking. However, Locke's defence contains the germ of a sustainability principle in that the right to exclude

---

[46] See Passmore, op. cit., ch.4. Sikora and Barry (eds.), *Obligations to Future Genera-tions* (Temple University Press, 1978). Des Jardins, op. cit., ch.4. Partridge (ed.), *Respon-sibilites to Future Generations* (Prometheus Books, 1980).

[47] See Sax (1970) 6 Mich LR 68. Cohen (1970) Utah LR 368. *Illinois Central Ry Co.* v. *Illinois* 146 US 337. *State* v. *Cleveland and P.R.R.* 113 NE 677, 682 (1916).

[48] *Duke of Devonshire* v. *Patterson* (1887) 20 QB 263 at 271. *Lord Fitzhardinge* v. *Purcell* (1908) 2 Ch.139 at 166–7. *Gann* v. *Whitstable Free Fishers* (1865) 11 HL Cas. 192. Cf. *Neill* v. *Duke of Devonshire* (1882) 8 App. Cas. 135 at 177.

[49] *Buckinghamshire C.C.* v. *Moran* [1990] Ch.623. Cf. *Leigh* v. *Jack* (1879) 5 Ex. D. 264.

others is, according to Locke, justifiable only where there is sufficient land left in common for others.[50]

Such common law doctrines as have been influenced by sustainability values have developed wholly in economic terms. The idea of nature as something of intrinsic value is wholly missing. Moreover, it must be remembered that even where obligations bind successive landowners, they can be released by the correlative right holder. Thus environmental protection can be bought out by private negotiation. For example the doctrine of waste is a preservationist principle. It prohibits a tenant of land from altering the land even by way of improvement (ameliorating waste). However, the duty is owed only to the landlord or other superior estate owner and concerns the economic value of the reversion. Letting cultivated land revert to nature is waste, firstly because it damages husbandry, and secondly because it may affect evidence of title, thereby clogging the market. Moreover waste is actionable only where there is economic damage to the inheritance.[51] Trees which are of economic value are protected but other trees can be freely destroyed unless planted specifically for human purposes.[52] Another example is that of water rights which I discussed earlier.

The development of land can be restricted indefinitely by means of a restrictive covenant. However, this must be tied to a specific benefit to neighbouring land owned by the covenantee or his successors in title. This benefit need not be narrowly economic in the sense of directly affecting the value of the land, but must be a benefit which a landowner could reasonably see as an advantage to him *qua* landowner.[53] The development of the law has been particularly influenced by the desire for conveyancing certainty in seeking to identify the benefited land and relate the covenant to it.[54] There seems to be little scope for broadening the purposes of the law. In the seminal case of *Tulk* v. *Moxhay*, Lord Cottenham justified binding successors in title to preserve an open space as a way of protecting the landowner's investment. In *LCC* v. *Allen*[55] the requirement that a covenant can be enforced only by a dominant landowner was applied with reluctance, but in *Re Gadd's Transfer*[56] the court accepted a minimalist dominant land requirement because of the economic consequences were the covenant not to be enforceable. The importance to the public of the environmental interest to be preserved is irrelevant.

---

[50] *Second Treatise on Government*, ch.5.

[51] See *Jones* v. *Chappell* (1875) LR 20 Eq. 539 at 541. *Doherty* v. *Allman* (1877) 3 App. Cas. 79. Blackstone Comm., vol.2, p.282.

[52] *Honywood* v. *Honywood* (1874) LR 18 Eq. 306. *Re Harkers W.T.* [1938] ch.323.

[53] *Wrotham Park Estates Ltd* v. *Parkside Homes Ltd* [1974] 1 WLR 798 at 808. *Re Foxe's Application* (1981) 2 BPR 9310 at 9312.

[54] (1848) 2 Ph. 774.

[55] (1914) 3 KB 602.

[56] [1966] Ch.56.

Apart from restrictive covenants the law is reluctant to recognize proprietary interests in fluctuating media such as air and water or in intangible rights such as the right to a view or to wander at large. These are too difficult to define as the subject matter of a grant for the purpose of conveyancing and hamper commercial development.[57]

The common law is also reluctant to recognize public rights unless clearly established by local custom or falling within the categories of charity. Once established, public rights do not seem to face a public-interest test but are vulnerable only to private-property interests.[58]

Private law liability

Nuisance law sets standards of reasonable use of land and so could serve as a basis for environmental rights. However, the law has concentrated upon the protection of property and in recent years has drawn closer to negligence liability, thus placing emphasis on the circumstances of the particular case and concepts of fault and less upon the achievement of socially desirable goals. Nuisance law has difficulty with intangible interests that do not involve personal injury, property damage or 'sensible' interference with health, comfort or convenience. It is relatively at home with pollution but does not protect amenity or aesthetic values. Indeed comfort and convenience are less well protected than damage to property. In the case of damage to property the character of the area is irrelevant. In the case of interference with comfort or convenience the level of protection is relative to the existing character of the neighbourhood, thus ruling out arguments based upon environmental improvement and, except in a weak sense, sustainability.[59] Things should not get worse but they need not get better. The thrust of the law is therefore in line with Garrett Hardin's well-known 'tragedy of the commons thesis'[60] in the sense that preservation depends upon keeping environmental goods in the hands of the minority who already have them rather than in redistribution according to the precepts of social justice even though there is a direct correlation between poverty and low environmental standards.

The courts have supported the power of planning authorities to alter the character of a neighbourhood for the purposes of the law of nuisance

[57] *Re Ellenborough Park* [1956] ch.131. *Bryant* v. *Lefever* (1879) 4 CPD 172. *William Aldred's Case* (1610) 9 Co. Rep. 576 at 586. *Harris* v. *De Pinna* (1886) 33 Ch.D. 238. See Gray, *Elements of Land Law*, 2nd edn, 1072. [1991] CLJ 252 at 261ff.

[58] *Goodman* v. *Saltash Corporation* (1882) 7 App. Cas. 633. See Barry Lady, *The Law of the Countryside: The Rights of the Public* (1987).

[59] *St Helen's Smelting Co.* v. *Tipping* (1865) 11 HLC 642 – damage to the plaintiff's trees and shrubs was recoverable as property damage, unrelated to the environment as such. See Malcolm, *A Guidebook to Environmental Law* (1994), 38.

[60] *Science* 162:1243 (13 December 1968). See Passmore, op. cit., 63–4, 104–5. O'Riorden, *Environmentalism*, ch.1.

by upgrading or downgrading, for example in a development plan or by a series of planning decisions.[61] This might result in environmentally friendly uses being driven out of the area.

No weight is attached to the interests of nature conservation. A landowner has a right to abate a trespass or nuisance by cutting back vegetation or chopping out roots even if there is no damage to his land.[62]

Common-law liability rules cannot easily accommodate the precautionary principle nor the rectification-at-source principle. The civil burden of proof places the onus on whoever asserts the environmental interest to show that damage is more likely than not. In the present state of ecological knowledge this is a difficult burden to discharge. The precautionary principle by contrast requires us to act in the face of scientific uncertainty. A more sophisticated risk-assessment approach based upon epidemiological techniques would possibly be preferable to the common-law approach. In the *Cambridge Water* [63] case the House of Lords restricted the precautionary and rectify-at-source principles by requiring that the damage be foreseeable at the time of the actual escape and by exempting the polluter from liability once the pollutant becomes irretrievable even if it remains on the polluter's land. This applies even to what was hitherto the strict liability rule in *Rylands* v. *Fletcher*.[64] Their Lordships regarded *Rylands* v. *Fletcher* as an application of nuisance law. Strict liability remains where the defendant creates a nuisance as regards the initial escape.

A significant aspect of *Cambridge Water* is that the authorities were previously inconclusive so that the House was free to decide the issue on principle. Their Lordships were influenced partly by reluctance to usurp the legislative function in a complex and controversial area, but also by a desire to support commercial values, in particular the consequences in terms of business overheads of liability for unforeseeable damage.[65] Thus the polluter pays principle was rejected, illustrating that there is no such thing as a policy of non-intervention. In litigation there is always a winner. The court is necessarily taking sides.

Public-law liability

Many of the weaknesses of the common law have been combated by legislation, relating to pollution, water abstraction and preservation, or by requiring public decision-makers to take into account environmental

---

[61] *Gillingham B.C.* v. *Medway (Chatham) Docks Co. Ltd* [1992] 3 WLR 449.

[62] *Lemon* v. *Webb* [1895] AC 1 — but no right of action without damage. *Smith* v. *Giddy* [1904] 2 KB 408.

[63] [1994] 1 All ER 53.

[64] (1868) LR 3 HL 330.

[65] Loc. cit. above note 63 at 75.

concerns.[66] These statutes form the corpus of environmental law, and fall to be interpreted by the courts in their public law mode as reviewers of the legality of government action.

The functions of the common law are different as between private and public law. In private law the common law directly imposes its own values albeit often modified by the superior commands of the legislature. In public law the role of the court is secondary. It is to ensure that those charged with fulfilling the purposes of the legislature do so fairly and rationally and within the terms of their mandate.

Environmental values are diverse and conflicting. They cannot easily be reduced to concrete rights and duties and their potential beneficiaries are the subject of hot debate. Against this setting public-law ideas of interest representation, proportionality and rationality seem to be more fruitful than private-law concepts of right. Two questions are especially important. Firstly, to what extent do broad environmental concerns have standing to challenge government action in the courts. Secondly, how far will the courts attach special weight to environmental concerns treating them as superior to other interests?

Both aspects can be illustrated by town and country planning law. This is the forum where development and preservationist interests directly clash. Planning authorities must take environmental factors into account and must sometimes carry out an environmental-impact assessment, but the purposes for which planning decisions can be made are matters of political policy. They can be to encourage or direct development as much as to restrict it. Subject to broad requirements of relevance to the proposed development and reasonableness, the general law will allow environmental benefits to be provided by developers as a condition of planning permission, but will equally endorse a restrictive policy under which such benefits will be taken into account only where they are needed to overcome an objection to granting permission.[67]

The attitude of the courts to environmental matters is broadly neutral. For example in R v. *Poole Borough Council ex parte Beebee*[68] planning permission was granted for housing development which affected an SSSI, one of the last English habitats of certain reptile species. European law probably required an environmental impact assessment. No formal assessment was undertaken, but the authority did consider the question of preserving the habitat. It was held that despite the special status of the site and notwithstanding the failure to carry out a formal assessment, the planning permission was valid. The court emphasized that the balancing

---

[66] E.g. Coal Industry Act 1994 ss.53 and 54. Town and Country Planning Act 1990 ss.12(3A), 31(3), 36(3), 71A, 190.

[67] R v. *Plymouth City Council ex parte Plymouth and South Devon Co-operative Society Ltd* (1993) 67 P and C.R. 78. *Tesco Stores Ltd* v. *Secretary of State* [1995] 2 All ER 636.

[68] [1991] 3 JEL 293.

of competing interests was a matter for the authority and that it was unnecessary to insist upon formal compliance with impact requirements provided that the authority's attention had been directed to the environmental issues. Indeed, in the absence of contrary evidence, it would be presumed that all relevant factors had been considered. This exemplifies the traditional reluctance of the law to weigh competing considerations even where the context suggests that environmental concerns are especially important. Similarly in *R* v. *Swale Borough Council ex parte RSPB*[69] the court exercised its discretion not to quash a planning permission which affected an important habitat on the ground that the applicants had not sought review promptly (even though within the statutory time limit) and the financial interests of contractors would be at risk if the permission were quashed.

Except where a decision is grossly unreasonable or where there is statutory or published policy guidance, the courts will not concern themselves with the weight to be attached to competing considerations, although they seem to recognize a presumption in favour of development.[70] Occasionally, however, the court will take a hesitant initiative. For example where a proposed development raises environmental problems, a planning authority must sometimes seek an alternative site.[71]

On the other hand the courts will respond to a clear lead from Europe. *R* v. *Secretary of State ex parte RSPB*[72] concerned an important bird sanctuary in the Thames estuary. The court upheld the Secretary of State's decision not to designate the area as a special protection area in accordance with the European Community Birds Directive,[73] holding that he was entitled to take the view that economic factors outweighed environmental ones. The case law of the European Court of Justice distinguished between initial designation of a habitat and subsequent decisions to modify the habitat. In the latter case, only health and safety factors would override the environmental considerations. The court was prepared to follow this. Moreover, Rose LJ emphasized that there might be cases where a habitat was so important that designation would be required whatever the countervailing economic factors. It is the intervention of European principles that makes it legitimate for the court to depart from its usual neutral stance.

Environmental interests can draw some limited comfort from a recent

[69] [1991] JPL 39.

[70] *London Residuary Body* v. *Lambeth B.C.* [1990] 2 All ER 309 at 314, 315.

[71] *G.L.C.* v. *Secretary of State* [1986] JPL 193. Cf. *Vale of Glamorgan B.C.* v. *Secretary of State for Wales* (1986) 52 P and C.R. 418. *Trust House Forte* v. *Secretary of State* [1980] JPL 834.

[72] Unreported 8 July 1994. Co/464/94.

[73] Comm 79/409 [1979] OJ L103/1. See now Habitats Directive 92/43 [1992] OJ 4/206/7. Cf. *Commission* v. *Federal Republic of Germany* (Case 57/89R) [1991] 1 ECR 83. See Baldock 4 JEL 139. PPG 9 Nature Conservation (HMSO, 1994).

relaxation of the standing requirements for judicial review. A direct legal or financial interest is not required, but on the other hand neither individuals nor environmental groups have standing merely on the ground that the issues are of public importance. The test of 'sufficient interest in the matter to which the application relates' is a matter for the court's discretion to be decided in all the circumstances. The importance of the issues is a relevant factor, but the emphasis of recent cases where pressure groups have sought to challenge governmental decisions on environmental grounds seems to be upon whether the group in question is respectable and accepted in official circles – in other words standing in the sense of status. In *R* v. *Secretary of State ex parte Rose Theatre Trust*[74] Schiemann J refused standing to a group which was specifically formed to defend the remains of an Elizabethan theatre against development. His Lordship took the view that as individuals none of the group had any special interest in the matter (even though the group included expert professionals) apart from the general public interest. He also considered that a group can have no greater standing than the sum of its individual members.

This approach is similar to that taken by the US Supreme Court in *Sierra Club* v. *Morton.*[75] The association was required to show that its members included persons who would be affected by the development of a Disneyland in a wilderness area. This prompted Stone to argue that natural objects such as trees and landscapes should have standing represented by a human agent.[76] As we have seen, there is no legal or conceptual objection to this. From a private law perspective, it is doubtful whether the content of a right vested in a tree is sufficiently determinate to be a useful analytical tool, but from a public law standpoint where the issue is primarily one of access to the courts, the case is much stronger. On the other hand, conferring standing on a tree does not take us far. How do we decide who is the most appropriate human agent to speak on the tree's behalf? This throws us back to the basic problem of why we should value nature. Again, the absence of a consensus environmental ethic has practical implications for the law.

Pressure groups have often been given standing. This seems to depend primarily upon the status of the group and the extent of its economic involvement in the interests it pursues.

In *R* v. *Pollution Inspectorate ex parte Greenpeace (No. 2)*[77] Otton J gave Greenpeace standing to challenge a government permission to discharge

---

[74] [1990] 1 WLR 193.

[75] 405 US 727 (1972).

[76] *Should Trees have Standing? Towards Legal Rights for Natural Objects* (Los Altos C.A.; Kaufmann 1974).

[77] [1994] 4 All ER 329. See also *R.* v. *Foreign Secretary ex parte World Development Movement* [1995] 1 All ER 611. Cf. Law Comm. No. 226 (1994) advocating a public-interest test. See also *Woolf* [1992] PL 221. *Schiemann* [1990] PL 342.

nuclear waste. His Lordship recognized that Greenpeace was a well-established and responsible body acknowledged as such by international agencies, that its members include many people living in the area and directly affected by the issues, that Greenpeace could help the court by providing expertise and that unless Greenpeace were given standing there might not be any other way to bring the issues to court. His Lordship also stressed that, due to the involvement of Greenpeace, the issues had been narrowed, thus saving the court's resources.

In one sense this pragmatic approach supports the environmental cause. It also has a dark side. Otton J's approach favours well-resourced groups prepared to work with established authority. It also reflects private law concerns in privileging people directly affected. Many environmental concerns can effectively be promoted by such groups. But environmental concerns include radical ideas that challenge the existing political and economic structure. Pressure groups with limited resources, without official recognition and exposing unpopular or novel ideas are at a disadvantage. On the other hand, there is a chink of light in Otton J's recognition that without giving standing to a pressure group there might be no other way of getting the issues before the court.

In other public law contexts the attitude of the courts, while remaining anthropocentric, allows broad environmental issues to be canvassed. In *R v. Somerset County Council ex parte Fewings*[78] the local authority had banned deer hunting on its land for moral reasons. The Court of Appeal quashed the ban on the ground that the authority had not properly considered the statutory restrictions upon its powers as landowner. As a statutory body the authority could act only in accordance with a statutory remit whereas a private landowner can do anything that is not prohibited by statute. The governing statute[79] entitled the authority to 'appropriate' land for the purposes of 'the benefit improvement or development of their area'.

Their lordships accepted that 'benefit' could include moral considerations but the authority had erred in regarding itself as having the same powers as a private landowner and had not taken account of the statute at all. The Court of Appeal did not therefore directly confront the difficult issues of law for the members of a public authority using their powers to impose their own ethical principles. It is well established that elected bodies are not delegates of those who elect them and are therefore entitled to form their own judgements upon controversial issues. On the other hand the idiosyncratic preferences of individual councillors should surely not be taken into account. The matter depends rather upon identifying

[78] [1995] 3 All ER 20.
[79] Local Government Act 1972 s.120 (1) 6.

important issues of public controversy and forming a judgement upon them.

Law J at first instance[80] did tackle the issues squarely. He took the view, firstly, that an elected body is not entitled to a more liberal construction of its powers than a non-elected body. In both cases the scope of the power depends upon the purpose of the particular statute and there is no presumption in favour of democracy as such. His Lordship gave no reason for this other than the absence of authority. Secondly his Lordship, consistently with an individualistic anthropocentric philosophy, held that where an activity such as deer hunting is not prohibited by the general law, clear statutory language is required to enable a public authority to restrict that activity on moral or ethical grounds.

Because the Court of Appeal decided the case on other grounds it is not clear how far their Lordships would have permitted the council to impose its own moral views. Given the uncertain and controversial nature of environmental ethics it is doubtful whether the law can do more than make sure that relevant views are openly and fairly canvassed.

Conclusion

The common law has been forged out of disputes, mainly of an economic kind, concerning the short-term interests of persons. It regards land as an exploitable resource. For this reason it has not developed an environmental ethic. Unless commanded by the legislature it does not privilege environmental rights. Apart from pollution cases which involve quantifiable damage to well-recognized existing interests there is no adequate legal or moral foundation upon which society can reach a consensus about why and to what extent we should preserve or conserve nature or save resources for the future. The burden of environmental protection is therefore properly carried by the legislature, the only measure of 'rightness' being votes.

What role therefore can the common law play? Firstly, the common law contains concepts, notably the doctrine of waste, the charitable trust, the restrictive covenant and *locus standi* that could be developed as means of protecting non-economic environmental concerns. It is for lawyers to push forward these concerns in argument. Secondly, the law can ensure that a wide range of views can be expressed, even unpopular, novel or radical ideas. Thirdly, public law can balance competing values in a search for common ground, modifying the messianic fervour of the deep ecologists as much as the short-term interests of developers. Public law concepts such as proportionality which at present are undeveloped are capable of serving environmental purposes. Fourthly, the law can ensure openness

---

[80] [1995] 1 All ER 513.

and the disclosure of environmental information. More generally the common law can absorb the environmental concepts of European law without usurping legislative territory, since article 5 of the Treaty of Rome requires national courts to further European objectives.

The common law has certain obvious drawbacks as an environmental instrument. Firstly, it can develop only piecemeal and cautiously against a well-established conceptual structure largely hostile to environmental interests. Secondly, the adversarial judicial process is narrow and not well suited to canvassing a wide range of competing interests, particularly those not located in individual claims. Thirdly, cost considerations restrict access to the courts primarily to those with a vested interest in the economic status quo. The most fruitful way forward seems to be for political science to develop clear and well-understood justifications for conservation and preservation, and to reconcile these with our ideas of social justice.

2

Sustainable Management of Aquatic Ecosystems and the Law

WILLIAM HOWARTH AND DONALD McGILLIVRAY

Preface: A Signal Tale

The American signal crayfish was first imported into Britain to be cultivated in the summer of 1976. Since then, a modest industry in crayfish farming, producing an annual yield of around 10 tonnes, has been established.[1] Yet the environmental impact of the introduction of the signal, and other non-native species of crayfish, has had an ecological impact many would consider wholly disproportionate to the economic benefits of the industry.

The mobile signal crayfish is a carrier of crayfish plague, a disease fatal to the white-clawed or Atlantic stream crayfish, the only crayfish species native to Britain. Whole populations of native crayfish can be wiped out within days of contracting the plague, which can be transmitted without direct contact between native and alien species. Although not yet conclusively 'proven', strong scientific evidence links the import and distribution of signal crayfish with the occurrence of plague outbreaks, first identified in 1981. The larger signal crayfish, which occupies a similar niche in the aquatic ecosystem, may also out-compete or prey on the smaller Atlantic crayfish.[2]

The loss of native populations of crayfish is a relatively under-publicized ecological disaster. However, the story does not end there.

---

[1] MAFF, WOAD, SOAFD, DANI, *Multi Annual Guidance Programme for Aquaculture*, Report of the United Kingdom for 1992.

[2] Generally, see D. J. Alderman, J. L. Polglase and M. Frayling, 'Aphanomyces astaci pathogenicity under laboratory and field conditions', *Journal of Fish Diseases*, 10 (1987), 385–93; D. J. Alderman, D. M. Holdich and I. D. Reeve, 'Signal crayfish acting as vectors in crayfish plague in Britain', *Aquaculture*, 86 (1990), 3–6.

Crayfish play a vital role in the ecology of the freshwater environment. They provide food for fish and other aquatic fauna such as otters. By their feeding, they help reduce nutrient exchange and slow down enrichment ('eutrophication') resulting in excessive weed and algal growth. In their absence, lakes and rivers can therefore become 'choked' by excessive plant growth. But the introduction of the alien signal has not compensated for this, causing *excessive* destruction of weed cover and thus of fish spawning sites. Huxley's description of the crayfish as 'the freshwater health inspector' may therefore be true of native species but cannot be extended to introduced species.[3]

In many ways, the tale of the signal crayfish is the aquatic counterpart to that of the grey squirrel, whose arrival in the UK in the late 1890s has caused the native red squirrel to be brought close to extinction. Yet the problems faced by the native crayfish illustrate the broader issues that surround aquatic ecosystem conservation, and highlight the need for effective legal provisions to ensure sustainable management of aquatic flora and fauna.

This chapter seeks to show that sustainable management of aquatic ecosystems involves more than the relatively discrete regulatory systems and divisions of responsibility which presently exist. It contrasts the traditional purposes of selected aspects of water law, water quality, water resources and land drainage, the regulation of species introductions and planning controls, with the legal innovations necessary to achieve adequate levels of water ecosystem protection. The overall inference is that a more coherent approach to the regulation and administration of aquatic ecosystem protection is required.

International Obligations and Administrative Responsibilities

By signing the Convention on Biological Diversity at the United Nations Conference on Environment and Development (the 'Earth Summit'), both the UK and the European Union (EU) demonstrated a commitment to the conservation of 'the variability among living organisms from all sources ... [including] diversity within species, between species and of ecosystems'.[4] More broadly, Agenda 21 of the Summit committed governments to a comprehensive programme of action to achieve more sustainable

---

[3] Huxley (1875), quoted in A. Thompson, 'Plague – some lessons to be learned', *Fish Farmer* (May/June 1990), 54–6. Recent plans to protect the native crayfish note that 'protection of the whole aquatic ecosystem from the impact of introduced crayfish is also a consideration', hence the inclusion of some areas for protection where the native crayfish is absent (see note 127 below).

[4] Article 2, Convention on Biological Diversity. See A. Boyle, 'The Convention on Biological Diversity', in L. Campiglio, L. Pineschi, D. Siniscalco and T. Treves (eds.), *The Environment After Rio: International Law and Economics* (1994).

patterns of development. Clearly, these broadly formulated international imperatives need to be transposed into detailed national measures, through law, administration and policy, so that a confident assurance can be given that national provisions guarantee that biodiversity protection is comprehensively and stringently provided for and development is not allowed to take place at an unacceptable cost to the environment.[5]

At national level,[6] the National Rivers Authority (NRA), a non-departmental public body financed by a combination of grant-in-aid and, increasingly, cost-recovery charges,[7] has executive responsibility for a number of core functions relating to the water environment. These relate principally to water resources, water pollution, flood defence and land drainage, and fisheries. It may also have functions assigned to it by other enactments.[8] The NRA has general environmental and recreational duties to act so as to further the conservation of flora and fauna.[9] Subject to these, it has a discretionary duty generally to promote 'the conservation of flora and fauna which are dependent on an aquatic environment', though this rests alongside equivalent duties to conserve and enhance the amenity of inland and coastal waters, and associated land, and the use of such waters and land for recreational purposes.[10] The NRA also has a duty to 'maintain, improve and develop' fisheries.[11]

While its general environmental duties do not necessarily provide a peg on which to hang any activity deemed to be of environmental benefit, some form of 'environmental gain' may nevertheless be sought when projects are authorized. Where this duty is not prejudiced, the NRA may exercise its promotional duties for conservation projects such as pond restoration and creation.[12] As long as it acts in relation to 'the conservation of flora and fauna which are dependent on an aquatic environment', the NRA may therefore promote conservation although this is not one of its principal functions.

The NRA must also consult with English Nature, the Countryside Council for Wales (CCW) or National Parks or Broads Authorities before

---

[5] See Biodiversity, the UK Action Plan, Cm. 2428 (1994) and Sustainable Development, the UK Strategy, Cm. 2426 (1994).

[6] For a discussion of administrative responsibilities generally, see chapter by Alder.

[7] There is little conservation income. The NRA estimates its total spend on conservation to be in the order of £18 million annually (NRA, 93–94 Annual Conservation, Access and Recreation Report, 1994).

[8] S.2(1) Water Resources Act 1991. Notably, the NRA does not have assigned to it core functional responsibilities in relation to recreation or conservation, though these are usually referred to equally as functions.

[9] S.16 Water Resources Act 1991.

[10] Ibid. s.2.

[11] Ibid. s.114.

[12] A. Heaton, 'Conservation and the National Rivers Authority', in F. B. Goldsmith and A. Warren (eds), Conservation in Progress (1993), p.316.

carrying out or authorizing any potentially damaging works, operations or activities in areas of special interest notified to the NRA by these bodies.[13] Following prior consultation with the NRA and key conservation and recreation agencies, codes of practice may be approved by the minister in relation to the practical operation of these duties.[14] Under this power, a *Code of Practice on Conservation, Access and Recreation* has been approved.[15]

Under the Environmental Protection Act 1990, the nature conservation agencies in England and Wales exercise general and specific functions inherited from the former Nature Conservancy Council and (in Wales) the Countryside Commission. Although the 1990 Act does not specifically impose environmental or conservation duties on English Nature or the CCW, these may be contained in legislation which they administer. For example, Sites of Special Scientific Interest (SSSIs) must be notified where relevant criteria are met.[16] Ministers, government departments and public bodies also have a general duty to 'have regard to the desirability of conserving the natural beauty and amenity of the countryside' which extends to land covered by water.[17]

The Environment Agency

At the time of writing, the Environment Act 1995 has recently passed into law providing for the establishment of an Environment Agency for England and Wales.[18] On 1 April 1996, the new agency will come into operation with almost all the regulatory powers and duties presently exercised by the NRA along with the responsibilities of Her Majesty's Inspectorate of Pollution[19] and the waste management functions of local authorities.[20] The establishment of a unified agency, with the capacity to take an integrated

---

[13] S.17 Water Resources Act. 'In practice, this has involved notification of Sites of Special Scientific Importance by the NCC and its successor bodies, whilst the National Parks authorities have defined and notified the whole of their respective areas as being of "particular importance"', Heaton, ibid., p.304. In respect of local authorities and internal drainage boards exercising land drainage functions, see similarly s.61C Land Drainage Act 1991 (inserted by s.1 Land Drainage Act 1994).

[14] Ibid. s.18(1).

[15] See Water and Sewerage (Conservation, Access and Recreation) (Code of Practice) Order 1989, SI 1989 No. 1152. Ministers are under a duty to take into account contraventions of the code in determining how to exercise their powers under the Act (s.18(2) Water Resources Act 1991).

[16] Under s.28(1) Wildlife and Countryside Act 1981. See Ball, below, Chapter 4, pp. 89–110.

[17] S.11 Countryside Act 1968.

[18] Generally, see Part I Chapter I Environment Act 1995.

[19] Under Part I Environmental Protection Act 1990.

[20] Under Part II Environmental Protection Act 1990.

approach to pollution control, is to be welcomed, but certain aspects of the legislation providing for the Agency may give cause for concern.

The Environment Act 1995 raises some particular concerns as to the diminution of conservation duties presently imposed on the NRA. The Act has modified the scope of the present duty to 'further' conservation so that this will apply only to functions other than pollution control. In respect of pollution control functions, the corresponding duty is merely to 'have regard to the desirability of conserving' flora and fauna.[21] This may be seen as an attempt to make the general conservation role of the agency a more remote consideration in the formulation or determination of 'proposals'. There is no compelling reason why pollution control should be placed on a different footing in this respect, and concern about the reduction of the conservation duty regarding this function must remain.

Whilst it is to be a principal aim of the Agency to make a contribution towards attaining the objective of 'sustainable development' in discharging its functions, this is to be elaborated by guidance from the Minister to which the agency is to have regard.[22] Accordingly, no direct duty to act 'sustainably' is provided for and only a duty to 'further' conservation in following such guidance is envisaged.[23]

The 1995 Act also incorporates a general duty on the Agency, when exercising its powers, to take into account the costs that are likely to be incurred and the benefits that are likely to accrue unless it is unreasonable to do so. However, this duty is not to affect its other obligations.[24] Given the tight financial restrictions and scrutiny under which the NRA presently operates, and the attention to 'added value' that is already given by the Authority, the import of this provision, it is suggested, is best seen initially at a symbolic level. No provision is made for a code of practice to elucidate the duty. By promoting economic calculations in nature conservation, it may serve to place undue emphasis on the utility of cost-benefit analysis where this may be unreasonable in particular cases. Cost-benefit analysis will be impossible, given the difficulties in quantifying costs or benefits to the environment, and may give rise to a considerable amount of litigation where it is contended that the Agency has had insufficient regard to this duty.

Whilst there is a relatively short period before the Environment Agency comes into existence, there are a range of administrative and policy matters concerning the Agency that remain to be determined. It is somewhat speculative to suppose that it will continue to adopt the same approach

[21] S.7(1) and (2) Environment Act 1995.

[22] Ibid. s.4(1) to (4).

[23] Contrast s.1(1) Natural Heritage (Scotland) Act 1991; and see Department of the Environment, *Draft Guidance Issued to Environment Agency on Sustainable Development*, News Release 10, 17 January 1995.

[24] S.39 Environment Act 1995.

to the regulation of the aquatic environment as that of the NRA, but more speculative still to attempt to prejudge what particular changes will ensue. Consequently, the discussion which follows is based upon the existing arrangements with an appreciation that significant revisions may be in prospect.

Water Quality and Aquatic Ecosystem Protection

At best, the protection of aquatic ecosystems may only be seen as a secondary objective of the civil and criminal law relating to water pollution and water quality. An amount of rethinking is needed to refocus existing legal measures upon this objective.

Civil law

At civil law, only the private property rights of individual riparian owners are protected. There is no riparian right to a satisfactory aquatic ecosystem enforceable by a riparian owner against others who may cause damage to aquatic flora and fauna.

The nearest that the civil law comes to aquatic ecosystem protection is the protection of water quality and quantity of watercourses from 'sensible alteration'. Hence 'a riparian proprietor will be entitled to have the water of the stream on the banks of which his property lies . . . without sensible diminution or increase, and without sensible alteration in its character or quality.'[25] But this rough-and-ready formula of 'sensible alteration', used as a basis for civil actionability, provides only the most indirect protection for aquatic ecosystems where the harm which has been caused is of an extreme kind. Regrettably, in many instances, serious ecological harm may be caused without the civil law criterion being satisfied.

Even where a riparian owner is able to show 'sensible alteration', there are immense difficulties in using the civil law for effective protection of the aquatic environment. For example, in *Granby* v. *Bakewell UDC*,[26] the plaintiff brought a civil action in nuisance for damages and an injunction arising from the pollution of his trout fishery by coal tar and ammoniacal by-products discharged from the defendant's gasworks, following which numerous fish were seen dead or dying. The plaintiff succeeded in obtaining an injunction in addition to damages for harm caused to the fishery. The case is most illuminating for the judge's observations as to the calculation of damages to the fishery interest in such situations, being limited to the natural and probable consequences of the wrongful act.

[25] Per Lord Macnaghten in *Young* v. *Bankier Distiller Co.* (1893) [1891–4] All ER 439 at 440.
[26] [1923] 87 J.P. 105.

As wild creatures, the dead trout were not owned by the plaintiff.[27] Yet it was conceded that their loss was a compensatable claim and their value needed to be assessed. In calculating damages the court accepted that for every dead fish seen, at least two more were not seen but needed to be taken into account. However, the value of the dead fish was not merely the cost of their replacement by farmed fish, which had been artificially reared by hand-feeding in a stew pond, as these were not of the same sporting value as the wild fish which had been killed. Implicitly, therefore, the limitation of seeking to 'replace' wild creatures was recognized. Moreover, the poisoning of the river must have killed a quantity of the fish food in the river, especially the crustacea, molluscs and nymphs, and this too had to be taken into account when assessing the damages.

This head of damages is an exceptional instance of civil liability extending to compensation for aquatic ecosystem damage. Regrettably, however, no explicit account is given as to how a figure of damages was computed to represent this kind of loss. Presumably, the basis of recovery was that damage to the fish food could in some way be related to the commercial value of the fishery. It would be presumptuous to interpret it as indicating that the civil law will recognize non-commercially related damage to the aquatic environment as compensatable.

It is thought that *Granby* v. *Bakewell UDC* is a unique example of a civil court taking, albeit indirect, account of damage to an aquatic ecosystem in assessing a damages claim. Significantly, however, it is doubtful whether the plaintiff would have recovered if his claim had been for damage to crustacea, molluscs and nymphs alone. His success was attributable to the commercial value of that part of the damaged aquatic ecosystem for which damages were allowed. The clear implication, therefore, is that aquatic ecosystem damage will only be compensatable where consequent economic loss can be shown. This presents a considerable difficulty where the protection of the civil law is contemplated for an aquatic ecosystem. Moreover, the legal need for financial quantification of damage raises almost insuperable difficulties where a price has to be put upon ecosystem protection. This is a difficulty which *Granby* fails to address.

In summary, two key difficulties are evident. First, protection of the aquatic environment *per se* does not fall within any private right recognized by civil law. Secondly, even if such a right were to be recognized, the provision of financial compensation to the owner of the right infringed would not bring any actual benefit to the ecosystem. The underlying supposition of the civil law that compensation can in some way be used to purchase a new environment to replace that which has been destroyed is surely misconceived. The compensatory mechanisms of civil law prove inappropriate in addressing the problem, though it may be noted that in

---

[27] *Fitzgerald* v. *Firbank* [1897] 2 Ch.96.

Granby the situation was so extreme that the plaintiff was granted an injunction to prevent further pollution discharges, which may have had the desired effect.[28]

Criminal law

The application of the criminal law to aquatic ecosystem protection is similarly indirect. Whilst principal criminal offences arise in relation to causing or knowingly permitting the entry of poisonous, noxious or pollution matter and the discharge of trade and sewage effluent into controlled waters,[29] the relationship between these offences and ecosystem damage is far from clear. Significantly, the offences are primarily formulated in terms of the manner of emission rather than the effects of the substance emitted upon the aquatic environment. Hence, it is an offence to cause the *entry* of polluting matter regardless of whether any actual pollution of the receiving waters is suffered as a consequence.[30] Beyond this, the offences are almost exclusively relevant to discrete pollution incidents, rather than gradual emissions of pollutants which may have a damaging cumulative effect upon the quality of receiving waters and their ecosystems. This feature finds an echo in the prosecution policy of the NRA, which focuses on prosecution of major pollution incidents rather than addressing by prosecutions the less dramatic, but at least equally damaging, cumulative effects of diffuse emissions of pollutants.[31]

Even where an extreme polluting incident is made the subject of criminal proceedings the value of such proceedings to the protection of aquatic ecosystems is limited. For example, in *National Rivers Authority* v. *Shell UK Ltd.*[32] an oil pipeline fractured, resulting in over 30,000 gallons of heavy crude oil being discharged into the Mersey estuary. The ensuing oil slick caused extensive damage to wildlife feeding areas. An estimated

---

[28] As an alternative to damages compensatory powers may arise under statute. Hence, where a person is convicted of a water pollution offence (under s.85 of the Water Resources Act 1991) the court may make an order for the polluter to pay compensation under s.35 of the Powers of Criminal Courts Act 1973. This provides that 'a court . . . before which a person is convicted of an offence . . . may, on application or otherwise make an order . . . requiring him to pay compensation for any personal injury, loss or damage resulting from that offence or any other offence which is taken into consideration'. Alternatively, any damage caused by pollution may be remedied by the NRA by the exercise of the power to carry out anti-pollution works and operations, and recover costs reasonably incurred from the polluter (under s.161 Water Resources Act 1991, see discussion below).

[29] S.85(1) and (3) Water Resources Act 1991, and see s.104 for the definition of 'controlled waters'.

[30] See *NRA* v. *Egger (UK) Ltd* [1992] Env. LR 130, discussed in W. Howarth, 'Poisonous, noxious or polluting: contrasting approaches to environmental regulation' [1993] *Modern Law Review* 171. See also *R* v. *Dovermoss Ltd* [1995] Env. LR 258.

[31] See NRA, *Water Pollution Incidents in England and Wales – 1993* (1994).

[32] [1990] *Water Law* 40.

200 to 300 birds were killed outright and 2,000 others seriously endangered by the after-effects of the oil.

Given the strict liability associated with the charge of causing polluting matter to enter a controlled water,[33] the company was obliged to plead guilty. After giving his 'careful attention to every aspect of this case', including the enormous financial resources of the company, the judge imposed a fine of £1million, noting that were it not for the previously good record of the company on conservation and protection of the local environment the fine imposed would have been 'substantially greater'. Although the amount of the fine is by a sizeable margin the greatest that has ever been awarded in a pollution incident from a land-based source,[34] nevertheless, fundamental questions are raised as to the environmental utility of imposing large fines for water pollution offences.

Whilst the amount paid by the company by way of the fine passed directly to the Exchequer, bringing no benefit to the damaged environment, it was recognized that the company had undertaken an expensive clean-up operation[35] and had established and funded an expert body to advise on the restoration of the area harmed by the incident. Arguably, these extra-judicial remedies brought far greater benefit to the affected ecosystem than the imposition of the fine.

Recovery of anti-pollution works and operations

In a more typical instance, where a company is not in a position to devote trained staff to clean-up operations, the powers of the NRA to undertake anti-pollution works and operations will be the first line of defence for the aquatic ecosystem. Where these powers are used, the NRA can recover reasonable costs incurred from a person who caused or knowingly permitted the incident.[36] The extent of these powers is, however, far from clear, though the recent case of *Bruton and the NRA* v. *Clarke* may provide useful guidance.[37] The case is notable also because, in the accompanying civil action brought for loss of amenity to an angling association, the

---

[33] Contrary to s.32 of the Control of Pollution Act 1974, now s.85(1) of the Water Resources Act 1991, see *Alphacell* v. *Woodward* [1972] 2 All ER 475.

[34] The second largest being a fine of £200,000 imposed on British Steel in the case of *NRA* v. *British Steel plc* (1991) 199 *ENDS Report* 37). The largest fine imposed for a water pollution offence in 1993 was £15,000 (see above note 31, p. 56)

[35] Costing it some £1.4million at the time of the hearing and subsequently estimated to have cost £6million, see T. Merrett, 'False economies in compliance with environmental legislation' [1993] *Water Law* 202. The court may, however, have taken into account this expenditure in determining the amount of the fine to be imposed.

[36] Under s.161 Water Resources Act 1991, and see W. Howarth, 'Making water polluters pay: England and Wales' [1994] *Environmental Liability* 29.

[37] [1994] *Water Law* 145, and see P. Carty, 'Lessons to be learnt', *Fish* (October 1994), 35.

judge did not equate damage with loss of biomass, taking adverse effects on diversity into account.

Although recompense may be required for works and operations for the purpose of restoring the waters, including any flora and fauna dependent upon the aquatic environment of the waters, to their state immediately before the polluting matter became present, this is subject to the proviso 'so far as it is reasonably practicable to do so'.[38] Whilst this provision is frequently used to recover the costs of restocking fisheries after pollution incidents, there is relatively little that can be done by the NRA in practice to restore flora and fauna in a damaged aquatic ecosystem to their former state. Fortunately, rivers have a remarkable capacity for self-restoration following pollution incidents, and populations of flora and fauna will, in time, be restored. But for species placed below fish in the aquatic food chain the legal power to embark upon restorative operations will be of limited practical utility.

Preventive and strategic approaches

Clearly, reactive legal provisions are of less value in protecting aquatic ecosystems than measures which could prevent damage occurring in the first place. Increasingly precautionary requirements upon the storage of polluting matter, and changes in land use, are being required to protect the aquatic environment.[39] Legislation has also recently been enacted implementing EU requirements on greening the Common Agricultural Policy.[40] The Habitat (Water Fringe) Regulations 1994, which apply only to England, provide payments for the management of land adjacent to certain designated watercourses or lakes where detailed conditions are complied with. Payments from MAFF of up to £360 per ha may be made for twenty-year management agreements over water fringe taken out of agricultural production, the scheme being presently targeted on river and lake SSSIs in six pilot areas.[41]

At a more strategic level, water quality objectives may be established for individual rivers. Under EU law, the 'competent authority' must ensure that water directive requirements are met in practice, placing the NRA under a legal duty to use its powers to ensure that, so far as practicable,

[38] S.161(1)(b) Water Resources Act 1991.

[39] Ibid.ss.92 to 95 and the Control of Pollution (Silage, Slurry and Agricultural Fuel Oil) Regulations 1991, SI 1991 No.324, the Nitrate Sensitive Areas (Designation) Order 1990, SI 1990 No.1187 and the Nitrate Sensitive Areas Regulations 1994, SI 1994 No.1729.

[40] Council Regulation 2078/92 (OJ L215/85, 30.7.92) on agricultural production methods compatible with the requirements of the protection of the environment and the maintenance of the countryside. And see Rodgers, below, Chapter 5, pp. 111–37.

[41] SI 1994 No.1291. See also the Habitat (Salt-marsh) Regulations 1994, SI 1994 No.1293.

water quality objectives are met and maintained. The Water Resources Act 1991 provides for a strategy of setting statutory water quality objectives, according to statutory water classification systems, and obliges the NRA to ensure that they are met in practice.[42] A number of national water quality classification systems have since been devised which serve to implement European standards into domestic law.[43] Although no specific statutory water quality objectives have so far been established, there are indications that the commencement of this process is imminent.

The setting of statutory water quality standards for particular waters provides an important mechanism for the incorporating into law of conservation objectives in relation to water quality.[44] As yet, however, plans by the NRA to incorporate biological assessment into water classification regulations[45] have been rejected by government on the grounds, first, that for simplicity, standards should be measurable in accordance with objective parameters for each class, and second, that an appropriate working methodology has not yet been formulated.[46] Opposition also came from the nature-conservation agencies on the ground that biological assessments would not sufficiently identify the offending substances.[47] The recently enacted Surface Water (River Ecosystem) (Classification) Regulations 1994 omit any reference to biological parameters.[48]

Recently, however, the European Commission has committed itself to maintaining a high standard of ecological quality of surface freshwaters with a biodiversity corresponding as closely as possible to the unperturbed state of particular waters,[49] and a draft directive to this end has recently been published. The draft directive marks a notable change in policy in relation to EU water law. With increasing emphasis on translating the subsidiarity principle into practice, it focuses on procedural requirements rather than substantive obligations in relation to maintaining and

[42] Ss.82 to 84.

[43] See Surface Waters (Classification) Regulations 1989, SI 1989 No.1148, the Surface Waters (Dangerous Substances) (Classification) Regulations 1989, SI 1989 No.2286, and the Bathing Waters (Classification) Regulations 1991, SI 1991, No.1597.

[44] S.84(2) Water Resources Act 1991. However, the NRA's general duty to monitor the extent of pollution of controlled waters makes no reference to any power to undertake *biological* monitoring of waters. This contrasts with the special functions of the nature conservancy councils, discharged through the Joint Nature Conservation Committee, which include the establishment of common standards throughout Britain for the monitoring of nature conservation (s.133(2)(d) Environmental Protection Act 1990).

[45] NRA, *Proposals for Statutory Water Quality Objectives* (1991), and *Recommendations for a Scheme of Water Quality Classification for Setting Statutory Water Quality Objectives* (1992).

[46] Department of the Environment, *River Quality* (1992).

[47] Heaton, op. cit., 309.

[48] SI 1994 No.1057. See [1994] *Water Law* 114.

[49] European Commission, *Towards Sustainability* (5th Action Programme on the Environment) (1992) 23 Com(92) final Vol. II, 50.

improving the ecological quality of EU waters. This marks a significant contrast to previous water directives, which have traditionally stipulated that substantive water quality goals must be achieved.[50]

To summarize this section on water quality, it is evident that aquatic ecosystem protection is only a secondary or incidental feature of the civil or criminal law. Historically, the explanation for this may be that the importance of aquatic flora and fauna other than fish have been regarded as of little legal importance or it may have been assumed that if water was not polluted then the aquatic ecosystem was necessarily in good order. As greater knowledge is gained, however, it is evident that these views are tenuous, and the law needs to take greater account of the living constituents of water if serious loss of biodiversity is not to be occasioned.

A final example draws further attention to the difficulties. The British Isles provide the habitat for a number of endangered species of freshwater fish.[51] Llyn Padarn in north Wales is the home of the wild char, one of the rarest of these species. However, the species is presently threatened by changes in the ecological quality of the water due to an accumulation of phosphates deriving from a sewage treatment works discharging into the lake. Phosphate emissions may cause eutrophication as nutrient levels in the lake increase and the habitat becomes less suitable for a species that has inhabited it for thousands of years.

The legal response to this situation is likely to be a civil action brought by the Anglers' Conservation Association, but the outcome of that action is difficult to predict. Given the need to show 'sensible alteration' in water quality for liability to be established there may be difficulties where it is essentially the changes to the ecosystem that are the basis of the complaint. Moreover, it is not apparent that the discharges of phosphate are in breach of the discharge consent granted to the operators of the sewage treatment works, Welsh Water. Consequently, criminal proceedings would not be appropriate.[52] Despite the legal difficulties, however, the acute ecological problem remains. The situation graphically illustrates the traditional divide between pollution regulation and nature conservation, and demonstrates how conservation objectives are poorly served by a body of law which has significantly different objectives.[53]

[50] OJ L 1994 C222/1. See [1994] *Water Law* 172.

[51] Nature Conservancy Council, *The Conservation of Rare Freshwater Fish* (1991).

[52] Unlike some other jurisdictions, s.100 of the Water Resources Act 1991 provides that actions in civil law for water pollution are not frustrated by compliance with administrative requirements.

[53] See 'When water gets too rich', *ACA Review* (Summer 1994), 8; also 'Survey reveals threat to rare fish', *Water Guardians* (Newspaper of the NRA), (February/March 1994), 2, and see *Hughes* v. *Dwr Cymru* [1995] *ENDS Report* 247, 42.

Water Resource Problems

Alongside water-quality needs, an essential requirement for any aquatic ecosystem must be the supply of a quantity of water compatible with the maintenance of a variety of habitats needed for the survival of diverse species. Whilst reduced flow may initially reduce the dilution of effluent discharged into a watercourse and produce stagnation, further reduction in flow will result in serious ecological harm. In the most extreme cases, over-abstraction has resulted in the total dehydration of surface flow in previously healthy streams.

The NRA report, *Low Flows and Water Resources*, catalogues the extreme concerns about some forty locations in England and Wales where rivers have been identified as suffering from severe over-abstraction and measures are urgently needed to alleviate the problems. The report sets firm target dates for the implementation of improvement programmes and publicly reporting progress.[54] Nevertheless, the problem of low flows represents a serious challenge for the protection of aquatic ecosystems, and the initial identification of seriously depleted watercourses, as a priority for action, may represent only the tip of the iceberg. Despite exacerbation of the problems of low flows over recent years due to a series of consecutive dry summers, the NRA is decisive in identifying the major cause of the problem as excessive authorized abstraction of water, frequently from underground sources, rather than the result of drought conditions.

Typically, abstraction involves the removal of groundwater for water-supply purposes, resulting in groundwater seepage into surface waters being reduced or halted in some instances. Most of these abstractions have been authorized under licences granted under previous legislation which allowed existing abstractors the right to a licence regardless of the environmental consequences. Although the NRA can reduce or totally revoke existing abstraction licences, significant compensation payments may be required.[55] Alternatively, various technical measures can be used to surmount the problem. At one site in Norfolk, for example, boreholes were relocated where a wetland site and National Nature Reserve were in danger of drying out to the detriment of the great raft spider.[56] Each strategy for flow improvement has its costs and limitations, though a combination of measures may offer the most cost-effective and environmentally acceptable solution in a particular situation. The significance of cost-benefits is, however, a critical issue in determining the viability of any proposed solution, since any significant expenditure by the NRA

---

[54] NRA, *Low Flows and Water Resources* (1993), 63.
[55] See discussion of variation of abstraction licences below.
[56] 'Fen protection', *Water Guardians* (October/November 1994), 5.

in alleviating a low-flow problem will be subject to the approval of the Department of the Environment and the Treasury.[57]

Civil law controls

As a matter of theory, it has been noted that riparian landowners are entitled to the flow of the stream in its 'natural' state without sensible diminution of quantity.[58] However, the difficulties of proving sensible diminution, and that this results from an identifiable abstraction, make this principle of limited practical value. Only specific property rights are offered protection. Again, the protection of the aquatic ecosystem is, at best, a secondary consideration. Moreover, the likelihood is that any offending abstraction that is identified will be undertaken under and in accordance with an abstraction licence granted by the NRA and therefore be immune from civil action unless for negligence or breach of contract.[59] The scope for a civil action to prevent damage to an aquatic ecosystem through depletion of water flow is, therefore, extremely limited.[60]

Regulatory controls

Given these limitations, the regulatory role of the NRA in exercising its water resource function[61] is of paramount importance. Subject to its environmental duties, Part II of the Water Resources Act 1991 provides for a range of general and specific powers and duties in relation to general management of water resources, abstraction and impounding, and drought measures.

At a strategic level, in accordance with directions from the Secretary of State, the NRA must take necessary or expedient action for the purpose of conserving, redistributing or otherwise augmenting water resources and securing the proper use of those resources.[62] For these purposes, and so far as reasonably practicable, the NRA is to enter into arrangements with water undertakers for securing the proper management of waters which are available to be used by the undertakers for water supply purposes.[63] At the more specific level, it is a criminal offence to abstract water from any source of supply, or to cause another person to do so, except under and in accordance with an abstraction licence.[64] Whilst issues may arise as to what

[57] Above note 54, pp.1–2.
[58] Above note 25.
[59] S.48(2) and (4) Water Resources Act 1991.
[60] Generally see S. Jackson, 'Joe Public and dried up rivers' [1992] *Water Law* 153.
[61] Under s.2(1)(a) and Part II Water Resources Act 1991.
[62] Ibid. s.19(1).
[63] Ibid. s.20(1).
[64] Ibid. s.24(1) and see s.221(1) on the meaning of 'source of supply'.

precisely is to count as an 'abstraction' of water,[65] the criminalization of unlicensed abstraction of anything more than insignificant quantities of water [66] is clearly an important water resource management mechanism.

Minimum acceptable flows

'If it thinks it appropriate', and following consultation, the NRA may submit to the Secretary of State a statement providing for the determination of a *minimum acceptable flow* (MAF) for particular waters and detailing the manner in which that flow is to be measured.[67] In addition to the views of consultees, the NRA must have regard to stated matters including the flow of water from time to time, the character of the waters and their surroundings in the light of its environmental duties and any statutory water quality objectives which may be affected by the flow of water in question.[68] Regard is also to be had to the need to safeguard public health, for meeting the requirements of existing lawful users of the waters for agriculture, industry, water supply or other purposes and the requirements of navigation, fisheries and land drainage.[69]

The establishment of MAFs for watercourses appears a useful legal mechanism to combat problems of low flows. However, the discretionary power of the NRA to define MAFs has never been exercised, and the Secretary of State has never used his power to direct the NRA to determine an MAF for any waters.[70] It is apparent, though, that the NRA is in the process of developing a policy for river minimum flow objectives which should be complete by 1995.[71]

Despite the absence of defined MAFs, account must nevertheless be taken of such flows in the process of abstraction licensing by the NRA. In determining licence applications, the NRA must have regard to existing abstraction rights and take account of river flows. Where no MAF has been determined for the waters that may be affected by the abstraction, the NRA is bound to have regard to the considerations by reference to which an MAF for the waters would fall to be determined.[72] In effect, therefore, the concept of minimum acceptable flow is applied to new abstraction licences though, perhaps, without the degree of formality that was originally envisaged.

[65] See *British Waterways Board* v. *NRA* [1992] *Water Law* 165.
[66] See s.27(1) Water Resources Act 1991.
[67] Ibid. s.21(1),(2) and (3) and see s.23 in relation to the volume of inland waters.
[68] Ibid. s.21(4).
[69] Ibid. s.21(5).
[70] Under ibid. s.22(1).
[71] NRA, *1993/4 Corporate Plan* (1994).
[72] S.40(2) Water Resources Act 1991.

Variation of licences to abstract

Whilst the importance of securing an MAF is recognized where a new
abstraction licence is sought, this may be of little assistance where a
problem arises through the continuing effects of licensed abstraction. Although
specific provision is made for modification of licences on the application
to the Secretary of State by an owner for fishing rights in the water
concerned,[73] there are difficulties in registering such an application, since
the fishery owner must show that loss or damage directly attributable to
the abstraction of water has been sustained.[74] Presumably, this means
identifiable damage to the actual fishery must be shown rather than to
the general aquatic ecosystem which supports it. Thereafter, the fishery
owner must also establish that the damage sustained is not attributable to
exceptional shortage of rain, or to an accident or other unforeseen act or
event outside the control of the NRA.[75] It would seem, therefore, that
fishery owners may encounter significant difficulties in making use of
their powers in respect of modification of abstraction licences.

More hopefully, the NRA may itself commence proceedings for the
modification of an abstraction licence to be determined by the Secretary
of State where it has been found to authorize excessive levels of abstraction
with consequent harm to an aquatic ecosystem. The NRA may formulate
proposals to revoke or vary an abstraction licence, or it may be directed
by the Secretary of State to formulate such proposals.[76] Curiously, although
the procedures which must accompany a modification of an abstraction
licence are provided for in some detail, the substantive basis upon which
such a proposal may be formulated is not explicitly specified. They must
therefore be referable only to the more general duties upon the NRA in
relation to the environment and fisheries management.

The major practical difficulty here is the need to pay compensation to
the licence holder. Where a licence is revoked or varied and it is shown
that the holder has incurred expenditure in carrying out work which is
rendered abortive, or has otherwise sustained consequent loss or damage,
the NRA must pay compensation for the loss incurred.[77] Any question of
disputed compensation is to be determined by the Lands Tribunal in accordance with the Land Compensation Act 1961.[78]

The Secretary of State may indemnify the NRA in respect of compensation payable for the revocation or variation of an abstraction licence.[79]

---

[73] Ibid. s.55, and see s.62 concerning compensation for damage to a fishery.
[74] Ibid. s.55(3).
[75] Ibid. s.56(4)
[76] Ibid. ss.52 and 53.
[77] Ibid. s.61(1).
[78] Ibid. s.61(5).
[79] Ibid. s.63(2)(c).

Notably, however, there is no *duty* to do so. Thus, proceedings for modification of an abstraction licence are unlikely to be entertained by the NRA
without an assurance that indemnification will eventually be forthcom-
ing. Control over the NRA's purse-strings means that it is the Department of the Environment that has the ultimate say in determining the
pace at which low-flow problems may be tackled where this involves
modification of abstraction licences and compensation payments. However,
the Thames region of the NRA in particular has revoked a number of
licences of protected rights to abstract with compensation,[80] though it is
notable that the summary of that region's future water resource strategy
makes no mention of this policy option.[81]

Water resources and the water industry

In exercising any of its powers, the NRA must have particular regard to
the duties imposed on water and sewerage undertakers under Parts II to
IV of the Water Industry Act 1991 where these duties upon undertakers
are likely to be affected by the exercise of the power.[82] Given the duty
upon water undertakers to develop and maintain an efficient and economi-
cal system of water supply within their areas and provide supplies to
persons who demand them,[83] this must be a consideration of which the
NRA must take account in determining a course of action in relation to a
low-flow problem. Precisely how this duty is to be reconciled with the
competing demands of the conflicting conservation duties upon the NRA,
however, is a matter on which there is no clear guidance.

Low-flow works programmes and policy options

Following extensive concern about low-flow watercourses it appears
that many of the most serious problems that have been identified are
now being actively tackled by the NRA by extensive work programmes.
In particular, the government has given the go-ahead for a scheme to
restore flows to the River Darent in north-west Kent, one of the
watercourses most seriously affected during the droughts of the late
1980s. The approved plans for the Darent include building artificial
springs, while reducing the volumes abstracted for water supply from
boreholes near the river and measures for enhancing the water

[80] Heaton, op. cit., 313.
[81] See NRA, *Future Water Resources in the Thames Region: A Strategy for Sustainable Management*, Summary Document (1994).
[82] S.15(1) Water Resources Act 1991.
[83] Under s.37(1) Water Industry Act 1991.

environment as a whole. It is hoped that target flows for the river will be achieved by 1996.[84]

The problem of low flows is part of the broader collection of issues of appropriate water resource management addressed in the NRA's recently published policy document on the subject, *Water: Nature's Precious Resource*, which indicates the mechanisms by which increasing water demands in England and Wales will be met in the years ahead. Significantly, the NRA stresses the need for sustainable management of water resources so that there is no long-term deterioration of the water environment attributable to the overuse of water resources; the precautionary principle should be applied where the water resource management decisions need to be taken on the basis of incomplete information about their environmental consequences; and demand management measures, such as the reduction of wastage, should be adopted in preference to the development of large-scale water resource schemes. In particular, concerns are expressed about the ecological effects of augmenting water resources by inter-river basin transfers (for example, by transfer of water of differing chemical composition) and the need for preservation of 'natural' river systems.[85]

In summary, therefore, future discrete demands on water use appear satisfactorily provided for in law. When formally introduced, MAFs should allow ecosystem conservation to be taken fully into account in determining applications for new licences. In the mean time, the duty to take minimum flow into account in granting new licences already allows for conservation factors to be taken into consideration in the licensing process, though duties in relation to water supply need also to be weighed. In general, however, the legal position with regard to watercourse depletion is seriously deficient. Existing licensed abstractions are relatively well insulated from the operation of the civil law, and, because of the costs involved, from substantial modification or revocation. Improvements to conservation, therefore, are likely to focus on demand management and efficiency savings, so long as these remain the most effective in cost-benefit terms.

Flood Defence and Land Drainage

Action taken by private individuals has, since the earliest times, been the first resort in protecting land from flooding, and remains of great importance in relation to present-day land drainage activities. However, it has long

[84] 'Darent action plan given go-ahead', *Water Guardians* (February/March 1994), 5, and see NRA, *River Darent Catchment Management Plan Consultation Report* (1994).

[85] NRA, *Water: Nature's Precious Resource* (1994), 79. See also Department of the Environment, *Using Water Wisely* (1992); *NRA Water Resources Strategy* (1993); and J. Rees and S. Williams, *Water for Life: Strategies for Sustainable Water Resource Management* (Council for the Protection of Rural England, 1993).

been recognized that drainage and flood defence operations may benefit a more extensive area of land than that on which they are conducted. For that reason, public bodies with general responsibilities for flood prevention and coastal defences have a long history.[86]

The traditional purposes of land drainage and flood defence have been the protection of land or its 'improvement' for agriculture. However, there is a high correlation between river corridors and existing environmental designations, and especially SSSIs, and a relatively recent concern has been that drainage activities should be conducted with proper concern for aquatic flora and fauna. To this end, land drainage operations are now subject to environmental duties under the relevant legislation.[87]

In practice, however, assimilating conservation objectives into land drainage operations has not been without difficulty. For years the importance of maximizing the speed at which surface water is directed from land where flooding is perceived to be a hazard has been emphasized. The engineer's response to this has been to utilize the hydrologically optimum mechanisms for containment of watercourses by accelerating water flow in areas vulnerable to flooding. That is, they have responded to a supposed need to conduit natural watercourses or to construct hydrologically designed 'canals' which maximize the rate of flow whilst neglecting the differing needs of aquatic ecosystems. The demands of hydrological efficiency and aquatic ecosystem conservation have been perceived to be in direct conflict, and the results of engineering endeavours condemned for the loss of habitats they have caused through dehydration of wetlands, depletion of groundwater and unnatural acceleration of flow to the extent that, in some instances, it may actually serve merely to transfer a flooding problem from one location to another further downstream.

Regulatory responsibilities

The legal structure designed to reconcile the competing demands of hydrologically efficient land drainage with adequate provision for the protection of aquatic ecosystems is a relatively complex collage of administrative jurisdictions and powers reflecting the combination of national and local, coastal and inland, rural and urban and agricultural, industrial and residential interests involved.

In outline, the Ministry of Agriculture, Fisheries and Food is centrally responsible for determining national flood defence policy and in providing grant-in-aid for major flood defence works where these are approved in accordance with national technical, economic and environmental criteria. Although ultimately sponsored by the Department of the Environment,

[86] W. Howarth, *Wisdom's Law of Watercourses* (1992), 59 and ch.12 generally.
[87] Part IV Water Resources Act 1991 and Land Drainage Act 1991.

the NRA must exercise general supervision over all matters relating to flood defence and carry out surveys for this purpose,[88] but it is bound to delegate all its land drainage functions, except the imposition of levies and charges and the exercise of borrowing powers, to Regional Flood Defence Committees.[89] These may, in turn, delegate functions to Local Flood Defence Committees and Internal Drainage Boards having duties to exercise general supervision over all matters relating to the drainage of land within their district.[90] Local authorities also have powers to undertake works on certain watercourses, under the supervision of the NRA,[91] and exercise important powers under planning law in relation to development planning and development control in respect of flood defence projects.[92]

Beyond the duties to exercise general supervision over flood defence matters, a distinctive feature of this area of law is the evident lack of mandatory legal duties. Whilst a range of statutory drainage bodies can undertake various kinds of drainage works, almost invariably *powers* rather than duties to act are provided for. The underlying reality is that the exercise of these powers will be subject to broader policy considerations including, crucially, the availability of funding to undertaken priority projects.

Another key feature of land drainage law is the distinction which is drawn between major watercourses, termed 'main rivers', and minor watercourses, termed 'ordinary watercourses', as these terms are applied by the Secretary of State in definitive main river maps.[93] Key drainage functions are exercised by the NRA, primarily, in relation to designated main rivers, and by Internal Drainage Boards and local authorities in relation to ordinary watercourses and land which will derive benefit or avoid danger as a result of drainage operations on such watercourses. Respectively, the drainage bodies may maintain and improve existing works and construct new works, as these powers are specifically elucidated.[94]

Alongside the operational powers of drainage bodies, important powers exist to regulate the activities of others which may impact upon the drainage of watercourses or land. Hence, the consent of the appropriate drainage body is required for the erection of a structure in, over or under a watercourse, for the carrying out of work of alteration or repair on such a structure if the work is likely to affect the flow of water in the

---

[88] S.105(1) and (2) Water Resources Act 1991.

[89] Ibid. s.106.

[90] S.1 Land Drainage Act 1991.

[91] Ibid. ss.14 and 17.

[92] Under the Town and Country Planning Act 1990, see below.

[93] Provided for under ss.113 and 192 Water Resources Act 1991.

[94] S.165(1) Water Resources Act 1991 and s.14(2) Land Drainage Act 1991.

watercourse or to impede drainage work, or for the erection of a structure to contain or divert floodwaters.[95]

Conservation duties and land drainage practice

The combination of extensive permissive powers allowing drainage bodies to undertaken drainage work, and the regulatory powers over the activities of others which may impact upon land drainage, provides a relatively open-ended legal mechanism by which very generally stated objectives may be accomplished. As regards the conservation of aquatic ecosystems, however, and the situations in which this may override purely hydrological considerations, it may be noted that the flood defence function of the NRA must be exercised in accordance with its statutory duty to promote conservation and its general environmental duty.[96] Similarly, Internal Drainage Boards and local authorities are subject to a corresponding general environmental duty in formulating any proposal for a land drainage activity.[97]

The difficulty, however, lies in the translation of these generally worded obligations, discussed previously, into specific land drainage policies and applying them to the details of particular drainage projects. For example, how much of a change in land drainage practice will be required for adherence to these obligations and the utilization of more ecosystem-friendly drainage operations? Some guidance may be found in the *Code of Practice on Conservation, Access and Recreation*, referred to previously, which specifically lists an extensive number of 'practices helpful to nature conservation' such as tree retention and the avoidance of canalization.[98]

More recently, however, the Land Drainage Act 1994 has provided further elucidation of land drainage responsibilities. Following consultation with bodies including the NRA, English Nature and the Countryside Council for Wales, the Minister has been empowered to approve a code of practice relating to the powers of local authorities and Internal Drainage Boards.[99] Where, for example, code procedures are not complied with, the Minister may now also issue appropriate directions.[100] An assurance was given that directions would only be given on the advice of the relevant nature conservation agency and other bodies.

[95] S.109(1) to (3) Water Resources Act 1991, and similarly see s.23(1) Land Drainage Act 1991.
[96] See above notes 9 and 10, though under s.105(3) Water Resources Act 1991 the NRA must exercise its powers under Part IV with due regard to the interests of fisheries.
[97] S.61A and B Land Drainage Act 1991 (inserted by s.1 Land Drainage Act 1994).
[98] See S.18(1) Water Resources Act 1991, above n.14.
[99] S.61E Land Drainage Act 1991.
[100] S.61D Land Drainage Act 1991.

In enacting the 1994 Act, the government emphasized that the Act largely formalized existing good practice, and some evidence of conservationally sympathetic practice in action was already in evidence. In particular, drainage bodies have adopted a major shift of policy in relation to applications for authorization for culverting of watercourses.[101] The NRA now resists the culverting of watercourses for both hydraulic and environmental reasons since it is recognized that culverting is in direct conflict with the conservation and enhancement of watercourses.[102] More broadly, it appears that securing sustainable management of river wildlife corridors must be realized by the exercise of powers beyond those relating to water quality and quantity. The need for integrated catchment planning must be met through the conservation of catchment rainfall to sustain local wildlife and stream base flows through maintaining groundwater recharge, managing surface water run-off and protecting river morphology.[103]

A striking example of flood-defence work being carried out with conservation gain may be seen in the vicinity of the Wildfowl and Wetlands Trust site at Slimbridge. There, the spoil needed to enhance embankments was taken from the internationally renowned bird reserve, creating new habitat in the process. Additional attention was paid to the creation of landscape features favourable to birdlife.[104] In Norfolk, the Natterjack toad, one of Britain's most threatened species, has also benefited from sea-defence measures through the creation of ponds for breeding.[105] Both examples illustrate the ecosystem benefits that may be gained from conservationally constructive land drainage and flood defence work. However, it is suggested that more fundamental questions need to be asked of the regulatory regime surrounding the exercise of the NRA's operational flood-defence responsibilities, which account for around one half of the total expenditure of the NRA. This issue is taken up in more detail in the concluding discussion.[106]

Species Introductions

One of the tragedies of the signal crayfish saga referred to at the start of this chapter was that the threat to native species was recognized at the

[101] Required under s.109 Water Resources Act 1991, s.23(1) Land Drainage Act 1991 or s.263 Public Health Act 1936.

[102] Institution of Civil Engineers, *Land Drainage and Flood Defence Responsibilities* (1993), 67.

[103] See papers by J. L. Gardiner and J. D. Banks delivered at the Hydro Research and Development Conference, *CONFLOW 92 Integrated Catchment Planning and Source Control*, Oxford 1 to 2 June 1992, and Ward, Holmes and Jose, *The New Rivers and Wildlife Handbook* (1994).

[104] 'Flood work brings benefits all round', *Water Guardians* (February/March 1994), 3.

[105] 'Toads thriving again', *Water Guardians* (July/August 1993), 12.

[106] See also the discussion of planning below.

time of the first introductions.[107] However, the importation of such species could not be prevented, since the power to control imports did not extend to shellfish.[108] Since then, legislation has been passed which has sought to close this legal loophole, which may be applicable even within the context of the Single European Market.

Species introductions need to be carefully regulated if destruction to existing ecosystems, through the spread of disease (affecting either fish or other aquatic organisms) or ecological disruption, is to be avoided. As noted above, disease may be spread not merely through direct contact but also indirectly through, for example, parasites or water used in transfers. Disease control measures may therefore extend beyond merely controlling the movement of the introduced species, although this alone may be problematic.

Ecological damage may arise through disruption to the existing species balance of the ecosystem. Population growth of the introduced species may result in habitat competition, degradation or predation. Alternatively, the introduced species may create an imbalance in the existing dynamic equilibrium between predator and prey species. In Loch Lomond, for example, serious damage to native fish populations has been caused by the introduction of a non-native species of ruffe.[109] The potentially catastrophic effects of even deliberate introductions are dramatically illustrated by the extinction of more than 200 distinct species of fish in Lake Victoria following the introduction there of the Nile Perch as a source of food.[110]

The introduction of non-indigenous species or stock may also have a damaging effect on the genetic integrity of indigenous populations.[111] Less damaging in the longer term, but still a nuisance, is the frequent escape of farmed fish and the disruption this may cause to angling interests. In one recent case, for example, an angling club succeeded in an action for damages for loss of amenity following an escape of farmed rainbow trout into a brown trout fishery.[112]

---

[107] Representations had been made to MAFF by the (then) Nature Conservancy Council since 1977. See evidence of P. J. Boon (NCC) to the Agriculture Select Committee, *Fish Farming in the UK*, Fourth Report of the Agriculture Committee, Session 1989–90, HC 141-ll, p.118.

[108] See ss.1(2) and 10(1) Diseases of Fish Act 1937. Such powers were in any event exercisable only in respect of disease control, and would not have been appropriate to control adverse ecological interactions more generally.

[109] P. S. Maitland and K. East, 'An increase in the numbers of ruffe (*Gymnocephalaus cernau* (L.)) in a Scottish loch from 1982 to 1987', *Aquaculture and Fisheries Management*, 20 (1989), 227–8.

[110] *New Scientist*, 6 March 1986, p.24.

[111] See, for example, O. Skaala, G. Dahle, K. E. Jørstad and G. Nævdal, 'Interactions between natural and farmed fish populations: information from genetic markers', *Journal of Fish Biology*, 36 (1990), 449–60.

[112] *Brodrick and Brown* v. *Gale and Ainslie Ltd.* [1993] *Water Law* 127.

The Wildlife and Countryside Act 1981

Under the EU Habitat and Species Directive,[113] Member States must ensure that deliberate introductions to the wild of non-native species are regulated so as not to prejudice natural habitats or native fauna or flora.[114] In the UK, s.14 of the Wildlife and Countryside Act 1981 implements this obligation by prohibiting the release or escape into the wild of any animal of a kind not ordinarily resident in or not a regular visitor to Great Britain in a wild state, or any animal specifically listed.[115] Listing allows for restrictions on alien species, such as the signal and other non-native species of crayfish, already established in the wild. Licences are granted by the Secretary of State, or the relevant agriculture minister in relation to fish and shellfish introductions,[116] on the advice of English Nature or the CCW as appropriate. These bodies must also be consulted from time to time by the relevant minister as to the exercise of his functions.[117]

However, the extent to which 'animal of a kind' in this context differs from species, and what constitutes the 'release' of fish into the 'wild', has yet to be established.[118] For example, is a large ornamental lake, possibly several hectares in area, 'the wild'? In one recent case, for example, action following the unlicensed introduction of non-native landlocked salmon (*Salmo salar* Sebago) into a lake in Wales was not pursued, in part because of the uncertainty in establishing that the fish was not of a 'kind' ordinarily resident in the UK.[119]

Importantly, it is unclear whether accidental introductions are rendered unlawful by the prohibition on introductions, and what obligations exist to ensure that captive non-native species do not escape from possession. However, since the health status of the released species is irrelevant to the commission of the offence, it is clear that the rationale behind the offence is primarily ecological.

---

[113] Council directive on the conservation of natural habitats and of fauna and flora (92/43/EEC, OJ L206/7, 22.7.92). And see generally Ball, below, Chapter 4, pp. 89–110.

[114] Ibid. article 22.

[115] Under Part 1 of sched. 9.

[116] Ibid. s.16(4) and (9).

[117] Ibid. s.10.

[118] W. Howarth, 'Regulating the introduction of freshwater fish: the United Kingdom, the European Community, and beyond', *International Council for the Exploration of the Sea, Marine Science Symposium*, 194 (1992), 21–30. In light of article 2 of the Convention on Biological Diversity (see note 4 above) it is suggested that 'kind' should be given a more restrictive meaning.

[119] *Glas y Dorlan* (Journal of the Welsh Region of the NRA), 18 (Spring 1994), 16. Policy guidance has subsequently been issued by MAFF and English Nature on such introductions (*Trout News*, 18 (1994), 12).

Import of live fish and the Single European Market

The Import of Live Fish (England and Wales) Act 1980 permits the appropriate minister, by order, to forbid either absolutely or under a licence, the import into, or the keeping or the release in any part of Great Britain of live fish, including shellfish, or the live eggs of certain species of fish. The Act, and its Scottish equivalent,[120] was introduced following concerns that, whilst the importation of salmon eggs required a permit from the Secretary of State for Scotland under s.1(3) Diseases of Fish Act 1937, no legal powers existed to prevent the movement of the progeny of the imported eggs, which might have a negative impact on native stocks either through the transmission of disease, competition, predation or genetic integration.[121] The species to which the Act is directed are therefore those which in the opinion of the Minister might compete with, displace, prey on or harm the habitat of any freshwater fish, shellfish or salmon in Great Britain.[122] The licensing power is subject to a prior consultation provision, specifying that English Nature and the CCW and any other person considered appropriate must be consulted.[123]

The enabling power under the 1980 Act has never been exercised due to the creation of overlapping provisions in s.14 of the Wildlife and Countryside Act 1981.[124] Moreover, its use is now subject to the broader obligations imposed by the Single European Market, under which movement of fish and fish products into and within the EU is now regulated.[125]

Despite some initial concerns to the contrary, it now seems to be accepted in law that the new regime should not operate so as unduly to curtail the powers of the NRA and other conservation agencies to conserve native stocks, though this must be achieved within the wider framework of the extent to which any restriction of the fundamental trading freedoms of the EU may be imposed on environmental protection grounds. In a recent case concerning an import ban on live

---

[120] See below note 124.

[121] See W. Howarth, *The Law of Aquaculture* (1990), 77–80.

[122] S.1(1) Import of Live Fish (England and Wales) Act 1980.

[123] Although the NRA is not expressly included, an assurance was given that the government would 'seek advice from the widest possible range of interests, including fishing and fish farming interests' (407 HL Deb 1980 col.1230).

[124] Orders have been made under the equivalent Scottish legislation, the Import of Live Fish (Scotland) Act 1978. See the Import of Live Fish (Coho Salmon) (Prohibition) (Scotland) Order 1980 (SI 1980 No.376) and the Prohibition of the Keeping or the Release of Live Fish (Pikeperch) (Scotland) Order 1993 (SI 1993 No.1288).

[125] See Council Directive 91/67/EEC concerning the placing on the market of aquaculture animals and products (OJ L46/1, 19.2.91); Fish Health Regulations 1992 (SI 1992 No.3300) as amended; Shellfish and Specified Fish (Third Country Imports) Order 1992 (SI 1992 No.3301).

European crayfish into Germany, the ECJ affirmed that such restrictions, while permissible, had also to be proportionate and not unduly restrictive of intra-Union trade.[126] Though movement controls for disease-control purposes are now governed by Directive 91/56, this decision provides useful guidance about the use of the 1980 Act to protect native crayfish populations against non-indigenous species.[127] An Action Plan for Crayfish Conservation, drawn up by the Joint Nature Conservation Committee, proposes that the keeping of all species of non-native freshwater crayfish in the UK be regulated, and in particular that 'no-go' areas be recognized where the keeping of such species will be subject to licensing. It is recommended that regulations cover not only crayfish farms but also such places as pet shops, restaurants and aquaria, and the associated trade in crayfish.

Internal fish transfers

Prior to more general restrictions on species introductions being formulated, national fishery legislation provided for the possibility for restricting fish introductions in order to protect fisheries, in addition to long-standing provisions regulating close seasons, unlawful instruments, and other matters designed to ensure productive commercial and recreational fisheries.[128] However, the focus of such provisions has largely been the protection of fisheries, hence determinations will be made in accordance with the fishery duty of the NRA rather than the conservation duty.

Section 30 of the Salmon and Freshwater Fisheries Act 1975[129] makes it an offence, except as regards fish farms, to introduce any fish or spawn of fish into an inland water of England and Wales without the written consent of the NRA. Although the exemption for fish farms does not extend to shellfish farms, it appears to be the practice of the NRA not to insist on consents for the introduction of crayfish.[130] In theory, the power to restrict internal fish transfers is a broad one, imposing on the NRA the duty to give consent for all introductions which might impact on the

---

[126] Articles 30 and 100a(4), Treaty of Rome; *Procureur du Roi* v. *Dassonville* [1974] ECR 837; *Commission* v. *Germany* [1995] CMLR 278.

[127] See M. Palmer, 'Action plan for the conservation of the native freshwater crayfish *Austropotamobious pallipes* in the United Kingdom', JNCC Report No. 193 (1994).

[128] Prior to 1975, this was provided for through fishery by-laws.

[129] As amended by s.34 Salmon Act 1986.

[130] See W. Howarth and D. McGillivray, *The Regulation of Fish Farming by the National Rivers Authority* (NRA, 1994) (in draft). Moreover, it seems that it is farms where such shellfish are kept with a view to sale or transfer, rather than shellfish movements *per se*, to which the fish movement exemption does not extend. Those farms where both crayfish and finfish are kept or reared may, in theory, be subject to the imposition of movement restrictions in respect of all movements to such farms.

conservation of native stocks. However, a number of practical and legal difficulties may be identified.

For example, the NRA does not possess the resources to check every consignment of fish before introduction. Usually, it must rely on issuing general consents to reputable stockists, backed by periodic screening for disease. The scope for such a system to be abused was well illustrated in one recent criminal conviction where three concurrent nine-month sentences were imposed for the fraudulent passing off of fish as having valid consents and thus as being free of disease.[131]

Concerns also relate to the breadth of the exemption from the consent requirement given to fish farms. Despite the updating by MAFF of the register of fish farms,[132] some transfer stations for fish for angling purposes are still alleged to be taking unintended benefit from designation as 'fish farms'. In any event, the inadequacy of the register as regards geographical limits of sites, and the delay in providing regions of the NRA with this information, have also been criticized. The difficulties in trying to enforce s.30, without knowledge as to the precise boundaries of 'fish farms', should be readily apparent. As with s.14 of the Wildlife and Countryside Act 1981, s.30 is limited to deliberate acts of introduction rather than accidental escapes.[133]

Introductions and administrative divisions of responsibility

Aside from practical considerations, it is clear that the division of responsibilities between MAFF and the NRA may be subject to criticism, not least because of the impossibility of separating the farmed from the wild aquatic environment in the way that the legal provisions appear to envisage. This is manifested by a lack of openness, in part a consequence of provisions relating to commercial confidentiality, between MAFF, whose primary responsibility is to producers, and the NRA, which has much broader responsibilities. Moreover, it might be questioned why MAFF should exercise licensing powers over introductions of fish and shellfish, but not other species reared for agricultural purposes.

More generally, it is increasingly incongruous that freshwater fisheries should still be segregated from the rest of the aquatic environment, given that a primary use of inland watercourses has long ceased to be the production of fish for food. It might be more rational to transfer responsibility

---

[131] See *R* v. *Brown and White (Sandholme Fisheries)*, Isleworth Crown Court, 1993, unreported.

[132] Under the Registration of Fish Farming and Shellfish Farming Businesses Order 1985, SI 1985 No.1391, made under s.7 Diseases of Fish Act 1983, all farms where fish are kept for sale or transfer must be registered.

[133] There appear not to be any reported cases where action under s.30 was taken in respect of fish escapes, though where such action was contemplated, the evidential connection between the escapees and their origin could not be made.

for all introductions to the freshwater aquatic environment to the relevant nature conservation authority. If this were to be done, then there would be a good case for the NRA to be involved earlier in the authorization stage. Confronted with a situation where a licence to introduce has been granted, it may be that the NRA feel under pressure to authorize fish introduction.

Planning Controls

As has been illustrated, effective protection for the aquatic environment must involve preventive measures. Two aspects of planning for conservation must be distinguished: first, controls administered by local planning authorities under the Town and Country Planning Act 1990, and second, NRA-led planning for river catchments, which may straddle planning authority boundaries.

Substantial progress towards integrating conservation considerations into the planning process has been made at both the development planning and the development control stages. Generally, there is now clear evidence of a closer working relationship between the NRA and local planning authorities. Since 1991, the NRA has been a statutory consultee in the preparation of development plans,[134] and involvement in development planning is increasingly emphasized by the NRA further to the enhanced status of the development plan.[135] In some cases, this has involved the NRA drawing up model policies for local planning authorities to incorporate. Thames Region, for example, has been successful in encouraging the adoption of policies creating a general presumption against development with an adverse impact on the water environment, and more specifically the promotion of river corridors for conservation purposes.[136]

Recently, more general guidance for local planning authorities seeking to outline the concerns of the NRA about the potential impact of development on the water environment has been produced.[137] This illustrates the increasing importance accorded to a more proactive approach by the NRA, working in partnership with planners, as against a reactive planning role as a consultee in the planning process.[138] In some regions it is now NRA practice routinely to inspect submitted planning applications. That one

[134] Town and Country Planning (Development Plans) Regulations 1991, SI 1991 No.2794, Regulation 10.

[135] Ss. 70(2) and 54A, Town and Country Planning Act 1990.

[136] Heaton, op. cit., 314.

[137] NRA, *Guidance Notes for Local Planning Authorities on the Methods of Protecting the Water Environment through Development Plans* (1994).

[138] See also NRA, Association of County Councils, Association of District Councils and Association of Metropolitan Authorities, *Memorandum of Understanding: Development and Flood Risk* (1994), in response to Joint Circular on *Development and Flood Risk* (DoE 30/92, WO 68/92, MAFF FD 1/92).

region recorded a tenfold increase in applications commented on following the introduction of such a 'visitation' system indicates that there are many more planning applications on which the NRA would wish to comment than those forwarded to it as a statutory consultee for certain developments.[139] In respect of flood defence, for example, the NRA is encouraged to copy the results of surveys undertaken,[140] as they become available, to local planning authorities.[141]

Catchment management planning

In a similarly proactive vein, a national programme for preparing catchment management plans is being implemented. As well as providing a useful input to the planning process, the making of such plans offers an opportunity for public participation in developing NRA policy. The NRA may also encourage public participation in conservation of the aquatic environment through involvement with local conservation initiatives. This may involve sponsorship by the NRA alongside bodies such as the Countryside Commission and local councils, but equally provides a focus for co-ordinating voluntary efforts.

Environmental assessment

A further legal constraint upon undesirable developments may be imposed, and enhanced public participation procedures provided for, through environmental assessment (EA) being required under the Environmental Assessment Directive.[142] Where projects are likely to have significant effects on the environment, an environmental statement must be prepared. The Directive has largely been implemented through the Town and Country Planning (Assessment of Environmental Effects) Regulations 1988.[143] EA may either be compulsory (Schedule 1 projects) or discretionary (Schedule 2 projects) according to criteria established by Member States.[144]

As with planning generally, EA may offer greater scope for aquatic

[139] Under the Town and Country Planning (General Development Procedure) Order 1995, SI 1995 No.419. See Howarth and McGillivray, op. cit., 33. The NRA *Conservation Strategy* suggests that screening of development proposals need not be restricted to situations where the NRA is a statutory consultee (p.13).

[140] Under s.105 Water Resources Act 1991.

[141] Joint Circular, above, note 138, para.7.

[142] See Council Directive 85/337/EEC on the assessment of the effects of certain public and private projects on the environment (OJ L175/41, 5 July 1985).

[143] SI 1988 No.1199. See also the Land Drainage Improvement Works (Assessment of Environmental Effects) Regulations 1988, SI 1988 No.1217.

[144] *Environmental Assessment,* Joint Circular, Department of the Environment 15/88, Welsh Office 23/88. See also A. King and P. Wathern, *Environmental Assessment Methodology,* NRA R and D Report (1991).

ecosystem protection than water legislation presently provides for, though in the absence of an assessment being required under the EA Regulations, the NRA may be able to use its incidental general powers to require, in effect, full EA.[145] Unlike civil law, for example, EA and planning law focus less on private rights than the broader public interest. The opportunity to place more general concerns about ecosystem protection on the legal and political agenda, offered by the planning process, may further the conservation both of individual areas of concern and of aquatic ecosystem conservation generally.

The Future for Sustainable Management of Aquatic Ecosystems

Conservation considerations clearly appear to be enjoying particular prominence in the exercise of the NRA's powers and duties. However, this cannot be attributed solely to the general environmental and specific conservation duties placed on the NRA. Such duties were also placed on the water authorities by the Wildlife and Countryside Act 1981.[146] Rather, integration of conservation concerns has occurred both through internal and external policy changes since the formation of the NRA. Internally, these seek to ensure that the potential impact of all NRA operational and regulatory activities are assessed by conservation staff in consultation with other functions, and that information and policy on conservation are disseminated across all functions. Externally, as has been noted, links with statutory and voluntary bodies, both locally and nationally, are being fostered, attributable in part to changes to the town and country planning system.

It is also clear, however, that aquatic ecosystem conservation may straddle the jurisdiction of the nature conservation agencies. It may also be dependent upon decisions taken by the NRA in the exercise of its operational functions. Two separate but related issues must therefore be considered: first, the effectiveness of the present division of responsibilities for nature conservation between the NRA and English Nature and the CCW, and second, the legitimacy of maintaining, to some extent, 'poacher/gamekeeper' functions. Both have been considered in the deliberations surrounding the establishment of the new Environment Agency for England and Wales.

The NRA as poacher and gamekeeper

Particularly in balancing the operational duties of the NRA such as land drainage or flood defence works with its conservation duties, the poacher/gamekeeper problem of a regulatory body possessing conflicting

---

[145] Under s.4(1)(a) Water Resources Act 1991.
[146] See s.48 Wildlife and Countryside Act 1981.

operational duties may persist. That is, the NRA may be required in law to perform a function which it is also obliged not to do where this has an unacceptable effect upon the aquatic environment.

Separating operational and regulatory functions of the NRA was one of the options put forward by the Department of the Environment as part of the consultation process prior to final publication of the government's proposals for the new Environment Agency.[147] Ultimately, however, the view prevailed that all existing functions of the NRA should be transferred to the Agency. However, the debate focused more directly on whether the NRA's pollution control functions could be separated from its other responsibilities; the undesirability or impossibility of separating off conservation (and other non-pollution) duties was largely uncontroversial. Implicitly, it was accepted that integrated catchment management requires conservation duties to be exercised alongside other responsibilities for the aquatic environment.

Boundaries of aquatic conservation responsibilities

The government's consultation paper contained no suggestion that English Nature or the CCW should form part of the new agency. Although the extent to which the functions of the nature conservation agencies could be integrated with those of the NRA, Her Majesty's Inspectorate of Pollution (HMIP) and the local waste regulation authorities was aired before the House of Commons Environment Select Committee, this was without serious conviction. The then Environment Secretary, Michael Heseltine, stated that there was no demand for such a move in stating, 'I think they are better left as free-standing organizations. They are small organizations . . . If they were brought within they would lose something of their popular identity and something of their political influence',[148] a view supported by the Committee.

Conclusion

The general conclusion from the preceding discussion must be that, at best, the protection of aquatic ecosystems is for most purposes a secondary consideration within the areas of law that have been considered. Whilst incidental conservation objectives are served by the laws relating to water quality, water resources and flood defence, species introduction regulation and planning control, for the most part the sustainable management

---

[147] See Department of the Environment, *Improving Environmental Quality* (1991), Draft Environment Agencies Bill, Department of the Environment (1994).

[148] Evidence to House of Commons Environment Committee, First Report Session 1991–22, *The Government's Proposals for an Environment Agency* (HC 1991–2 55) (1992), 5.

of aquatic ecosystems is subsumed to other priorities. Given the background of international commitments to biodiversity and sustainable development, the legal mechanisms for securing these objectives must be placed under ever closer scrutiny. In those areas that have been considered in this chapter the limitations of the law have been highlighted and the need for improvements emphasized.

Whilst substantive legal changes are desirable in many respects, there is an additional requirement that conservation responsibilities should be allocated to appropriately constituted administrative and regulatory bodies possessed of adequate powers and duties. In some respects, it has been illustrated, the duties which presently exist need to be strengthened and clarified. In other respects, the problems of interrelationship between bodies that have conservation as their primary responsibility and those that have conservation as a contingent duty in relation to other water functions need to be stated with greater transparency. Although, the establishment of a new Environment Agency provided an ideal opportunity for reconsideration of the mechanism by which this may have been achieved, the changes which have been introduced have not encompassed the comprehensive review of conservation duties that is needed. Regrettably, this is a missed opportunity to place the sustainable management of aquatic ecosystems upon a more secure legal and administrative footing.

3

Law and Policy for Marine
Protected Areas

LYNDA M. WARREN

The main characteristic of marine nature conservation law in the United Kingdom is that it has followed the model of terrestrial conservation law. Because of the failure to take account of the scientific, practical and legal differences between marine and terrestrial sites, however, marine conservation law has not been as effective as its terrestrial counterpart. Since the last major wildlife statute was enacted in 1981,[1] however, there have been several significant developments that point towards a change in policy for marine nature conservation. The EC Habitats Directive[2] will have the most direct effect as its implementation necessitates increasing the amount of protection currently enjoyed by protected areas. Its approach, however, is in the same style as the earlier EC Birds Directive[3] which formed the basis for much of the Wildlife and Countryside Act 1981. The Convention on Biological Diversity,[4] however, makes a break with the traditional view that conservation issues can be dealt with simply by setting aside a few special areas and applying special protection measures for endangered species. Although the convention acknowledges the importance of protected areas and of species conservation measures,

[1] Wildlife and Countryside Act 1981.

[2] Council directive on the conservation of natural habitats and of wild fauna and flora (92/43/EEC, OJ L206, 22.7.92. p.7). And see Ball, below, Chapter 4, pp. 89–110.

[3] Council directive on the conservation of wild birds (79/409/EEC, OJ L103, 25.4.79, p.1).

[4] The Convention was opened for signature at the United Nations Conference on Environment and Development (Rio, June 1992) and came into force in December 1993, ILM, 31 (1992), 818.

it is primarily concerned with the maintenance of biological diversity through sustainable use. It acknowledges for the first time what marine conservationists have been claiming for years, namely that conservation is not an activity on the same level as, for example, farming or industry but a fundamental philosophy forming an integral part of the sustainability concept. Similar thinking has stimulated renewed interest in the concept of coastal zone management which seeks to place marine protected areas within the context of a broader integrated management policy for the whole of the coast.

The final development has been the increase in public and political awareness of marine environmental issues, especially the potential health hazards of marine pollution. One consequence has been a proliferation of ideas for offshore marine protected areas designed to protect environmentally sensitive areas from pollution.

In this chapter I shall examine the case for marine protected areas, review existing types of marine protected areas and consider the likely effectiveness of current proposals for new mechanisms for marine nature conservation.

What Needs Conserving?

Until recently it has been assumed scientific wisdom that species diversity in the sea is much lower than on land. One estimate, for example, is that of 5 million living species in the world only about 250,000 are marine.[5] Recent research, however, suggests that the number of deep-sea species may have been grossly underestimated in the past.[6] Furthermore, if the diversity is measured at higher levels of classification, the relative importance of marine biodiversity increases considerably. Depending on which classification system is used there are some fifty plant and animal phyla[7] of which virtually all are found in the sea. Terrestrial environments, on the other hand, are dominated by a small number of phyla, notably the vertebrates and the arthropods. Shepherd[8] has addressed this disparity. He concludes that the old-style methods of determining biodiversity by counting numbers of species and assessing population abundance are not appropriate for

[5] Figures quoted in R. S. K. Barnes and R. N. Hughes, *An Introduction to Marine Ecology*, second edition (Blackwell Scientific Publications, Oxford, 1988), 17.

[6] J. F. Grassle and N. J. Maciolek, 'Deep-sea species richness: regional and local diversity estimated from quantitative bottom samples', *American Naturalist*, 139 (2), (1992), 313–41.

[7] A phylum is a major grouping of similar organisms used in biological classification systems. Examples include the vertebrates (i.e. fish, amphibians, reptiles, birds and mammals) and the flowering plants.

[8] C. Shepherd, 'Marine biodiversity: meaning and measurement', in B. Earll (ed.), *Marine Environmental Management: Review of Events in 1993 and Future Trends* (Bob Earll, Kempley, Glos), 23–6.

the development of a policy geared to conserve biodiversity.[9] The UK Biodiversity Action Plan[10] tacitly admits this by including several measures designed to conserve marine biodiversity. Fifteen of the fifty action points in the plan are of particular relevance to marine nature conservation.[11]

Unfortunately, because of the practical difficulties and costs of conducting marine survey work, knowledge of marine species, habitats and ecosystems in British waters is far from complete despite a long-term programme of work undertaken by the Nature Conservancy Council and its successor, the Joint Nature Conservation Committee.[12] What is clear, however, is that the UK has a particularly rich and diverse marine flora and fauna because of its position in relation to the main ocean currents. The British Isles are affected by cold boreal waters from the north, by the North Atlantic drift and by warm Lusitanian currents originating in the Mediterranean. As a result, our wildlife contains elements of both warm- and cold-water assemblages with several representatives of species at the extreme limits of their ranges. The varied geology of the British Isles is a further factor in increasing the variety of marine wildlife through its effects on substrates. Virtually all the major marine habitat types, with the exception of mangroves and coral reefs, can be found in British waters.

What are the Threats?

Pollution

The main threats to marine flora and fauna are from pollution, especially organic pollution and oil pollution. Organic pollution is caused by the discharge of sewage and sewage sludge into the sea and by agricultural run-off entering the sea via rivers. The effect of even moderate levels of organic enrichment is to raise the level of nutrients in the seawater so that the productivity of marine phytoplankton increases, that is to cause

[9] The Convention on Biological Diversity defines biological diversity as 'the variability among living organisms from all sources including, *inter alia*, terrestrial, marine and other aquatic ecosystems and the ecological complexes of which they are part' and specifically includes 'diversity within species, between species and of ecosystems' (Article 2).

[10] *Biodiversity: The UK Action Plan* (1994), Cm.2428 (London: HMSO).

[11] K. Hiscock, 'The UK Biodiversity Action Plan', *Marine Scene*, 4 (1994), Joint Nature Conservation Committee, p.8.

[12] The Marine Nature Conservation Review was started in 1987 to survey and assess coastal marine habitats from the lower limit of terrestrial flowering plants out to territorial sea limits. The emphasis is on the benthos (i.e. wildlife living on or in the seashore or seabed rather than water column).

eutrophication.[13] This can lead to plankton blooms and, if appropriate species are involved, so-called toxic tides. Eutrophication of the marine environment is largely restricted to enclosed and semi-enclosed areas where there is a long flushing time. Although parts of the North Sea, for example, are affected, the Department of the Environment (DoE) reported[14] that eutrophication was only experienced in a small number of localized inshore seas. Sewage disposal at sea has a similar effect but carries with it the added complication of potential damage to human health. Dumping of sewage sludge at sea has a more extreme, but localized, effect on marine life resulting from smothering and from oxygen depletion in the immediate vicinity of the dump site. The gross effects on the distribution and abundance of marine organisms, especially those living in or on the seabed, have been well documented.[15] Sewage disposal at sea also adds to the load of heavy metals in sea water. Similarly rivers may bring organic chemicals used in farming. Small concentrations of toxic chemicals are believed to have a chronic effect on marine wildlife and have been implicated as causal factors in fish lesions and seal deaths.[16]

Control of pollution in UK marine waters is governed by a combination of international conventions, European directives and commitments made at the North Sea Ministerial Conferences. For organic pollution regulation is exercised by the National Rivers Authority under the Water Resources Act 1991. Oil pollution at sea is tackled by the Department of Transport, and local authorities are involved in clean-up operations for coastal pollution incidents.

Physical changes

In coastal waters, especially the intertidal zone and estuaries, development pressures have an indirect effect on wildlife through destruction of habitat. Examples in recent times include marinas, infrastructure associated with the offshore oil industry, and port developments. To these may be added barrages such as that under way in Cardiff Bay. Until recently authorization for such developments took the form of planning permission where the affected land was within a local authority boundary or

[13] Eutrophication is defined in the Council directive concerning urban waste water treatment (91/271/EEC, OJ L135, 30 May 1991, 40) as 'the enrichment of water by nutrients, especially compounds of nitrogen and/or phosphorus, causing an accelerated growth of algae and higher forms of plant life to produce an undesirable disturbance to the balance of organisms present in the water and to the quality of the water concerned'.

[14] *Third International Conference on the Protection of the North Sea: UK Guidance Note on the Ministerial Declaration* (DoE, July 1990).

[15] See, for example, R. B. Clark, *Marine Pollution*, third edition (Clarendon Press, Oxford, 1992), p.18.

[16] For a review, see The Irish Sea Study Group, *The Irish Sea: An Environmental Review: Part Two Waste Inputs and Pollution* (Liverpool University Press, 1990).

else a private Act of Parliament. The Transport and Works Act 1992 now provides that the necessary consents for operations are to be obtained by ministerial order.

Offshore oil exploration has a limited effect on wildlife, principally through bird strikes and through seepage into surrounding sediments and waters, but also carries a small risk of major accidental pollution. Dredging for minerals has a more serious effect in that vast quantities of substrate are removed destroying habitat and adding to sediment loads. Dredging is currently controlled through a non-statutory procedure administered by the Department of the Environment.[17]

Fishing

The fishing industry is one of the major human impacts on marine ecosystems. Over-fishing not only affects the target species itself but has a knock-on effect on other species in the food web although, because of our lack of knowledge, it is not always possible to prove a direct correlation. The population crash of sea-bird populations in Shetland, for example, appears to be related in some way to the decline in sand eels which are caught as factory fish. Fisheries law in the UK is largely dictated by the European Common Fisheries Policy.[18]

Disturbance

For some particularly sensitive species and habitats, the mere presence of people can have a detrimental effect. Obvious examples include the use of noisy pleasure craft which can frighten birds and mammals, but even quiet pursuits such as bait digging can keep birds away from feeding grounds and may cause irreversible damage to the infaunal communities. For the most part there are no direct controls over access to the seashore or the sea itself. There is an assumed right of access to beaches and a legal right to fish in the sea and to navigate in tidal waters.

Comparison between Marine and Terrestrial Protected Areas

Prior to the enactment of the marine nature reserve legislation there was considerable debate as to the efficacy of any sort of marine protected

[17] DoE issued a consultation paper on the review of licensing arrangements for minerals dredging in England and Wales in April 1994.

[18] For further details of conservation aspects of fisheries policy see I. Lutchman, *A General Overview of European and UK Fisheries* (WWF-UK, Godalming, 1991).

areas as a means of furthering marine nature conservation.[19] With the
subsequent difficulties arising from implementation of this legislation,
the issue has remained on the agenda.[20] Given the success of terrestrial
protected areas, it is useful to analyse the similarities and differences
between protected areas in the marine and terrestrial environments.

Natural characteristics

The obvious difference, of course, is that the sea is a buoyant fluid medium
in motion. It is tempting, therefore, to suggest that the protected area
concept is meaningless at sea because of the inability to confine the water.
In fact, though, only 2 per cent of marine organisms live permanently in
the water body; the rest are firmly associated with the bottom for part of
their lives, at least. Given adequate scientific knowledge it is possible to
mark out the boundary of an area of seabed on a map and to indicate its
position using marker buoys. Many larval stages are planktonic and may
leave the protected area, but then terrestrial protected areas are not prisons
either. Nobody suggests that a nature reserve is a waste of time because
some of its species migrate. As Norse[21] points out, despite the differences, terrestrial and marine areas show a number of similarities that
suggest that the protected area concept is applicable. Most significantly,
it is possible to select certain sites as being of greater ecological value
than others – an important consideration for any protected area system.

Threats

The types of threats suffered by marine and terrestrial sites are broadly
similar; it is the relative importance that differs. A marine site that is of
particular nature conservation importance may be under threat from all
or any of the following. It may be at risk from pollution from an accidental oil spill and from a general increase in organic matter and siltation
as a result of riverine inputs, sewage outfalls, ship discharges and dredging. If it is a site of recognized conservation interest it is less likely to be
affected by infrastructural developments[22] but it is likely to attract visitors and the disturbance that they bring. For a terrestrial site the major

[19] See R. Mitchell, 'Marine wildlife conservation', *Progress in Underwater Science.
Report of the Underwater Association*, 2 (ns) (1977), 65–81.
[20] The Joint Marine Group, consisting of representatives of the statutory conservation
agencies and various non-governmental organizations, have discussed this matter at some
length.
[21] E. A. Norse (ed.), *Global Marine Biological Diversity: A Strategy for Building
Conservation into Decision Making* (Island Press, Washington, 1993).
[22] But note the decision of Parliament to sanction the total destruction of the Cardiff
Bay SSSI for the purposes of constructing an amenity barrage (Cardiff Bay Barrage Act
1993).

threat is a change in land use, be it building or infrastructural developments, afforestation or simply a change in farming practice. Disturbance
can also be a problem, especially where very rare and attractive species
are concerned. Pollution is not generally perceived as a particular problem
for which special measures over and above those applying elsewhere are
needed. This is presumably because protected areas are usually situated
in the countryside far from the obvious effects of industry. In reality,
however, protected sites are affected, especially by air-borne pollution.[23]
Protected area status provides no safeguards against pollution for either
marine or terrestrial sites. Only in the case of the former, however, is it
seriously suggested that a protected area is worthless because of this.

Managerial differences

Concerns over the differences between the nature of marine and terrestrial sites and the threats facing them has detracted from the far more
important differences in the legal framework governing the regulation of
activities on land and at sea and in practical management. The main
legal differences are the relative unimportance of land ownership for marine
sites, the public rights, real and assumed, enjoyed over marine lands, and
the absence of any equivalent to the town and country planning regime.
Practical management is also very different. Working at sea is expensive,
time-consuming and is less straightforward than equivalent terrestrial work.
This has important consequences for the identification of potential protected
areas and the enforcement of legal provisions.

The UK Approach to Marine Protected Areas

The first legislation for nature reserves and Sites of Special Scientific
Interest (SSSIs), in the National Parks and Access to the Countryside Act
1949,[24] was a spin-off from the revision of the planning system. Given
the emphasis on land use controls, it is not surprising that marine conservation was ignored. Subsequently attention focused on damage to the
countryside from changes in agricultural practice and, again, marine sites
were excluded. In 1971 the Natural Environment Research Council set
up a working group to examine the case for additional conservation measures
for marine wildlife. It concluded[25] that there was insufficient evidence to
assess the priority for such action. Not until the publication of a joint

---

[23] See, for example, C. Sketch and S. Bareham, *Terrestrial SSSIs at Risk from Soil
Acidification in Wales* (CCW, Bangor, 1993).

[24] See ss.19 and 23.

[25] *Marine Wildlife Conservation* (NERC Publications, Series B, No. 5, 1973).

Nature Conservancy Council/Natural Environment Research Council report[26] just prior to the publication of the Wildlife and Countryside Bill was a scientific case for marine protected areas made out. The government concluded that, despite the apparent scientific justification for taking action, the complexities of marine protected areas warranted further attention before legislation could be drafted.[27] In the event, fears that the opportunity would be lost fuelled the lobby for marine nature reserves and the government gave way. The resulting legislation, however, is no more than a watered-down version of the national nature reserve provisions. In retrospect, it might have been better to forgo this window of opportunity and take the time to draft a bill tailor-made to deal with the particular legal and practical complexities of marine protected areas. It is the failure to take these things into account, more than anything else, that accounts for the ineffectiveness of existing marine protected area mechanisms.

Sites of Special Scientific Interest

An SSSI is an area of land that is recognized as being of such a high level of interest that its importance is worth noting with a view to safeguarding it.[28] A site may be important because of its wildlife or for physical qualities of land form or geology. The scope is thus very broad, and encompasses the full range of what might be termed natural, as opposed to cultural, heritage. Nevertheless, the SSSI is of little relevance to our marine natural heritage and SSSIs are not generally notified below low-water mark. The National Parks and Access to the Countryside Act 1949 s.23 provided that the Nature Conservancy[29] must notify the local planning authority of any site of special scientific interest. The sole purpose of notification was to draw the planners' attention to matters of science of which they might not otherwise be aware. The Act did not impose any requirement on the part of the planning authority to attach any particular weight to the scientific value of the site. As local authority jurisdiction and, thence, local planning authority jurisdiction, generally extends only to the low-water mark of medium tides, SSSIs have no application for subtidal sites. This was not simply an oversight brought about by a failure on the part of Parliament to appreciate the limits of local planning authority jurisdiction but is a natural consequence of the purpose behind the

[26] *Nature Conservation in the Marine Environment* (NCC and NERC, 1979).

[27] [416] HL Debs, col. 1094, 16 December 1980, *per* Lord Avon.

[28] See D. A. Ratcliffe (ed.), *A Nature Conservation Review* (Cambridge University Press, 1977), which gives an inventory of the country's wildlife and identifies key sites.

[29] The predecessor of the Nature Conservancy Council (NCC), itself replaced by English Nature, the Countryside Council for Wales, Scottish Natural Heritage and the Joint Nature Conservation Committee.

legislation. The National Parks etc. Act is, essentially, a piece of special-ist land use planning legislation. It arose from an extensive planning review[30] and followed a major revision of planning law.[31] And, to cut it down to its simplest basic component, planning law is about regulating the use of land by private persons for the best advantage of the public as a whole. In the immediate past, if not now, the concept was meaningless for land covered permanently by the sea because there was no develop-ment of marine land.

Even in the intertidal zone, where there are many SSSIs,[32] the reason for notification is seldom because of the scientific importance of the in-tertidal invertebrate animals or the seaweeds. Instead it is because the site is important as a feeding ground for birds, or for its saltmarsh flora, or for its geological features, such as fossil exposures. The reason for this paucity of 'marine' intertidal SSSIs is, in part, that there is no clear guidance to assist nature conservation agency staff in the identification of sites. For terrestrial and freshwater sites, there is a series of guidelines for the assessment of the importance of a site[33] based on a number of established criteria.[34] In theory, it is possible to adapt the Ratcliffe criteria to marine sites.[35] In practice, the exercise is greatly hampered by the lack of scientific knowledge of British marine wildlife.

The Wildlife and Countryside Act 1981 s.28 dramatically altered the SSSI concept and elevated it from a mere source of information to a mechanism for controlling land use. Notification of planning authorities remains a requirement, so that subtidal sites are still mainly excluded, but, in addition, the owner and occupier of the land are also notified and furnished with a list of potentially damaging operations that are not to be undertaken in the short term without permission. The standard list includes some things that can only apply to intertidal sites, such as bait digging in

---

[30] See L. M. Warren, 'Conservation – a secondary environmental consideration', in R. Churchill, J. Gibson and L. M. Warren (eds.), *Law, Policy and the Environment* (Basil Blackwell, Oxford, 1991), 64–80.

[31] Town and Country Planning Act 1947.

[32] Some 7,800 sq. km of land and intertidal water in England have been notified as SSSIs of which 2,980 sq. km, or 38 per cent, is within the coastal zone. See House of Commons Environment Committee, Session 1991–2, Second Report, *Coastal Zone Protection and Planning*, HC-17, published March 1992, evidence of English Nature, at p. 151.

[33] *Guidelines for Selection of Biological SSSI* (Nature Conservancy Council, Peterborough, 1989).

[34] First described in Ratcliffe, op.cit. The ten criteria are size, diversity, naturalness, rarity, fragility, typicalness, recorded history, position in ecological/geographical unit, potential value and intrinsic appeal.

[35] R. Mitchell, *Conservation of Marine Benthic Biocenoses in the North Sea and the Baltic* (Council of Europe, Strasbourg, 1987) describes how this can be done. S. Gubbay, *Using Sites of Special Scientific Interest to Conserve Seashores for their Marine Biological Interest* (WWF, Godalming, 1989) takes the process one step further by setting guidelines for selecting sites.

intertidal areas and collecting marine life from intertidal areas. The restrictions only apply to owners and occupiers, however, and, given the open public access to most beaches, are largely ineffective. The inevitable conclusion, therefore, is that SSSIs are of little relevance for marine wildlife because (1) the marine environment was outside the purposes of the Act and the policy behind it; (2) at the time the legislation was enacted there was no perceived threat to its integrity; and (3) marine wildlife has always been less well known than terrestrial wildlife.

The SSSI is regarded as the cornerstone of site protection in this country and its absence from the marine scene leaves a large gap. Opinion differs as to how to remedy this defect. Several witnesses to the Environment Committee's inquiry into coastal protection and planning commented on the UK's failure to implement some international conservation agreements properly because subtidal sites could not be protected by SSSI notification.[36] The RSPB advocated the extension of the SSSI to spring low-tide mark.[37] Estuaries and intertidal mudflats are important feeding areas for birds and the present limit of mean low-water mark creates an artificial boundary. The Chief Executive of English Nature[38] was in favour of a proposal to extend an SSSI-type mechanism offshore so as to enhance compliance with the international agreements. The DoE, on the other hand, dismissed SSSIs as a mechanism for implementing the Habitats Directive offshore.[39]

Marine Nature Reserves

Statutory marine nature reserves (MNRs) were introduced in the Wildlife and Countryside Act 1981 following fierce debate in both Houses of Parliament. The legislation is broadly similar to that for nature reserves on land but differs in a number of ways that have made effective implementation difficult. An MNR may be declared for the purpose of

(a) conserving marine flora and fauna or geological or physiographical features of special interest in the area; or
(b) providing, under suitable conditions and control, special opportunities for the study of, and research into, matters relating to marine flora and fauna and the physical conditions in which they live, or

[36] See, for example, evidence submitted by the Marine Conservation Society, the Royal Society for the Protection of Birds (RSPB) and the World Wide Fund for Nature (see above note 32) at pp. 84, 120 and 136 respectively.

[37] See above note 32. Evidence at p. 120. Note that in Scotland planning jurisdiction already extends to spring low-water mark.

[38] See above note 32, Question 400.

[39] See below note 61.

for the study of geological and physiographical features of special interest in the area.[40]

Just as for National Nature Reserves (NNRs), a designated MNR may be protected by by-laws made by the nature conservation agency. However, the list of relevant authorities whose activities cannot be interfered with by such by-laws is much longer than that applying to NNRs. In the case of NNRs, rights of access by the main utilities are protected but otherwise there are few exclusions. For MNRs there are far more statutory bodies involved in regulating activities whose fields of responsibility must be left intact. Most problematic has been the role of sea fisheries committees which are charged under the Sea Fisheries Regulation Act 1966 with making by-law for the conservation of fisheries. As a consequence any by-law affecting fish and shellfish that is considered necessary for the protection of an MNR must be made by the sea fisheries committee using procedures governed by European policy and must be confirmed by the Ministry of Agriculture, Fisheries and Food (MAFF), not the DoE.

Because of the opposition to the introduction of MNRs, the scope of the by-laws has been further limited by excluding certain activities, notably access by shipping. Although the Act expressly provides for by-laws to be made controlling or prohibiting access,[41] this provision is qualified by the statement that by-laws shall not interfere with the right of navigation of any vessel, other than a pleasure boat.[42] The motive for this exclusion was concern on the part of the Foreign Office that attempts to control navigation would be in breach of international law. Although the term 'pleasure boat' is not defined it was presumably intended to apply to small locally based vessels carrying the national flag and hence under direct control.[43] Lobbying by the Royal Yachting Association weakened even this control by leading to the inclusion of a proviso that access could not be denied from the whole reserve for all of the year.[44] Given that there is also a public right of fishing which includes the ancillary right to collect bait,[45] the result is that powers to control access to and within an MNR and to limit activities carried out therein are limited.

There have also been considerable practical difficulties in designating MNRs. While NNRs are declared by the nature conservation agencies themselves, for MNRs their role is relegated to making a submission to

---

[40] Wildlife and Countryside Act 1981 s.36(1).

[41] Ibid., s.37(2).

[42] Ibid., s.37(3).

[43] For further details see J. Gibson. 'Marine Nature Reserves', *Journal of Planning and Environmental Law* (1984), 699–706.

[44] Wildlife and Countryside Act 1981 s.37(3)(b).

[45] This matter was considered in *Anderson* v. *Alnwick District Council* (1993) 3 All ER 613.

the Secretary of State who makes the final decision. The reasons for this are obvious in that NNR status is dependent on managerial control of the site having being obtained[46] which generally means that the land is either owned or leased by the nature conservation agency or is in the hands of a sympathetic public body or non-governmental organization, so that all the usual rights accruing to ownership can be used for conservation purposes. Although the Crown Estate owns most of the seabed, ownership does not carry with it the same degree of control as on dry land and many other parties without any proprietary rights in the site have, or consider themselves to have, a right. Unfortunately, the government made a promise during the passage of the Wildlife and Countryside Bill through Parliament that no MNR would be declared without a consensus of opinion in its favour.[47] This has meant that the nature conservation agencies have had to spend a considerable amount of time and staff resources in negotiations with a wide variety of interested groups in an attempt to obtain approval for designation. As a result only two MNRs have been declared[48] and the by-laws made for their protection are not as strong as would have been preferred. One other site, the Menai Strait, is currently under consideration by the Welsh Office.[49]

Marine Consultation Areas

In response to the ineffectiveness of the marine nature reserve legislation, the government issued a consultation paper[50] on Marine Consultation Areas (MCAs) with a view to providing effective protection of the nature conservation interest of coastal waters outside MNRs. The paper was produced in fulfilment of an undertaking in the White Paper on the Environment[51] rather than in response to the Habitats Directive, which was always intended to operate separately.

The scheme was designed to operate as an early-warning system. Sites of marine conservation interest were to be formally identified and listed and all bodies taking decisions that might affect that interest were to be asked to consult the conservation agencies at the earliest feasible stage. Any advice given by these bodies was to be given due weight by the decision-makers, and the conservation agencies were to be told of decisions taken. The scheme was to be subject to regular monitoring. The scheme was to be voluntary but this was not regarded as a problem because the public bodies affected would be answerable to government anyway.

---

[46] Wildlife and Countryside Act 1981 s.35.
[47] [424] HL Debs, col. 524, 15 October 1981, per Lord Avon.
[48] Lundy, in 1986, and Skomer and the Marloes Peninsula, in 1990.
[49] A submission was made in March 1994.
[50] Issued jointly by DoE and the Welsh Office in February 1992.
[51] This Common Inheritance: Britain's Environmental Strategy (1990, Cm. 1200), para.7.69.

The statutory nature conservation agencies were broadly in favour of the proposals, although they had concerns over the costs involved. The majority of non-governmental organizations were less enthusiastic and tended to regard the proposals as an attempt to divert attention from the failure of the MNR legislation to deliver the goods without actually rectifying the problem.

In the event the promised circular on MCAs was never produced and the government decided to drop the scheme,[52] allegedly because of substantial advances in coastal policy and practice since the original proposals were made and because of the overlap between MCAs and Special Areas of Conservation (SACs) under the Habitats Directive.

Marine Protected Areas

In March 1991 a group of conservation organizations which were becoming increasingly dissatisfied with the lack of progress in marine conservation held a series of brain-storming sessions which led to the publication of proposals for Marine Protected Areas (MPAs).[53] These suggested that a new legal framework was needed in order to provide the required degree of protection and to ensure integration. One of the key advantages claimed for the approach was that it brought together conservation of wildlife, seascape, commercial species and archaeological features under a simple unified system. The proposal was for a two-tier system of MPAs. Type 1 areas would be sites given strict protection where there would be a presumption against any activity unless authorized. This type of MPA would be broadly equivalent to an MNR but with a higher level of protection. For Type 2 areas there would be a legal regime permitting unrestricted use with the exception of activities expressly prohibited or regulated. It was envisaged that these might be large areas such as sea-loch systems or large bays comparable in size with the Marine Consultation Areas subsequently proposed by government. The whole system was dependent on management which was to be administered by a statutory authority.

Coastal Zone Management

Coastal zone protection and planning

One thing that the MPA and MCA approaches had in common was recognition of the need to manage marine activities. In 1991–2 the House of Commons Environment Committee conducted an inquiry into management

---

[52] A statement to this effect was included in *Managing the Coast*, see below note 59.

[53] L. M. Warren and S. Gubbay (eds.), *Marine Protected Areas: A Discussion Document* (WWF-UK, Godalming, 1991).

of the coastal zone[54] which reached specific conclusions concerning marine conservation. The Committee[55] expressed disappointment that there had been no progress with protecting marine conservation areas since a previous report of the Committee had recommended changes seven years previously. In particular, it expressed dissatisfaction with MNRs and MCAs and recommended that government give consideration to the wider concept of Marine Protected Areas. There was also concern that the land/sea divide was hampering conservation because it prevented terrestrial designations from applying at sea. It recommended that the government should consider the option of extending SSSIs below low-water mark.

On broader issues, the Committee considered that the current legislation for activities in the coastal zone is too diffuse to provide an integrated or efficient framework for coastal zone protection and planning.[56] It also drew particular attention to the need to balance fisheries with conservation[57] and to the need to improve co-ordination between bodies with responsibilities in the coastal zone.[58]

Government consultation papers

In October 1993 the government issued two consultation papers[59] in fulfilment of the commitment that it made in its response to the Environment Committee.[60] Marine conservation was not a central issue in either paper because the government had also issued a consultation paper [61] on the implementation of the Habitats Directive which covered most of these issues, and had also promised to replace the existing circular on nature conservation[62] with a Planning Policy Guidance note. 'Managing the coast' was concerned with coastal management plans. It was drafted in accordance with the government's strategic aim of promoting the sustainable use of the coast. The government is not in favour of mandatory coastal management plans but expects statutory bodies to co-operate and work together on a

[54] House of Commons Environment Committee, Session 1991–2, Second Report, *Coastal Zone Protection and Planning*, HC-17, published March 1992.

[55] Ibid., para.101.

[56] Ibid., para.19.

[57] Ibid., para.113.

[58] Ibid., para.32

[59] *Managing the Coast: A Review of Coastal Management Plans in England and Wales and the Powers Supporting Them* and *Development Below Low-Water Mark: A Review of Regulation in England and Wales*, issued jointly by DoE and the Welsh Office.

[60] *The Government's Response to the Second Report from the House of Commons Select Committee on the Environment − Coastal Zone Protection and Planning* (Cm. 2011, July 1992).

[61] *Implementation in Great Britain of the Council Directive on the Conservation of Natural Habitats and of Wild Fauna and Flora (92/43/EEC), 'The Habitats Directive'*, issued jointly by DoE and the Welsh Office in October 1993.

[62] DoE Circular 27/87 *Nature Conservation*.

voluntary basis. For sites covered by the Habitats Directive, however, the possibility of mandatory plans was left open, suggesting that confidence in voluntary co-operation is not absolute. The theme running throughout the paper is that management is best done on a sectoral basis by those bodies with the knowledge and expertise to deal with a particular set of interests, but that this management should be in some way co-ordinated with the efforts of other bodies. The companion paper on 'Development below low-water mark' concluded that policies for environmental protection should be integrated into decision-making yet adopted a sector-by-sector approach to its analysis. There is no specific reference to conservation.

Marine Protection under the Habitats Directive

The main aim of the EC Habitats Directive is to promote the maintenance of biodiversity.[63] The primary mechanism for doing this is to establish a network of protected areas throughout the European territory of Member States to be known as Natura 2000. The network will consist of sites designated as Special Protection Areas (SPAs) under the EC Birds Directive[64] and SACs designated under the Habitats Directive. Sites are to be selected on the basis of the representation of specified habitat types and habitats of specified species in each Member State. Annex III lays down criteria for selecting sites eligible for identification as sites of Community importance and subsequent designation as SACs. Natura 2000 sites are to be afforded the highest level of protection. Member States are required to take appropriate steps to avoid the deterioration of habitats and the disturbance of the species.[65] Any proposal for plans or projects likely to have a significant effect on an SAC is to be subject to assessment and shall, with certain exceptions, be approved only where it is concluded that the integrity of the site will not be adversely affected. The exceptions apply where a plan or project is necessary for imperative reasons of overriding public interest, including those of a social or economic nature.[66] In such cases Member States are required to take all compensatory measures necessary to ensure that the overall coherence of Natura 2000 is protected.[67] There is also a positive aspect to protection in that

---

[63] See above note 2, article 2(1).

[64] See above note 3.

[65] Article 6(2), Directive 92/43/EEC.

[66] Article 6(4), ibid.

[67] Article 6(4), ibid. Where the site has been designated because it has 'priority' habitat or the habitat of a 'priority' species, the only considerations that may be raised to justify overriding the basic protection are those relating to human health or public safety, to beneficial consequences of primary importance to the environment or where the Commission so decrees.

Member States are required to establish the necessary conservation measures involving, if necessary, appropriate management plans and appropriate statutory, administrative or contractual measures corresponding to the ecological requirements of the habitats and species.[68]

Annex I lists natural habitat types of Community interest whose conservation requires SAC designation. The list is based on a hierarchical habitat classification produced by the CORINE Biotopes Project.[69] The list includes several coastal and marine habitats, some of which are found in the UK.[70] Annex II lists animal and plant species of Community interest whose conservation requires SAC designation.[71]

The government published draft regulations for the implementation of the directive in June 1994,[72] having published a consultative paper on implementation in October 1993.[73] The delay in publishing the draft regulations, which means that the UK is technically in breach of the directive, was at least partly caused by difficulties in devising a mechanism for the protection of marine SACs.

The principle guiding the regulations is that the present system for nature conservation in the UK is sound and should be interfered with only to the extent that this is necessary because of the need for higher levels of protection. The case of marine SACs would appear to be a prime candidate for such a departure. The consultation paper proposed that conservation of marine habitats as required by the directive should be secured without interfering unnecessarily with the legitimate pursuit of activities such as navigation, fishing and recreation. The aim was to control activities only to the extent that they posed a potential threat to nature conservation interests. MCAs were expressly excluded as a mechanism for implementing the directive; existing provisions for MNRs were considered inappropriate and it was not thought feasible to extend an SSSI-type legislative system offshore. It might be thought,

[68] Article 6(1).

[69] Council Decision 85/338/EEC on the adoption of the Commission work programme concerning an experimental project for gathering, co-ordinating and ensuring the consistency of information on the state of the environment and natural resources in the Community (OJ L176, 6 July 1985, 14). There is concern by some that the classification is not properly geared to northern European habitat types and is more attuned to habitat sub-divisions of southern Europe. For a summary account of CORINE see M. Clark, 'Better knowledge, better management – the story of CORINE', *Ecology and Environmental Management in Practice*, 3 (1992), 4.

[70] These include large shallow inlets and bays, lagoons and saltmarshes.

[71] The list of animals includes a number of marine species found in British waters such as grey and common seals, bottle-nosed dolphins, harbour porpoises and various fish. No British marine invertebrates are listed and there are no marine plants.

[72] The Conservation (Natural Habitats etc.) Regulations 1994, made under the European Communities Act 1972 s.2. The regulations came into force in October 1994 as SI 1994 No. 2716.

[73] See above note 61.

then, that a new legislative framework would be proposed and, indeed, this is claimed in text accompanying the draft regulations.[74] In practice, however, neither the proposals nor the regulations go that far. Instead the government placed a duty on bodies with jurisdiction in the marine environment to use their existing statutory powers and to perform their duties in ways that will safeguard the interests of Natura 2000 sites. No new body was proposed and no lead agency. Instead the relevant authorities[75] are to work together voluntarily, following best practice for coastal management plans with the prospect of statutory reserve powers for Ministers to require relevant bodies to work together[76] being invoked upon failure to co-operate.

The regulations deal with special provisions for 'European marine sites' separately from the other provisions. Essentially the new scheme is based on revised MNR powers and a broadened responsibility for conservation management. Regulation 33 enables the appropriate nature conservation body to install markers to indicate the existence and extent of the site. This is comparable to a similar power to mark MNRs under the Wildlife and Countryside Act 1981 s.36. This power has never been used. Once a site has become a European marine site the nature conservation body must advise other relevant authorities of the conservation objectives for the site and of any operations that may cause deterioration of natural habitats or the habitats of species or disturbance of species for which the site has been designated.

Under Regulation 34, the relevant authorities, or any one of them, may establish a management scheme for the site under which their functions shall be exercised so as to secure compliance with the directive. Such functions are deemed to include by-law-making powers. Only one such management scheme is to be made for each site. Once it has been made it is to be circulated to the appropriate nature conservation body.

European marine sites may be protected by by-laws made by the appropriate nature conservation agency under s.37 of the Wildlife and Countryside Act 1981, i.e. MNR by-laws.[77] All of the constraints that apply to MNR by-laws shall also apply to these by-laws including the proviso that nothing shall interfere with the exercise of any functions

---

[74] Compliance Cost Assessment, para.28.

[75] Relevant authorities are defined in Regulation 5 and include nature-conservation agencies, local authorities, the National Rivers Authority, water and sewerage undertakers, navigation authorities, harbour authorities and sea fisheries committees.

[76] Regulation 35. Such directions may, *inter alia*, require specific conservation measures to be included, may appoint one of the relevant authorities as a co-ordinator and may set a time limit. The minister may also give directions for the amendment of a management scheme.

[77] Regulation 36.

of a relevant authority, any functions conferred by or under any enactment (whenever passed) or any right of any person (whenever vested).[78]

In addition, under Regulation 3(3), any competent authority having functions relevant to marine conservation must exercise those functions so as to secure compliance with the directive. Competent authorities are broadly defined in Regulation 6 as any minister, government department, public or statutory undertaker, public body of any description or person holding a public office.[79]

The regulations must be read in conjunction with other measures designed to bring various statutory bodies in line. From the marine perspective, the most important of these are the enhanced powers given to sea fisheries committees, enabling them to make fisheries by-laws for environmental purposes outside sites covered by the directive.[80]

The changes are in line with the government's stated philosophy for coastal management. The key features of the approach are reliance on a voluntary approach to achieve conservation goals coupled with placing a duty on a wide variety of public bodies to use their powers for environmental purposes.

The full lists of proposed marine SACs have not yet been made publicly available but there are already some SPAs below low-water mark. The nature conservation agencies are likely to experience some difficulty in defining the limits of sites in accordance with Annex III criteria because there is not sufficient information available. In many cases the seaward boundary is likely to be arbitrary.

Another Sort of Marine Protected Area?

Although protection from pollution is not regarded as a prime function for marine protected areas in coastal waters, there is growing interest in the identification of areas of open water that need to be given some sort of special protection against the risks of pollution from shipping. This protection might take the form of more stringent pollution controls, routeing measures or just the provision of information to assist mariners in adopting the best environmental options. The focus of

---

[78] Wildlife and Countryside Act 1981 s.36(6). 'Relevant authorities' for these purposes include the same bodies as under the regulations (see s.36(7) of the Act).

[79] Note that this definition includes the Crown Estate Commissioners who, as landowners of much of the seabed, have an important part to play in the management thereof but are excluded from the list of relevant authorities who may instigate the development of management plans.

[80] Environment Act 1995 s.103.

attention at the moment is on the identification of the sites rather than their protection.

Marine Environmental High Risk Areas

In January 1993 an oil tanker went aground on the Shetland Islands. The incident prompted the government to set up an inquiry, chaired by Lord Donaldson, into the risk of pollution from merchant shipping. The report of the inquiry[81] included among its recommendations proposals for the establishment of Marine Environmental High Risk Areas (MEHRAs) defined as 'comparatively limited areas of high sensitivity which are also at risk from shipping'.[82] The idea behind the proposals is to single out environmentally sensitive areas so that mariners are made aware of them and can take their sensitivities into account in deciding routeing. A particular site would only be eligible for consideration as a MEHRA if it met two sets of criteria, one dealing with environmental considerations and the other with maritime considerations. So not all of the best marine conservation sites in British waters would necessarily be eligible for MEHRA status. To qualify they would also have to be at risk from pollution from shipping. The suggested environmental criteria[83] encompass high conservation status as evidenced by designation as an SAC or SPA, the existence of commercially exploitable biological resources and public recreational amenities.

The report does not recommend any specific protective measures to follow automatically from MEHRA status but follows the government view that, if mariners are given the necessary information, they will act correctly without the need for statutory controls over routeing. Such a conclusion avoids the difficulty of tackling the possibility of infringement of international rights of navigation.

Particularly Sensitive Sea Areas

The Law of the Sea Convention embodies the principle of freedom of navigation of vessels in the high seas and the right of innocent passage of vessels in the territorial waters of other states. Any restraints on these freedoms are subject to agreement with the International Maritime Organization (IMO). The IMO has introduced several voluntary measures on grounds of safety including Areas to be Avoided and Vessel Traffic Schemes. In addition it has negotiated a regime for discharges

[81] *Safer Ships, Cleaner Seas* (1994, Cm.2560).
[82] Ibid., para.14.120.
[83] Ibid., para.14.123–4.

from vessels under the MARPOL Convention.[84] In 1992 IMO further agreed to a new type of area, known as a Particularly Sensitive Sea Area.[85] This bears many similarities to a MEHRA in that it is merely an identification of an area of sea that is vulnerable to shipping activities because of its environmental qualities. Identification carries with it no automatic special protection.

Marine Environmentally Sensitive Areas

In 1993 the European Council invited Member States to identify Environmentally Sensitive Areas in their national territory[86] as a prelude to determining adequate standards for ships sailing through such areas. The responses, although incomplete, suggest that Member States believe most of the European Union coastline and adjacent seas to be environmentally sensitive. The UK response stresses that site selection must be based on a balance between the environmental interests in need of protection, the implications of any proposed restrictions on the free movement of shipping and the degree of risk involved. The government did not submit a definitive list, therefore, because no indications have yet been given as to the level or type of protection to be applied. At the most general level, however, it was concluded that there was no part of the United Kingdom coast where it can be assumed that no consideration should be given to additional protection against pollution from shipping.

Conclusions

As with any other type of nature conservation law, the main purpose of marine nature conservation legislation must be to protect marine wildlife from undue human interference. The traditional device for protecting nature conservation interests is the protected area. This is good for controlling access and for regulating the use of land. Even where the land is not in sympathetic ownership, the system works on the basis that there is a responsible owner or occupier who can be required to control the use to which his or her land is put. It is precisely because of its proprietary nature that the traditional protected area system is ineffective for marine conservation. It cannot accommodate the public and international rights and it is greatly complicated by the involvement of so many statutory bodies and government departments. Hence the failure of both the SSSI

[84] International Convention for the Prevention of Pollution from Ships 1973 and its 1978 Protocol, UKTS 27 (1983) Cmnd. 8924.

[85] IMO Assembly 17 Resolution 720 adopted 6 November 1991.

[86] Council Resolution of 8 June 1993 on a common policy on safe sea (OJ C271, 7 October 1993, p.1).

and the MNR to further marine conservation. An additional problem with both of these, especially the SSSI, is that they are essentially information-led. The SSSI, after all, is first and foremost a notification of the scientific interest of a site and MNR submissions must be based on a detailed submission from the appropriate nature conservation agency including a scientific justification for designation. In most cases, however, our knowledge of the marine environment is far from complete. Even for the statutory MNR at Skomer, for example, only a small percentage of the sea bed has been properly explored. The traditional protected area system, therefore, fails to provide for use of the precautionary principle in the sense of protecting areas before their conservation importance has been evaluated.

So what is the alternative? The idea of integrated coastal management has been canvassed for years[87] but has only recently come into prominence within government thinking. Advocates of coastal zone management want a system of integrated management of all activities within the coastal zone under the administration of a statutory agency or other authority.[88] Management is envisaged as being plan-led with a hierarchy of plans at national, regional and local levels. The essence of management is that activities will be balanced with a view to sustainability. This gives a high profile to conservation considerations, including conservation of resources as well as wildlife. It is possible to incorporate a system of MPAs within a wider system of coastal zone management as was proposed by the Marine Protected Areas Working Group.[89]

Despite broad endorsement by the Environment Committee the government has not been supportive of such a far-reaching approach.[90] This is not surprising on political grounds in that the existing proposals for coastal zone management are all based on increased regulation, legislative reform and, inevitably, increased bureaucracy. This is very much against the government's favoured voluntary approach. Even if there were the political will to place coastal management on a stronger statutory footing, there would still be the problem of establishing a suitable administrative framework and, in particular, of deciding what form the managing authority should take.[91] There would also be a problem with such tight

---

[87] See, for example, R. B. Clark, *The Waters Around the British Isles: Their Conflicting Uses* (Clarendon Press, Oxford, 1987), especially ch.IX, 'Development and conservation on the coast'.

[88] See, for example, S. Gubbay, *A Future for the Coast: Proposals for a UK Coastal Zone Management Plan* (Marine Conservation Society and WWF, Godalming, 1990.)

[89] See above note 53.

[90] See above note 60.

[91] Note that the Marine Protected Areas Working Party (see above note 53) deliberately avoided this issue.

regulation of coastal activities of squaring the measures with international obligations and rights.

The government has, however, conceded that management is necessary in some cases, especially for SACs where it is virtually mandatory, and that there must be co-operation if not integration. It is strongly supportive of management plans produced in various contexts and has promised to take action to highlight good practice on coastal management plans.[92] Its proposals for MCAs were a first attempt at moving towards a sustainability-led conservation policy away from treating conservation as a sectoral interest. Since then, largely in response to the obligations under the Habitats Directive, it has recognized the need to make legislative changes. The path it has chosen to take is to impose additional purposive powers and duties on statutory bodies so that they use their statutory powers for nature conservation purposes.

The result is a hybrid. We have a move towards integration but without any lead. With the exception of European marine sites, there is no intention to make any one body responsible for drawing up or implementing management plans and even in this case it is expected that co-operation will be voluntary. When the Habitats Directive regulations were debated in the House of Commons there was a broad welcome for the measures but concerns were expressed that the voluntary approach would not work without considerable financial input that appeared to be lacking.[93] It is very unclear how these various bodies are to decide who is to take the lead and what part the nature conservation agencies are expected to play. It might be thought that for European marine sites they would be the appropriate body to draw up the management plan in every case but it is clear that this is not what is intended. If co-operation cannot be achieved the Secretary of State will be able to require it. The fear here is that at best the outcome will be a compromise. Giving sea fisheries committees express powers to make by-laws for environmental purposes does not mean that they will necessarily agree with the nature conservation agency as to how to exercise them. The addition of a few environmentally qualified members to a sea fisheries committee[94] will not remedy this. Sea fisheries committees and nature conservation agencies approach nature conservation from different starting points and are answerable to different sectors of government. The present proposals make no provisions for conflict resolution.

[92] [246] HC Debs Written Answer col. 781–3, 15 July 1994, Mr. Atkins.
[93] [247] HC Debs col. 239–61, 19 July 1994.
[94] Environment Act 1995 s.102.

With the exception of the consultation paper on 'Managing the coast',[95] the impact of individuals, rather than bodies, has been completely overlooked. The MNR by-laws, which are to form the basis of any by-laws made for European marine sites, cannot prevent damage resulting from the thoughtless action of a few individuals. Neither is there any provision to deal with international aspects of navigation despite the acknowledged need manifest in the various proposals for identifying offshore areas.

Despite these apparent deficiencies in the proposed legislation there is a fear that the European Marine Site will become the most important, if not the only, statutory marine protected area. Certainly the amount of effort that will need to be put into it will inhibit the nature-conservation agencies from making much progress with other initiatives. There is already evidence that MNRs will be regarded as surplus to requirements and too costly to be justified. This is unfortunate because the purposes of MNRs are broader than those for SACs. The latter are purely a protective mechanism whereas MNRs are also appropriate for educational and research purposes. The proposed Menai Strait MNR, for example, can be justified on the grounds that it would provide an opportunity to inform the public about marine wildlife, and a recent international review of the Skomer MNR has recommended that it should be developed as a major research base.

Following the enactment of the 1981 Act there was criticism that the government was placing far too much reliance on the voluntary approach. In terms of progress with MNR designation these criticisms can be seen to be justified. The criticism to be levied at the government's present approach to marine conservation and, particularly, its approach to implementing the Habitats Directive, is that it has added complexity to the existing problems. Even assuming that the various bodies will be able to co-operate together to draw up a suitable management plan for a European Marine Site there is nothing to guarantee that it will be implemented. There is a danger that management plans will be a good displacement exercise, diverting attention from the immediate task of addressing the problems rather than planning to address them.

The need to implement the Habitats Directive provided the government with an ideal opportunity to review site protection in the marine environment and come up with a form of statutory protection that could meet the needs for conservation post-Rio. Both the conservation agencies and DoE are questioning the need for all the present types of protected areas and are considering possible rationalization. The European Marine Site merely adds to the confusion. It is too narrowly defined to replace MNRs and goes far beyond the requirements of an SSSI. Because international navigation is left out, it is only a matter of time before one

[95] See above note 59.

of the proposed offshore designations fills this gap and adds a further complication. The government's concessions to coastal zone management are unlikely to win much support either, because of the continued reliance on the voluntary approach in the absence of clear guidance and direction.

4

Reforming the Law of Habitat Protection

SIMON BALL

Introduction

Ever since most of the recommendations of the landmark report of the Huxley Committee[1] were accepted by the government of the day, the protection of habitat has been central to nature conservation law in the UK.[2] The National Parks and Access to the Countryside Act 1949 created two types of designated site which are still with us – the nature reserve and the site of special scientific interest (SSSI) – although in the case of SSSIs the scope of the legal powers applicable to them, and hence their function, has changed virtually out of all recognition since then.

At the same time, the Huxley report and the resulting legislation established a clear distinction between nature conservation and amenity protection. Of particular note was that nature-conservation law and policy was based firmly on scientific, ecological principles, whilst amenity and recreational matters were seen in more human-centred terms.

Over the years the centrality of habitat protection has been reinforced regularly, and, despite recent institutional changes and the growth in interest in nature conservation as a recreational activity, the scientific basis of

---

[1] Wildlife Conservation Special Committee, *Conservation of Nature in England and Wales,* Cmd. 7122 (1947); for Scotland, see the similar recommendations of the Scottish Wildlife Conservation Committee (the Ritchie Committee), *Nature Reserves in Scotland,* Cmd. 7814 (1949).

[2] For a fuller discussion of the law relating to habitat protection, see Reid, *Nature Conservation Law* (W. Green, 1994), esp ch.5, or Ball and Bell, *Environmental Law* (Blackstone, 3rd edn; 1995), ch.16.

the law remains. In terms of changes in the legislation there have been two major advances. First, Part II of the Wildlife and Countryside Act 1981 introduced a more detailed regime for habitat protection, effectively establishing notification as an SSSI as the mechanism which provides the basic legal protection for important nature-conservation sites.[3] In the main, this was a reflection of the need to comply with Directive 79/409/EEC on the conservation of wild birds (the Birds Directive) and the Council of Europe Convention on the Conservation of European Wildlife and Habitats 1979 (the Berne Convention), both of which placed great emphasis on habitat protection, but it also reflected the clear inadequacy of the existing law when it came to protecting nature from agricultural as well as urban development threats.[4]

Second, Directive 92/43/EEC on the conservation of natural habitats and of wild fauna and flora (the Habitats Directive), agreed in 1992 after many years of argument within the EC, further reinforced the place of habitat measures. Building on the principles established in the Berne Convention, the directive requires (ultimately) the designation of special areas of conservation which will make up, together with the special protection areas for birds classified under the Birds Directive, a system of European sites known as Natura 2000. The UK government has implemented the directive through the Conservation (Natural Habitats etc.) Regulations 1994,[5] which came into force on 30 October 1994.

Questions about the reform of the law of habitat protection can perhaps be grouped into two main categories, reflecting the two major periods of legislative development.

(a) Has the Wildlife and Countryside Act 1981 worked? Does it actually provide an adequate basis of legal protection for important nature-conservation sites? Could it be improved?

(b) What changes does the Habitats Directive make? Will it improve the legal protection of habitat? In any case, has it been implemented fully in the UK?

There is, however, a third set of issues which relate to whether the current shape of the law requires wholesale rethinking in the light of the concept of sustainable development. Some deeper questions about the whole purpose and direction of nature conservation law are thus raised. All these questions will be discussed further below.

[3] The Wildlife and Countryside Act 1981 applies to the whole of Great Britain; similar provisions applicable to Northern Ireland are laid down in the Nature Conservation and Amenity Lands (Northern Ireland) Order 1985.

[4] See Moore, *Loss and Damage to SSSI* (NCC, 1981), which showed the SSSI series to be 'under very serious threat', with between 10 and 15 per cent of SSSIs suffering significant damage or loss in 1980 alone.

[5] SI 1994 No. 2716.

Habitat Protection and Property Rights

The emphasis on habitat protection creates a fairly obvious potential conflict between nature conservation laws and property rights. At common law, owners of land can do what they like with it. In principle, this means they can use the land as they wish, exclude others from it, sell it, or damage or destroy it. Plants (and also rocks, fossils, etc.) are part of the land until severed from it, so have no protection against the owner, though the owner could take steps to protect them against others. Wild animals and birds are in a sense even worse off: whilst they belong to nobody, they have no legal rights of their own and thus are essentially unprotected. Of course, there are some inherent common law restrictions on what owners can do, but these relate to the protection of other owners' rights (for example, through the law of nuisance), or the protection of personal or financial interests (for example, through the law of negligence), rather than to the protection of the environment. The idea of a wider concept worthy of protection in its own right, such as a habitat or a landscape, is foreign to the common law.

Legislation which seeks to restrict property (or private) rights is normally justified in terms of the public interest. The process is seen most clearly in the planning system, where the public interest is effectively decided by a democratically elected body (the local planning authority or, on appeal, the Secretary of State) and includes such things as the need for economic development and financial resourcing questions as well as cultural, environmental and amenity factors. In other words, the competing private and public interests are balanced against each other.

Inevitably, the balancing process leads to compromise. In relation to nature-conservation sites, the assumption has always been that some sites will have to be sacrificed in the furtherance of the public interest – again this is seen most clearly in the relationship of the planning system to SSSI protection, but it is also apparent throughout environmental law.

Is this position acceptable? It is strongly arguable that the ecological interest, which is traditionally seen as only one part of the wider public interest, deserves greater protection. Whilst this gets little support from traditional legal approaches because of the absence of any entrenched rights given to the environment, it may seem to follow from the scientific/ecological basis of the legislation referred to above. Support can be drawn from the current debate on sustainable development. The Brundtland Commission defined sustainable development as 'Development that meets the needs of today whilst not affecting the ability of future generations to meet their own needs',[6] which implies that global environmental resources (or 'capital') should be measured to ascertain

[6] *Our Common Future*, Report of the World Commission on Environment and Development (1987).

whether they have been depleted over time. Pearce[7] suggests there is a distinction between 'weak' and 'strong' sustainability. Whilst weak sustainability treats the environment as simply one interchangeable form of capital (i.e. it is acceptable to deplete environmental resources/capital if there is equivalent investment in substitutes), on the strong view of sustainability some environmental resources are critical to survival in the sense that losses 'may threaten the primary life support functions of ecological systems'.[8] Potential examples of such 'critical natural capital' are the ozone layer and the carbon cycle, but arguably the clearest example is biodiversity. The argument is that *any* loss of this capital is unsustainable and thus deserving of absolute protection.

The Legal Protections

In the current law the two main protective devices for nature conservation are SSSI designation and planning law. However, as shown below, both systems reflect compromise – planning law because ecological/ environmental issues are seen as just one part of the public interest, SSSI protection because of its essentially voluntary nature. There are no real absolutes in either system. The big difference that the Habitats Directive makes is to suggest, in line with the arguments set out above, that there may be some sites where there is no balance to be drawn – where protection is to be something close to absolute.

SSSIs

The key legal protection for nature-conservation sites (and indeed for geological and geomorphological sites) is the site of special scientific interest (SSSI). SSSIs are notified by the appropriate national nature-conservation agency (English Nature, Scottish Natural Heritage or Countryside Council for Wales – for ease of explanation, the text will hereafter refer simply to English Nature) on *scientific* criteria.[9] Land-ownership is unaffected, but restrictions are imposed on the owners and occupiers of sites, who have to notify English Nature before they carry out any of the 'potentially damaging operations' that were specified in the notification to them. It is a criminal offence to fail to notify English Nature before carrying out a potentially damaging operation, or to fail to wait four months once English Nature has been notified. The objective of this four-month period is to enable English Nature to try to enter into a management agreement with the owner or occupier under which

---

[7] Pearce et al., *Blueprint 3: Measuring Sustainable Development* (Earthscan, 1993).
[8] Ibid., p.16.
[9] Wildlife and Countryside Act 1981, s.28(1).

compensatory payments will be made in return for not damaging the site.[10] The sum total of SSSI protection is thus a four-month ban on owners and occupiers carrying out potentially damaging operations.

A further protection is that, under s.29 of the 1981 Act, the Secretary of State can make a nature conservation order. This involves a number of slightly stronger protections, such as that the restrictions and the offences apply to non-occupiers, English Nature has some limited rights of entry to the land, the maximum fine is unlimited and a restoration order may be made. However, the essential nature of the protection is the same as for SSSIs in that a temporary ban is imposed on specified potentially damaging operations, in this case the ban being for twelve months rather than four.

It is also possible for English Nature to declare a site a national nature reserve,[11] in which case the land will be managed by English Nature and a limited range of protective by-laws may be imposed.[12] These national nature reserves normally require the agreement of the landowner (either to sell or lease the land to English Nature, or to enter into a nature reserve agreement). There is a power of compulsory purchase,[13] but the use of this power has been very rare, no doubt mainly because of the resource implications.

Has Part II of the 1981 Act worked?

In looking at the adequacy of the habitat protection provisions in Part II of the Act, the philosophy underpinning them must be understood. The general philosophy adopted by the Conservative government is one of voluntariness. This can be summarized by saying that landowners are offered incentives to act in accordance with agreed nature-conservation policies, rather than subjected to compulsory, regulatory controls over their activities. The approach is exemplified by the central position given to the management agreement in the legal regime. This philosophy can be seen as part of a general shift in the 1980s towards neo-liberal solutions based on contract, but it also means that, looked at in terms of the competing interests referred to earlier, the private interest is fully protected,

[10] Management agreements over SSSIs are made under the Countryside Act 1968, s.15, as amended by the Environmental Protection Act, sched. 9, para.4, which allowed them to be agreed with the owners of the land 'adjacent' to an SSSI. Nature reserve agreements are made under the National Parks and Access to the Countryside Act 1949, s.16. Agreements relating to the wider countryside may be concluded under the Wildlife and Countryside Act 1981, s.39.

[11] Wildlife and Countryside Act 1981, s.35: as Reid, op.cit., points out at pp.150–1, the word 'national' was technically only added by s.35, previous sites simply being nature reserves.

[12] National Parks and Access to the Countryside Act 1949, s.20.

[13] National Parks and Access to the Countryside Act 1949, s.17.

whilst the ecological interest is not. The effect, to quote Lord Mustill, is clear:

> it needs only a moment to see that this regime is toothless, for it demands no more from an owner or occupier of an SSSI than a little patience . . . In truth the Act does no more in the great majority of cases than give the Council a breathing space within which to apply moral pressure, with a view to persuading the owner or occupier to make a voluntary agreement.[14]

This is not to say that the ecological interest is *wholly* unrecognized, but it is not given any entrenched protection. In addition, it has to be protected within financial and other constraints. In relation to SSSI management agreements, the level of compensation reflects the arguably generous measure of the profits forgone by the owner or occupier.[15] It is hard to amass firm evidence, but it must be suspected that there have been cases where the potential cost of the management agreement has led to a decision to allow damage to a site (or even to a policy decision not to notify the site in the first place, which would appear to be unlawful under s.28(1)).[16] A more telling criticism is that management agreements tend to be negative – they pay the owner not to do something and do not provide positive incentives to act in a particular environmentally friendly manner.[17] In this context, the question must be asked whether these agreements are cost-effective, especially when it is realized that each SSSI management agreement effectively has to be negotiated afresh, unlike those in systems which provide for off-the-shelf measures (for example, in environmentally sensitive areas).

However, at the simplest level, the answer to the question whether the Act works can be provided by looking at the statistics on loss and damage to protected sites. These suggest that, whilst there may have been *some* improvement since 1981, the position is still not at all healthy for SSSIs. For example, the National Audit Office has reported that, using English Nature figures, 869 SSSIs (over 20 per cent of the total number of SSSIs in England) suffered loss or damage between 1987 and 1993, although there was some double counting as some sites were damaged year after year.[18] Similarly, in a major report published in 1991, Wildlife Link reported significant loss and damage to SSSIs, suggesting that each

[14] *Southern Water Authority* v. *Nature Conservancy Council* [1992] 3 All ER 481 at 484.

[15] See Wildlife and Countryside Act 1981, s.50 and DoE Circular 4/83.

[16] See *R* v. *Nature Conservancy Council, ex parte London Brick Property Ltd.* [1995] ELM 95.

[17] Although this is being addressed through English Nature's Wildlife Enhancement Scheme.

[18] *Protecting and Managing Sites of Special Scientific Interest* (National Audit Office, 1994).

year around 5 per cent of all SSSIs suffered loss or damage.[19] These figures raise the question of what, if that is the position in relation to the most important sites, is happening in the wider countryside.

Can the 1981 Act be improved?

Given the adoption of a voluntary approach, has the Act been implemented as successfully as it might have been? For example, are there any gaps which could be plugged, or any drafting difficulties that could be improved? In this context it is relevant to note that the provisions of Part II of the 1981 Act were originally drafted in a fair degree of haste and, structural problems aside, provide a number of difficult matters of interpretation. For example, *Southern Water Authority* v. *NCC*[20] illustrates a situation where the House of Lords was unwilling to diverge from the precise words of the Act even when they produced a clearly unintended and undesirable result.

The following problems can be noted:[21]

(a) The Act does not apply below the low-water mark, which means that many of the UK's most important habitats are unprotected.[22] In legal terms, this is a consequence of requiring, under s.28(1), that the local planning authority be notified of the designation of an SSSI. However, it also follows from the reliance on management agreements, since below the low-water mark there are no owners or occupiers with whom to enter into an agreement.

(b) The restriction only applies to the initially specified potentially damaging operations and not to all activities that may damage the site: it would be simple to amend the law so that it covered all damaging activities, unless exempted.

(c) Neglect and lack of management, significant causes of damage to SSSIs, are not covered by the phrase 'potentially damaging operations'. In other words, English Nature has no powers under the SSSI legislation to combat inactivity or neglect by a landowner. This reflects the general way that the legislation is worded so as to compensate for not doing something, rather than for doing

[19] Rowell, *SSSIs: A Health Check* (Wildlife Link, 1991).

[20] Loc.cit.

[21] Further discussion of the defects of the Act is provided by Ball, 'Protected nature conservation sites and the water industry', [1990] *Water Law* 74, and Hughes, *The Habitats Directive and the UK Conservation Framework and SSSI System*, House of Commons Research Paper 94/90, 15 July 1994.

[22] The protection of coastal and marine areas is covered by the chapter by Lynda Warren in this collection. Accordingly, this important topic will not be dealt with in this chapter except in passing.

something positive (though, increasingly, other pieces of legislation address this problem).

(d) In *North Uist Fisheries Ltd* v. *Secretary of State for Scotland*,[23] it was decided that the word 'likely' (actually as used in s.29) meant that something had to be probable rather than merely possible. If this is correct (and this writer would argue that it is not in the context of the Act) and also applies to s.28, it would drive a coach and horses through the limited protection provided by the Act by reducing the list of potentially damaging operations on each site.

(e) The maximum fine is only £2,500. It is hard to see why the maximum fine should be less than, for example, under the Town and Country Planning Act 1990, where the maximum fine on summary conviction is £20,000. In addition, under that Act the profit to the defendant has to be taken into account in determining the amount of the fine,[24] an idea that could usefully be copied.

(f) S.28 only restricts the activities of owners and occupiers. Apart from some continuing lack of clarity about the meaning of an occupier, even after *Southern Water Authority* v. *Nature Conservancy Council*[25] decided that it requires some form of stable relationship with the land, this means that third parties, such as trespassers and temporary visitors using the site for recreational purposes, are not affected. Indeed, the *Southern Water* case, which concerned a water authority carrying out drainage works on an SSSI in a manner that the House of Lords termed 'environmental vandalism', is a good example both of this problem and of another one − the difficulty of controlling statutory undertakers and other public bodies.[26]

(g) Off-site problems, such as pollution migrating on to the site or drainage by surrounding landowners, are difficult to address directly because s.28 only applies to owners and occupiers of the SSSI (although there is now a power for English Nature to enter into management agreements with adjacent owners and occupiers).[27]

Points (e), (f) and (g) do not apply to sites where a s.29 nature conservation order is in force. However, the main criterion for designation under s.29 is that the site is of 'national importance'. Despite the highly plausible argument that SSSIs are part of a representative series and are logically

[23] [1992] JEL 241.

[24] Town and Country Planning Act 1990, s.179(9).

[25] Loc.cit.

[26] Under the Water Resources Act 1991, s.17 bodies in the water industry are subject to specific duties in relation to SSSIs, but these are ultimately enforceable only through judicial review.

[27] Environmental Protection Act, sched. 9, para.4, though why the power is limited to *adjacent* owners only is unclear.

all of *equal* (and thus arguably of national) importance, it is clear that the Secretary of State has interpreted this requirement as ruling out the application of s.29 to many SSSIs.[28]

Returning to the statistics on loss and damage to SSSIs, it is clear that a significant number of cases of damage are caused by these largely unnecessary gaps.[29]

Nature Conservation and Planning Permission

There are certain protections for nature within the town planning system. Apart from the general duty to include environmental considerations in development plans, Planning Policy Guidance (PPG) Note 9, *Nature Conservation* (October 1994), lays down some fairly clear policies about the protection of the nature conservation interest of sites and emphasizes the use of conditions or planning obligations to avoid damaging impacts (for example, bunding requirements, translocation, or safeguard of part of a site). The presence (and importance in national and international terms) of something of nature conservation interest on a site is clearly a material consideration which must be taken into account. At a procedural level there is a duty to consult with English Nature before a planning decision is made on an SSSI or in a surrounding consultation area.[30]

Of course, many activities which may damage the nature conservation interest of a site do not require planning permission. However, even where they do, the ecological interest is, as mentioned earlier, only one interest amongst many. The decision whether to grant permission is a discretionary one based on a balancing of *all* material factors. The limitations of planning law in protecting ecological interests are illustrated by *R v. Poole DC, ex parte Beebee*[31] and *R v. Swale BC, ex parte RSPB*,[32] where in each case planning permission was granted in the face of fairly strong nature-conservation grounds that it should be refused.

In addition, acting in accordance with a planning permission is a defence to a prosecution for damaging an SSSI or a s.29 site.[33] In other words, once granted, a planning permission outranks an SSSI designation. In one sense this is a significant gap in the legislation relating to SSSI protection. But what it does is transfer the power to protect the site to the

---

[28] See Withrington and Jones, 'The enforcement of conservation legislation: protecting sites of special scientific interest', in *Agriculture, Conservation and Land Use*, ed. Rodgers and Howarth, 93–6.

[29] See Hughes, op.cit.

[30] Town and Country Planning (General Development Procedure) Order 1995 (SI 1995, No. 419), article 10.

[31] [1991] JPL 643.

[32] [1991] JPL 40.

[33] Wildlife and Countryside Act 1981, ss.28(8) and 29(9).

planning system. A decision to grant planning permission is effectively a decision (by an elected decision-maker) that the general public interest is more important than the ecological interest reflected in the SSSI designation.

One specific situation where the balancing process always produces an unacceptable result relates to past planning permissions, which are treated exactly the same as any other permission for this purpose. For example, perpetual planning permission was granted for peat extraction on Thorne Moors, the largest lowland raised bog in the country, in the late 1940s, when the nature conservation interest of the site was little understood (or maybe simply little accepted). Because compensation has to be paid where a planning permission is revoked, it would be very expensive to revoke or buy off this permission. In this situation, the private interest is protected through the compensation right. So is the public interest, though this is as it was originally defined in the 1940s and things have changed radically since then. The ecological interest is ignored.

The Birds Directive

The Birds Directive includes two separate obligations relating to habitat. Article 3 imposes a general obligation on Member States to act so as to preserve, maintain or re-establish a sufficient area of habitat for all the species of wild birds listed in Annex I[34] and to strive to avoid pollution or deterioration of these habitats. Article 4 requires further conservation measures for Annex I birds, in particular the classification (i.e. designation) of suitable sites as *special protection areas* for the conservation of these species (hereafter SPAs). In recognition of the importance of western Europe for migratory species, this duty also applies to key breeding, moulting, wintering and migration sites for *all* regularly occurring migratory species. In *Commission* v. *Spain*,[35] the European Court of Justice decided that the Spanish government was in breach of the directive by failing to designate an important wetland area, the Santoña Marshes. In essence, this case establishes that there is a duty to designate an area as an SPA where it fulfils the objective ornithological criteria laid down in the directive.

In relation to SPAs, Member States are required to take, under article 4(4), 'appropriate steps to avoid pollution or deterioration of habitats or any disturbances affecting the birds, in so far as these would be significant having regard to the objectives of this Article'. In *Commission* v. *Germany*,[36] in an important judgement concerning an area known as Leybucht Dykes,

[34] Annex I includes 175 species or sub-species and is by no means limited to the rarest birds.
[35] Case C355/90.
[36] [1991] ECR 883; [1992] JEL 139.

the European Court of Justice decided that the only exceptions to article 4(4) were where the works were necessary for reasons of public health or public safety (which was actually the situation in the case itself), and that works could not be permitted for economic or recreational reasons. The immediate effect of this decision was reversed by article 7 of the Habitats Directive, which brought the Birds Directive into line with the less restrictive exceptions laid down in article 6 of that directive (see below), but it illustrates the tendency of the European Court of Justice to take a fairly robust interpretation of environmental directives. The point is reinforced by the *Santoña Marshes* case, which suggested that article 4(4) is sufficiently clear to be directly effective in relation to the duty to avoid pollution or deterioration of SPAs, although it appears that the duty to classify in article 4(4) is sufficiently clear to be directly effective in relation to the duty to avoid pollution or deterioration of SPA s, although it appears that the duty to classify in article 4(1) is not directly effective.[37]

Notwithstanding the partial reversal referred to above, the implication is clear – SPAs (whether actually classified or merely fulfilling the criteria) are to be given very strong protection, although it does fall short of absolute protection.

The Habitats Directive

The main focus of the Habitats Directive is on the creation of a 'coherent ecological network of special areas of conservation' to be called Natura 2000. In other words, although there are some significant provisions on the protection of species, the emphasis is on the protection of the designated sites. Natura 2000 is to be made up of three types of site:

(a) those hosting the natural habitat types listed in Annex I to the Directive;
(b) those comprising the habitats of the (rare) species listed in Annex II;
(c) the SPAs designated under the Birds Directive.

The general idea is to maintain (or where appropriate restore) these habitat types and species' habitats to a position where for the foreseeable future they are stable or increasing.[38]

Leaving aside the SPAs (which are discussed above), the procedures for producing the list of Natura 2000 sites are complex.

(a) By 5 June 1995, Member States were required to send the Commission a list of proposed sites, identifying whether they are in

---

[37] See Somsen, 'Member States' obligations under directive 79/409', [1993] *Water Law* 209.
[38] Article 3(1).

category (a) or (b) above. This list was to be drawn up by reference to the criteria laid down in Annex III (Stage 1): in relation to Annex I sites this covers such things as the representativeness, area, degree of conservation and global importance of the site for the habitat type concerned, whilst in relation to Annex II sites it covers the size in national terms, degree of isolation, degree of conservation and global importance of the site for the species concerned. In *Biodiversity: The UK Action Plan*,[39] it is estimated that some seventy-five habitat types and forty taxa of animals and plants occur within the UK.

(b) The Commission is then under a duty to draw up, by 5 June 1998, a draft list of 'sites of Community importance'. This selection process will take account of the criteria set out in Annex III (Stage 2): these include such things as the relative national importance of the proposed site, its geographic location, its area, and the global ecological value of the site in respect of the biogeographical region it is in.[40] In other words, not all the sites proposed by a Member State will be listed by the Commission. In addition, the Commission will produce a separate list of those sites which host one or more of the *priority* habitat types or species which are identified in Annexes I and II (these sites can be termed 'priority sites'). According to Annex III (Stage 2) such sites *must* be considered as sites of Community importance, with the proviso that, under article 4(2), a Member State which has more than 5 per cent of its territory covered by priority sites may request the Commission to apply the criteria more flexibly.

(c) Under article 21 the draft list is to be considered by a committee of representative experts appointed by the Member States before adoption by the Commission – the EC Council will arbitrate over any disagreements between the Commission and the committee.

(d) Article 5 provides for a bilateral consultation process between the Commission and a Member State where the Commission considers a priority site has been left off a Member State's list. In the event of a dispute over a site remaining unresolved, the EC Council will decide the matter. However, since this decision can only be taken unanimously, the usefulness of this procedure must be questioned, as the Member State concerned will presumably veto the selection of the site.

(e) Once the Commission has adopted the list of sites of Community importance, under article 4(4) Member States are under a duty to

---

[39] Cm. 2428 (January 1994).

[40] Article 1(c)(iii) lists five biogeographical regions: Alpine, Atlantic, Continental, Macronesian and Mediterranean.

designate any site on the list as a *special area of conservation* (SAC) as soon as possible and no later than six years from the adoption of the list. The full list of SACs will therefore be in existence by 5 June 2004 at the latest.

(f) There are some continuing procedural duties under the directive. Under article 9 the Commission is under a duty to review the Natura 2000 list in the light of the directive's objectives (this could include de-classifying a site), whilst under article 17 detailed implementation reports are required from the Member States and the Commission. Finally, the Annexes can be altered by a qualified majority vote in the EC Council (article 19).

Protection provided by the Habitats Directive

Article 6 contains the central protections laid down by the directive. The two following duties apply to sites *adopted* by the Commission as sites of Community importance and to SPAs designated under the Birds Directive:

(a) under article 6(2), Member States are required to take appropriate steps to avoid the deterioration of the sites and 'significant' disturbance of the species for which the areas have been designated (this duty also applies on an interim basis to sites subject to the article 5 consultation procedure); and

(b) under article 6(3), 'any plan or project not directly connected with or necessary to the management of the site but likely to have a significant effect thereon . . . shall be subject to appropriate assessment of its implications for the site . . . [T]he competent national authorities shall agree to the plan or project only after having ascertained that it will not adversely affect the integrity of the site concerned . . .'

However, article 6(4) provides for an exception. If (and only if) there is no alternative solution, a 'plan or project' affecting a site may be carried out for 'imperative reasons of overriding public interest, including those of a social or economic nature'. For priority sites the exception is more limited – only three types of exception can be relied upon:

(a) considerations relating to human health or public safety;

(b) considerations relating to 'beneficial consequences of primary importance for the environment', which is not defined;

(c) other reasons of overriding public interest only if they are accepted by the Commission.

This appears to retain the position set out in the *Leybucht Dykes* case for priority sites, whilst watering the protection down for other sites.[41]

In any situation where the exception in article 6(4) is relied on, the Member State has to take any compensatory measures necessary to ensure the protection of the overall coherence of Natura 2000 and must inform the Commission of those measures. In addition, a wider obligation to adopt necessary conservation measures (which may include a management plan for the site) arises once a site is formally designated by the Member State as an SAC. Rather oddly, this obligation does not apply to SPAs designated under the Birds Directive.[42]

Finally, two other articles of the directive require a mention. Article 10 requires Member States to 'endeavour, where they consider it necessary', to encourage the management of certain important features, such as linear features (i.e. rivers, hedges, field boundaries, etc.) or areas functioning as stepping stones (e.g. ponds, small woods or areas of fragmented heath).[43] Article 11 places Member States under a general duty to monitor the conservation status of *all* habitats and species.

The regulations

The Conservation (Natural Habitats, etc.) Regulations 1994[44] seek to implement the provisions of the directive in British law. In general terms, the government has sought to 'continue to work as far as possible under the voluntary principle, seeking the involvement and active co-operation of those involved who live and work in rural areas and at sea'.[45] Its approach has been a minimalist one in which it has tried to engraft on to existing mechanisms the additional protections that are required by the directive. In essence, this means that, although there are *some* additional controls and restrictions, there is a continuing reliance on the twin systems of SSSI protection and planning control. As pointed out above, these are both systems with an in-built tendency towards compromise. It also means that the existing defects in these systems identified earlier may doom such an approach to failure from the start, irrespective of any extra measures that may be added.

[41] One anomaly which is of importance for the UK is that there are no priority bird species, thus reducing the possibility of birds benefiting from the stronger controls applicable to priority sites.

[42] This is perhaps as well, since SI 1994/2716 does not include a reference to management plans for terrestrial sites, although in *Biodiversity: The UK Action Plan* (Cm. 2428), ch.4.64, it is stated to be government policy that a summary management plan be produced for each biological SSSI by 2004.

[43] This obligation is implemented in SI 1994/2716, article 37.

[44] SI 1994, No. 2716.

[45] *Draft Conservation (Natural Habitats etc.) Regulations 1994 Compliance Cost Assessment.*

The regulations are made under the European Communities Act 1972, s.2(2). As such they can do no more than simply implement the directive. It also means that they must be interpreted in the light of the directive.[46] In recent years it has become government practice to avoid the difficulties involved in correct transposition of directives into domestic law and the resultant threat of infringement proceedings for non-compliance by simply repeating the words of the directive. One result is that implementing regulations such as these tend to include phrases of unparalleled opaqueness and unintelligibility. Another is that it puts the onus of ascertaining whether implementation has been adequate on to those who wish to challenge the government's (or any other public body's) interpretation, who must bring appropriate judicial review actions. A third result is that responsibility for interpreting the directive shifts from the government (i.e. through the transposition process) to the courts. In the first instance this means the UK courts, though obviously the intention is that the domestic courts will take the opportunity to refer suitable matters to the European Court of Justice under article 177 of the EC Treaty.[47]

The regulations stick to the procedures and timetable set out in the directive fairly closely. For example, regulation 7 requires the Secretary of State to propose a list of sites on or before 5 June 1995,[48] whilst regulation 8 requires the Secretary of State to designate sites adopted by the Commission as SACs 'as soon as possible and within six years at most'. Regulation 10 establishes the concept of a 'European site' and, in accordance with the directive, defines it to mean:

(a) an SAC;
(b) a site adopted by the Commission as a site of Community importance;
(c) an SPA designated under the Birds Directive;
(d) a site subject to consultation under article 5 of the directive (although in this last case the protection is limited in the same way as under the directive).

The Secretary of State will draw up a public register of European sites

---

[46] Regulation 1(3); see also, von Colson [1986] 2 CMLR 430; Marleasing [1992] 1 CMLR 305.

[47] This is exactly what happened (ultimately) in the case of the RSPB's challenge to the non-designation of Lappel Bank as an SPA (see the Guardian, 10 February 1995). However, the general impression in environmental cases has been that the lower courts are very reluctant to make references under article 177 – see, for example, R v. Poole DC, ex parte Beebee (loc.cit.), R v. Swale BC, ex parte RSPB (loc.cit.) and Twyford Parish Council v. Secretary of State for Transport [1992] JEL 273. In each of these cases it is strongly arguable that the judge was incorrect in his interpretation of EC law, yet did not make a reference.

[48] On 31 March 1995, the government issued A List of Possible Special Areas of Conservation in the UK for consultation, though this was clearly incomplete as it omitted proposed river sites.

(article 11) and notify them to English Nature (article 12), which will then notify local planning authorities, owners and occupiers and anyone else the Secretary of State may direct (article 13).

Amendments to nature conservation law

The regulations then proceed to lay down the protective measures that apply to European sites. Essentially, these mirror existing nature conservation controls, repeating their structure and only adding extra controls where necessary. Thus, regulations 16 and 17 provide for management agreements over European sites and adjacent land; under regulation 28, by-laws may be made for terrestrial European sites as if they were nature reserves (in fact there is a slight extension to the law here, as the by-laws may also cover surrounding or adjoining sites); and regulation 32 provides compulsory purchase powers.

Regulations 18–21 mirror the SSSI system. In keeping with the voluntary principle, no absolute restrictions are imposed, but there are three significant alterations to s.28 to fit in with the directive.

(a) English Nature may amend the original list of potentially damaging operations (thus extending the protection afforded to the site);
(b) the process through which English Nature grants consent for potentially damaging operations is structured;
(c) existing consents must be reviewed and may be withdrawn or modified.

In relation to an application for consent to carry out a potentially damaging operation, if it appears to English Nature that a *plan or project* is likely to have a significant effect on the site, it must carry out an appropriate assessment and may only give consent if the plan or project will not affect the integrity of the site. If it considers there is a risk that the operation will be carried out anyway (i.e. without consent), it must notify the Secretary of State, who may choose to make a special nature conservation order (see below). In accordance with article 6(3) of the directive, these duties do not apply where the operation is directly connected with or necessary to the management of the site, which will exclude a large number of potentially damaging operations.

It is important to recognize what has *not* changed. Even for European sites there is only a four-month temporary ban on potentially damaging operations; only owners and occupiers are restricted in their activities; the maximum fine for breach of the law remains £2,500; and a planning permission still outranks the nature conservation status of the site. Compared with the existing law on SSSIs, the changes are pretty minor. Accordingly, it must be asked why these minor changes could not have been made for all SSSIs.[49]

Special nature conservation orders

Regulations 22–7 mirror the law on s.29 nature conservation orders by creating 'special nature-conservation orders'. In this case there is a major change, which is that the ban on potentially damaging operations is permanent. This is arguably the central feature of the whole body of regulations, since it means that for the first time there is such a thing as a designation that may stop a damaging activity completely.

However, it is not quite as simple as that. At the outset, the Secretary of State has a discretion whether or not to make a special nature conservation order, although this discretion is not unfettered because regulation 3(2) requires all nature conservation functions to be exercised so as to secure compliance with the directive.

Once a special nature conservation order has been made, regulations 22–9 lay down the following, somewhat tortuous, procedures.

(a) If it appears to English Nature that a *plan or project* is likely to have a significant effect on the site, it must carry out an appropriate assessment and *must refuse* consent if the plan or project will affect the integrity of the site. Reasons must be given for a refusal.

(b) The owner or occupier must then refer the matter to the Secretary of State, who may direct English Nature to grant consent, but only if (1) there are no alternative solutions and (2) the plan or project must be carried out 'for imperative reasons of overriding public interest' (these are defined as in the directive and include the more restrictive test for priority sites). If consent is granted, appropriate compensatory measures are required. The all-important corollary is that consent must be refused if either (1) or (2) is not satisfied.

The effect is that there is now a mechanism through which absolute protection can be ensured, but there are some tricky hurdles to negotiate and its operation is seen very much as a last resort.

Amendments to planning and other controls

The regulations also make some important amendments to planning and other regulatory controls in relation to European sites. The following

---

[49] In this context, it is important to understand that all European sites will already be SSSIs.

requirements apply in similar fashion to such things as planning permissions, discharge consents, pollution authorizations,[50] waste management licences, procedures relating to the construction of highways or roads and consents for pipelines and electricity works.[51]

(a) Under regulation 48, where a plan or project is likely to have a significant effect on a European site, before giving permission the relevant regulatory agency is required to consult with English Nature and to carry out an appropriate assessment of the implications of the plan or project for the site.

(b) The agency must only agree to the plan or project if it will not adversely affect the integrity of the site, unless the provisions of regulation 49 are satisfied. These repeat the exceptions laid down in article 6(4) of the directive. If the agency proposes to rely on article 49 it must inform the Secretary of State, who may prohibit the plan or project, either temporarily or permanently. Under regulation 53, compensatory measures must also be taken.

(c) Existing consents, permissions, etc. must be reviewed as soon as reasonably practicable. This review should look at the position as if the application had just been made. If the integrity of the site is adversely affected, the agency should use its normal powers of revocation or modification, paying compensation if that would be the usual position. There is a special set of regulations to similar effect where planning permission would otherwise be granted by a development order, or in an enterprise zone or simplified planning zone.[52]

Three practical criticisms may be made of these very wide powers. First, the process of reviewing existing consents will be very time-consuming for the regulatory agencies concerned. Second, the liability for compensation where existing rights are revoked may prove very significant.[53] Third, many of the powers rely on the agencies anticipating a likely effect, which may prove beyond them, particularly in relation to developments some way away from the protected site.

In relation to applications for planning permission, the regulations are supplemented by Planning Policy Guidance Note 9 (PPG 9).[54] This creates some additional protections as a matter of policy, for example, in paras. 13 and 38, which state respectively:

[50] For example, under the Environmental Protection Act 1990, Part I.

[51] For example, under the Pipe-lines Act 1962, the Transport and Works Act 1992 and the Electricity Act 1989.

[52] See regulations 60–7.

[53] The high cost of compensation is exactly why no action was taken for many years over the damage to Thorne Moors (incidentally, at one time a candidate SPA).

[54] *Nature Conservation* (October 1994).

For the purpose of considering development proposals affecting them, potential SPAs and candidate SACs included in the list sent to the EC Commission should be treated in the same way as classified SPAs and designated sites.

Environmental assessment will normally be required where a Ramsar site or a potential or classified SPA, or a candidate, agreed or designated SAC could be affected.

But, more importantly, the regulations and PPG 9 create what is in practice a presumption against development on a European site. Such a presumption has been seen by some commentators as 'semi-confiscatorial',[55] because it effectively prevents an owner realizing the development value of the land. This raises an important issue concerning the relationship between the protection of nature-conservation sites and private interests, since it is arguable that if owners' rights are to be abrogated in this way, they should have formal rights to object to a designation and rights to compensation. Interestingly, whilst there are no such rights in relation to SSSIs and European sites, they do exist where an s.29 nature conservation order or a special nature conservation order is made.[56]

Has the directive been implemented fully?

It is very difficult to give a definite answer to this question.[57] The regulations appear formally to satisfy the requirements for the designation of SACs and to ensure that the important protections in articles 6(3) and 6(4) of the directive are transposed into domestic law. However, it remains unclear whether some of the wider obligations in the directive are covered properly. Articles 6(3) and 6(4) (and the regulations that implement them) only apply to *plans and projects*, when much that is damaging to sites occurs in a more unplanned manner. Article 6(2), which deals more generally with deterioration of habitats, is not dealt with specifically. Instead, it is implemented through the general obligations imposed on regulatory agencies (i.e. regulation 3(4)), which simply requires all agencies to 'have regard to' the requirements of the directive, and regulations 48–53). As noted above, there are some practical difficulties concerning these regulations, which call into question whether full protection will happen in practice.

There is another angle to the question. Reasoning from the *Santoña*

---

[55] Hockin, Ounsted, Turner and Lund, 'Conservation of migratory birds and protection of their habitat' [1992] LMELR 178.

[56] Wildlife and Countryside Act 1981, sched. 11 and s.30; SI 1994/2716, sched. 1 and regulation 25.

[57] Except in relation to marine sites, where the essentially administrative (as opposed to legislative) and voluntary mechanisms for ensuring implementation appear to fall a long way short of adequate implementation.

Marshes case,[58] it is probable that the procedure whereby the Commission draws up the final list of sites of Community importance will deprive the requirement to designate sites of direct effect. However, the requirement under article 6(2) to avoid deterioration of habitats is effectively the same as in article 4(4) of the Birds Directive, so it is likely to be of direct effect. The potential implications of this point for a situation where a European site actually suffers damage are immense.

This question of practical implementation also raises some other issues. For example, the success of the one mechanism for absolute protection, the special nature conservation order, depends on the willingness of the Secretary of State to make such orders, whilst the success of the whole system depends on the initial identification of SPAs and candidate SACs. Critics could be forgiven for thinking that, given the minimalist legal approach to implementation adopted by the government in the regulations, there will also be a minimalist policy approach when there are specific threats to sites. In this context it is relevant to note that the whole structure of the regulations ensures that the appropriate mechanism for challenge to any decision is judicial review, which is prohibitively expensive for many potential objectors and fraught with evidential difficulties.

Have the directive and the regulations improved the legal protection of habitat? Notwithstanding the above qualifications, there is little doubt that the law is stronger than it was before the regulations were made, at least as far as very important sites are concerned. However, by creating special protections for European sites, resources (both financial and human) will arguably be channelled into the protection of those sites at the expense of 'ordinary' SSSIs. The creation of a category of sites with a higher protection also has the effect of downgrading other sites in the minds of decision-makers, which would be a retrograde step.

Conclusion

The following conclusions can be suggested:

(a) The voluntary principle embodied in the 1981 Act does not recognize sufficiently the ecological interest implicit in nature conservation legislation.

(b) Even in its own terms the 1981 Act does not work properly, as the loopholes, gaps and figures on loss and damage illustrate.

(c) The government has chosen to improve the protection for European sites without plugging these gaps and loopholes. It does not seem sensible to engraft a new regime on to one that does not work. It

[58] Loc.cit.

would have been better to draft wholly new legislation in which all sites were protected to a higher standard, As it is, the legislative protection is improved for the most important sites only: it is arguably downgraded in practice for some of the others.

(d) The Habitats Directive and the regulations give a greater recognition to the ecological interest than before, in particular by providing a form of absolute protection for certain key sites. It appears that in formal legal terms, the main obligations in the directive relating to terrestrial sites have been implemented.

(e) However, it is clear that in practice the government will adopt the least onerous solution which is consistent with compliance with the directive – absolute protection will only be afforded where it is absolutely necessary.

(f) Given the above attitude, the history of the failure of the 1981 Act and the fact that many of the powers in the regulations rely heavily on an unrealistic level of ability to anticipate problems before they happen,[59] it is unlikely that the directive will be fully implemented in practice. This could give rise to challenges based on both UK and EC law.

(g) But perhaps the real conclusion takes us back to sustainable development. Despite the rather bland set of principles for sustainable development set out in chapter 3 of *Sustainable Development: The UK Strategy*,[60] it is clear that any acceptance of the concept, and especially of the idea of critical natural capital, involves a radical programme, with new institutions, new mechanisms and new concepts. There has to be a change in philosophy rather than a tinkering around with the current inadequate mechanisms. This applies as much to legal concepts as it does to other discourses and would probably involve the development of such things as environmental rights, a specialist environmental court and mechanisms to allow actions to be brought on behalf of the environment, rather than a continuing emphasis on the protection of property and economic interests. For example, the precautionary principle requires a complete rethink of traditional legal values relating to certainty and proof. The relationship between the ecological, public and private interests also needs to be clarified, because the protection of the environment inevitably conflicts with certain personal freedoms. In working out that relationship, the law should concentrate on the substantive nature of the various interests rather than on procedural questions

---

[59] For example, regulation 20(4), which envisages English Nature anticipating a risk that a damaging operation will be carried out without consent.

[60] Cm. 2426 (January 1994); see also, Winter, 'Planning and sustainability: an examination of the role of the planning system as an instrument for the delivery of sustainable development', [1994] JPL 883.

relating to whether the process has been carried out properly, which it tends to emphasize at present. The year 1995, appropriately designated European Conservation Year, would have been a good time to start.

5

Environmental Gain, Set-aside and the Implementation of EU Agricultural Reform in the United Kingdom

CHRISTOPHER P. RODGERS

Agricultural Reform and 'Sustainable' Conservation

A number of the other chapters in this book deal with specific nature-conservation measures, e.g. protection of wildlife in coastal zones,[1] and implementation of the EC Habitats Directive and the 'Natura 2000' pro-gramme.[2] We now have a not inconsiderable body of legislation – both European and domestic – which seeks to protect endangered species and vulnerable wildlife habitats. More recently, the recognition has been grow-ing that, in order to be successful, specific conservation provisions must be supplemented with broader measures creating a legal framework within which *sustainable* conservation of the character of the rural environ-ment, and its important features, can be achieved. A wider framework of protective measures is needed to conserve a sympathetic rural environ-ment in which specific wildlife initiatives can be pursued.

The momentum for the adoption of broader measures to underpin specific nature conservation initiatives has grown considerably since 1992. Legisla-tive policy hitherto has favoured the designation of specific habitat sites for protection, and the use of management contracts and stricter planning

---

[1] See L. Warren (ch.3) at p.65ff. above.
[2] Council Directive (EEC) No.43/1992 on the Conservation of Natural Habitats and of Wild Flora and Fauna. See further S. Ball (ch.4) at p.89ff. above.

controls within protected zones to achieve the required degree of site protection sought, for example, in Sites of Special Scientific Interest (SSSIs) or Areas of Outstanding Natural Beauty. This approach has been widely used in the United Kingdom, and has also been used by the European Community's 'Habitats Directive' as the means of implementing the Europewide 'Natura 2000' programme – by the designation of Special Areas of Conservation (SACs) representative of specific European habitat types, in which development and land use will be strictly controlled.[3] To be fully successful, however, zonal programmes must be underpinned by wider measures which recognize the interdependence of protected wildlife habitats with the countryside surrounding them, and the effects of migration and genetic exchange of protected species. This is recognized by the Habitats Directive itself, article 10 of which obliges EC member states 'where they consider it necessary', through their land-use planning and development policies, to encourage the management of features of the landscape which are of major importance for wild flora and fauna 'with a view to improving the ecological coherence of the Natura 2000 network'. The features to be protected are those which are essential for the 'migration, dispersal and genetic exchange of wild species'.

The 1992 reform of the Common Agricultural Policy has created a unique opportunity to introduce policies to foster wider countryside protection. The agreement of the European Agri-environment Regulation[4] as part of the 1992 reform package, in particular, has placed greater emphasis on sustainable conservation – and the choice of legal techniques for achieving it. The Agri-environment Regulation established a Community aid scheme to promote, *inter alia*, the use of farming practices which reduce the polluting effects of agriculture, the development of ways of using agricultural land 'which are compatible with protection and improvement of the environment, the countryside, the landscape, natural resources, the soil and genetic diversity', long-term set-aside for environmental reasons, and land management for public access and leisure activities.[5] These objectives are to be met by means of zonal programmes of at least five years' duration, providing for grant aid to farmers within fixed limits of Community cofinancing. 'Environmental' set-aside programmes must be for a minimum twenty years' duration to qualify for Community aid.[6]

[3] Articles 4 and 6, Council Directive EEC/43/92 providing for the designation of 'Special Areas of Conservation' by Member States and requiring the adoption of measures to 'avoid ... the deterioration of natural habitats and the habitats of species as well as disturbance of the species for which the areas have been designated' (article 6.2). See further S. Ball (ch.4) at p.101ff. above

[4] Council Regulation (EEC) No.2078/92, OJ L215/85, 30.7.92.

[5] Council Regulation (EEC) 2078/92, article 1.

[6] Ibid., articles 3 and 4. And see below p.132ff. for environmental set-aside in the UK under these provisions.

In the United Kingdom, implementation of the Habitats Directive – and particularly the wider countryside protection requirements of article 10 – is being pursued by a wide variety of initiatives, and similar measures are also being introduced under the aegis of the Agri-environment Regulation.

Cross-compliance

It has, since 1992, been made a precondition for the receipt of several EC agricultural subsidies that producers promise not to undertake environmentally damaging practices. This is an important departure, and introduces a new legal technique of considerable potential. One problem which has aroused controversy in the past is the extent to which agricultural price support policies have increased the cost of implementing conservation measures. The cost of implementing land management agreements in SSSIs, for instance, is increased by the payment of output subsidies, the loss of which is a hidden ingredient increasing the 'compensation' payable for the adoption of less intensive farming practices. Conservation policy and agricultural price support policy are, in other words, often pulling in opposite directions. One way to bridge the gap is to link the receipt of price support or subsidy payments to the adoption of environmentally beneficial farming standards, i.e. to make the payment of public subsidy conditional upon the giving of undertakings as to land management by the private party (the producer).[7] The concept needs, for its application, the existence of a system of standard support payments to individual producers. This type of support exists within the Common Agricultural Policy (CAP) for, *inter alia*, arable production (in the form of arable area payments for cereals) and for livestock (e.g. suckler cow premiums and Hill Livestock Compensatory Allowances). There is therefore considerable scope for the application of the concept within the CAP to impose general environmental standards of land management, e.g. by reducing overgrazing in the uplands where this is damaging unimproved grassland.

Cross-compliance is a major feature of the new set-aside management rules for arable land, and is also reflected in the new overgrazing conditions for the receipt of Hill Livestock Compensatory payments. As a result of UK pressure, the extension of the concept to Sheep Premiums and Suckler Cow Premiums was agreed in December 1993. As part of its biodiversity programme, the government is committed to the application, where appropriate, of environmental conditions to support payments, and

[7] See generally D. Colman et al., *Comparative Effectiveness of Conservation Mechanisms* (1992) at 3.8ff., and I. Hodge, 'Incentive policies and the rural environment', 7 *Jo. of Rural Studies* 373 at 377–8.

to seeking further improvements to the CAP to secure this.[8] Set-aside payments and HLCAs are the first areas of agricultural support in which, it is claimed, environmental considerations have been successfully integrated into agricultural support policy.[9] Whether the legal regime for set-aside *does* in fact adequately integrate environmental controls is considered below.

Implementing the Agri-environment Regulation

The agri-environment package has been implemented in the UK largely by extending existing schemes, rather than the adoption of innovatory environmental measures. Six new Environmentally Sensitive Areas (ESAs) have been designated, in which management agreements and grant aid will be available for the adoption of environmental farming techniques.[10] Additionally, new public access opportunities in ESAs have been created by the introduction of additional grants for access under ESA management agreements.[11] New access opportunities have also been introduced for set-aside land under the aegis of the 'countryside access' scheme, with additional premiums for permitting public access to farmland. The long-term set-aside of land for environmental reasons, as envisaged by the Agri-environment Regulation, is provided for in a new 'Habitat Improvement Scheme' allowing for the voluntary set-aside of land for a twenty-year period.[12] Grants for the extensification of livestock grazing on moorland *outside* existing ESAs will be available under a new Moorland Scheme, aimed at improving heather and semi-natural vegetation habitats in moorland areas.

These measures will, it has been claimed, 'target specific environmental objectives in a coherent and complementary way'.[13] They are certainly necessary — especially cross-compliance within the CAP support regime — in order to provide a favourable context[14] in which successful conservation policies can be pursued. But how effective will the new measures be? And, in particular, how effective are the new legal *techniques* for

---

[8] See *Sustainable Development: The UK Strategy* (HMSO, 1994, CM. 2426) at 110.

[9] *Biodiversity: The UK Action Plan* (HMSO, 1994, Cm. 2428), 97ff.

[10] SI 1994/704 (Blackdown Hills), 1994/708 (Cotswold Hills), 1994/709 (Shropshire Hills), 1994/710 (Dartmoor, 1994/711 (Essex Coast) and SI 1994/712 (Upper Thames Tributaries). Also SI 1994/238 (Clwydian Range) and SI 1994/239 (Preseli).

[11] Implemented by amending the existing ESA designation orders. See variously, SI 1994/918 – SI 1994/933 (inclusive). And see A. Sydenham (ch.8) at pp.191ff.below.

[12] See below pp.132ff.

[13] Department of the Environment Consultation Paper: 'Implementation in Great Britain of the Council directive on the conservation of natural habitats and of wild flora and fauna' (92/43/EEC), para.4.1.

[14] 'Sympathetic wider countryside' is the phrase chosen by the DoE consultation paper on the Habitats Directive, para.4.1

enforcing environmental protection currently being introduced under the aegis of CAP reform? Consideration of the whole range of CAP reform measures is clearly beyond the scope of this chapter. Discussion will be confined, therefore, to the environmental potential (or otherwise) of the set-aside scheme for farmland introduced under the 1992 reforms. Set-aside is probably the most controversial aspect of the new CAP regime and has a high public profile as a 'flagship' of CAP reform. Moreover, its proponents have claimed that it offers the potential for a considerable 'green dividend' arising out of changes in the CAP.[15] And it provides a paradigm of the new legal techniques, such as cross-compliance, which are being introduced to further environmental goals within the framework of the CAP. The 'greening' of set-aside land management rules, and the introduction of long-term 'environmental' set-aside, are central features of both the UK's agri-environment programme and its biodiversity strategy.[16]

Set-aside – the Environmental Potential

The management rules for set-aside land provide one of the most important examples of 'cross-compliance' measures within the reformed CAP. A pilot set-aside scheme has been operating in the UK since 1988.[17] The 1992 harvest was the last in respect of which applications could be made for participation in the voluntary 'pilot' five-year scheme. The old scheme was criticized by environmentalists, *inter alia*, for encouraging the degeneration of fields left fallow without proper management ('paying farmers for doing nothing') and for encouraging the proliferation of non-agricultural development (golf clubs etc.) in the countryside.[18] Undoubtedly there were individual successes with environmental management but the environmental impact of the scheme was (overall) minimal. Whatever its merits or demerits, the pilot scheme achieved very little success in reducing production in the arable sector, as ministry statistics illustrate. The pilot scheme, together with the temporary one-year scheme offered in 1990/1, resulted in just under 5 per cent of total arable land being taken out of production. In the four years of the scheme to 1991, a total of 158,847 ha of land had been put into set-aside, with 4,583 producers

[15] See, for example, MAFF 255/93; 'Set-aside offers considerable environmental potential in terms of creating habitats for plants and wildlife; a "green dividend" which is made possible by the Community's policies to cut over-production' (Gillian Shepherd MP, Minister of Agriculture).

[16] See *Biodiversity: The UK Action Plan*, at pp.97ff.

[17] See Lennon, 'Set-aside of agricultural land', ch.2 in Howarth and Rodgers (eds.), *Agriculture, Conservation and Land Use* (University of Wales Press, 1992); Rodgers, *Agricultural Law* (Butterworths, 1991), ch.13.

[18] See e.g. Council for the Protection of Rural England (CPRE), *Agriculture and England's Environment* (1993), paras.6.1–6.4.

participating.[19] Of the five management options available under the pilot scheme, permanent fallow was overwhelmingly the most popular with producers – 82.3 per cent of land put into set-aside in 1991, for instance, went into permanent fallow. Of the other management options available under the old scheme, non-agricultural use was the only other which attracted significant support, e.g. 16.9 and 11.3 per cent of set-aside in 1990 and 1991 (respectively) was put to non-agricultural use.[20] Rotational fallow, grazed fallow and woodland (the other options) received little support.

The voluntary pilot scheme has now been replaced by the Arable Area Payments Scheme, a central plank in the reform package for the CAP agreed in 1992. A greater emphasis on environmental protection, and the introduction of cross-compliance measures to guarantee environmental management of set-aside land, are central features of the new scheme. Paradoxically, however, delays in formulating the detailed rules to be applied to set-aside land have been widely criticized for *encouraging* environmental damage – for instance, the destruction of nesting sites and nesting birds when land has been ploughed up under the new rotational set-aside (RSA) option. Management rules for non-rotational set-aside were only agreed in July 1993,[21] and the Arable Areas Scheme remains subject to ongoing change and development. A new Council regulation introduced in February 1994[22] made substantial changes to the scheme, reforming it to introduce greater flexibility into the land management options and permitting transfers of set-aside obligations. The transfer rules were introduced to 'protect' environmental gain on set-aside land, by allowing the transfer of set-aside obligations where land is sold or its occupation otherwise transferred. The new rules on land transfer are considered below.[23] Until recently the new set-aside rules were to be found principally in the directly applicable European legislation, and the Ministry of Agriculture's (MAFF) detailed rules implementing the European requirements were to be found in the MAFF guides to the Arable Area Payments Scheme. The law has since 1994 been made more accessible by the introduction of domestic regulations, those currently in force being the Arable Area Payments Regulations 1995,[24] which came into force on 31 July 1995. These now contain the land management rules applicable to both rotational and non-rotational set-aside land, and derogate from certain of the European provisions. The principal European legisla-

---

[19] MAFF release 456/91.

[20] For the statistics see MAFF release 456/91, tables 1 and 2.

[21] MAFF release 234/1993.

[22] Council Regulation (EEC) 231/1994, vol.37, OJ L30,3.2.94.

[23] See below pp.126ff.

[24] SI 1995/1738.

tion is to be found in Council Regulation 1765 of 1992,[25] Commission Regulation 762 of 1994,[26] and Council Regulation 231 of 1994.[27]

Area Payments – the Scheme

The CAP reform package agreed in 1992 included substantial reductions in support of prices for cereals over three years.[28] The Arable Area Payments Scheme was introduced by Council Regulation 1765 of 1992 with the dual aim of (a) reducing over-production by extending the concept of set-aside and making receipt of subsidy conditional upon it, and (b) of providing compensatory payments to offset (in part) the reduction in farming incomes occasioned by the phased withdrawal of production subsidies. The objective of the scheme, as stated in the preamble to the 1992 regulations, is 'to approximate the Community prices of . . . arable crops to the prices of the world markets and to compensate the loss of income caused by the reduction in the institutional prices by a compensatory payment for producers who sow such products'. The cereals compensatory payment is calculated by multiplying a 'basic amount' per tonne by the average cereals yield of a holding, determined by reference to a regionalization plan identifying the average yield for the region concerned. The basic amount, or multiplier, was initially set at 25 ECUs for the 1993/4 marketing year, rising to 45 ECUs for the 1995/6 marketing year onwards.[29] Payments are administered under two schemes – General Scheme payments, and Simplified Scheme payments for small producers.

General Scheme payments

Payments under the General Scheme are open to all producers. By virtue of article 2.5 of Council Regulation 1765/92, however, producers who apply for compensatory payments under the General Scheme are subject to an obligation to set aside part of the land they are holding from production. They will receive a separate payment for the set-aside land (for the 1994/5 marketing year this was fixed at 338.01 ECUs per ha). The set-aside requirement is, by virtue of article 7, normally to be 15 per cent of the area of a holding down to arable crops and left in set-aside. The European regulations provide for three types of set-aside: rotational set-

[25] OJ No. L181, 1 July 1992, p.12.
[26] OJ No. L90, 7 April 1994, p.9. This replaced Commission Regulation 2293/92 from the 1994/5 marketing year onwards (Comm. Reg 762/1994, art. 12).
[27] OJ No. L30, 3 February 1994, p.2.
[28] The common organization of the market in cereals is now established in Council Regulation (EEC) 1766/1992. For an account of the detailed changes in the areas support regime, with worked examples, see W. Nevill and F. Mordaunt, *A Guide to the Reformed Common Agricultural Policy* (1993), esp. chs.3 and 5.
[29] Article 4.2, Council Regulation (EEC) 1765/92.

aside (RSA), non-rotational set-aside (NRSA), and 'free' or 'mixed' set-aside (combining rotational and non-rotational uses of set-aside land). The 15 per cent requirement applies where RSA is chosen as the mode of management. If land is put into non-rotational or mixed set-aside, the requirement is for 18 per cent of the total area down to arable crops (arable plus set-aside) to be set-aside. The European rules also allow for the growth of non-food crops on set-aside land, in which case (also) the 18 per cent rule is applied. The higher figure for NRSA was fixed for 1993/4 onwards, and will be periodically reviewed. If NRSA is proven to be less effective in reducing production than RSA at 15 per cent, the proportion to be set aside could well be increased beyond the previous 18 per cent requirement. The set-aside rate, after a review by the Commission, was cut by 3 per cent to 12 per cent (RSA) and 15 per cent (for NRSA and 'mixed' set-aside) for 1995. Producers not wishing to reduce their set-aside will be permitted to treat the extra 3 per cent set-aside as voluntary set-aside.[30] It is likely, however, that the rate will increase again in future years if production is not reduced. Member States, when introducing management rules for set-aside land, are directed by article 7.4 to 'apply appropriate environmental measures which correspond to the specific situation of the land set-aside'. The rules adopted for managing land under the rotational, non-rotational, mixed and non-food crop options are discussed further below.[31]

Simplified Scheme payments

This is intended for small producers.[32] Small producers qualifying for participation are defined by article 8.2 of Council Regulation 1765/92 – not by reference to the size of the enterprise, however, but by reference to the size of the *claim* for arable payments made. The latter provision makes the simplified scheme available to producers who make a claim for compensatory payments for an area no bigger than the area which would be needed to produce 92 tonnes of cereals, having regard to the average cereals yield determined for that region under the scheme. It is possible, therefore, for a large producer to take advantage of the Simplified Scheme, simply by limiting his claim to the given number of hectares (calculated from the regional yield), even if cropping from a larger area than this. The significance of this is that no set-aside requirement is imposed as a precondition for payments under the Simplified Scheme.[33] It follows that cross-compliance with the new environmental management rules for

[30] MAFF/460/1994. And see generally N. Hawke et al., 'Set-aside: its legal framework and environmental protection', *Environmental Law and Management* (1993), 153–7.

[31] See below pp.120ff.

[32] Article 2.5, Council Regulation 1765/1992.

[33] Article 8.3, ibid.

set-aside land is also inapplicable. The Simplified Scheme therefore offers the small producer an exemption from set-aside altogether. It also offers exemption to the larger producer with a mixed enterprise, only a small portion of which is given over to arable. The *quid pro quo* for exemption is that a claim for payments under the General Scheme cannot be made, neither can a producer make more than one claim under the Simplified Scheme (even if he has two or more holdings). Payments under the Simplified Scheme are all made at the rate paid for cereals.[34] There would appear to be no justification on environmental grounds for exempting producers with a small arable output from the set-aside requirement. On the contrary, the anachronistic definition of 'small' producers offered by the European regulations affords an exemption from set-aside to any producer willing to limit his or her claim for subsidy to an area needed to produce 92 tonnes of cereals.[35] This emphasizes one feature of the new set-aside regime, to which we shall return below, viz. that the targeting and application of set-aside under the new scheme remains governed by the economics of agricultural production and subsidy, and not by environmental considerations.

Eligibility for set-aside

Where General Scheme payments are applied for, certain basic requirements are imposed in order for land to be eligible for entry into set-aside. The smallest block of land which can be entered into set-aside must be at least 0.3 ha in area, and all strips of land submitted must be at least 20m wide.[36] Land is ineligible for set-aside if it was under permanent pasture, forest, permanent crops or put to a non-agricultural use on 31 December 1991.[37] The land must have been cultivated for cereals in the year 1991/2 and, moreover, must have been farmed with the intention of producing a harvestable crop in the previous year. Land which was down to temporary grass or lucerne during 1991/2 cannot be entered into set-aside, even if used for producing hay and silage, and neither can land which was not used for *any* arable crop in 1991/2. These requirements all go to the central economic rationale of set-aside, viz. to reduce overproduction of arable crops within the CAP.

The European regulations impose a further qualifying requirement, stipulating that a producer cannot set land aside unless he has farmed it himself during the previous two years.[38] This is aimed at preventing the specula-

---

[34] Article 8.3, ibid.

[35] Article 8.2 ibid.

[36] Commission Regulation (EEC) 762/94, article 3.1.

[37] Council Regulation (EEC) 1765/92, article 9, 'Permanent' crops are those which occupy the land for five years, e.g. fruit trees and bushes.

[38] Commission Regulation (EEC) 762/94, article 3.4.

tive purchase or renting of poor land with the object of 'dumping' one's set-aside requirement on it. The UK has derogated from this requirement by introducing exceptions allowing for the entry into set-aside of land previously let on a variety of short-term arrangements.[39] As this goes to the question of avoidance of set-aside, and the effectiveness of the scheme as a tool of environmental policy, it is considered separately below.[40]

Environmental Management of Set-aside Land

Article 7(3) of Council Regulation 1765/92 requires Member States to apply 'appropriate environmental measures' corresponding to the specific situation of the land set-aside. This is amplified by the relevant Commission regulations laying down the detailed rules for implementing the set-aside scheme.[41] The latter direct Member States to apply 'appropriate measures' corresponding to the specific situation of the land so as to ensure protection of the environment,. The measures applied can provide for the establishment of a green cover, but the detailed requirements are left to Member States for decision and implementation. The European regulations provide for, essentially, four types of set-aside: RSA, NRSA, 'free' set-aside (a mixture of the two), and for the growth of non-food crops on set-aside land. The management rules for NRSA were, after prolonged uncertainty, only finalized for the 1993/4 harvest onwards. The management rules implementing the European scheme in the UK are now to be found in sched. 2 of the Arable Area Payments Regulations 1995.[42] In response to criticism of the old five-year set-aside scheme, the new regime applies more stringent environmental controls on the use of set-aside land. It is on these that any 'green dividend' offered by set-aside depends.

Certain basic environmental controls are applied by the 1995 regulations, whichever management option is chosen. So, for example, producers must not damage, destroy or remove environmental features (including archaeological sites) which are sited either on, or 'immediately next to' set-aside land. Environmental features protected by this injunction include vernacular buildings, stone walls, existing hedges, rows of trees, ditches, ponds and lakes.[43] Further, no fertilizer or manure can be applied to set-aside land. To this rule there are two exceptions. Fertilizer can be applied if a farmer satisfies the ministry that the land is situated in an area known to be used as a feeding area for over-wintering geese, and it is, accord-

[39] See sched. 1, Arable Area Payments Regulations 1995, SI 1995/1738.
[40] See below pp.128ff.
[41] Commission Regulation 762/94, articles 3.2, 3.3.
[42] SI 1995/1738.
[43] Sched. 2 para.26, SI 1995/1738.

ingly, to be managed as a winter feeding area for geese.[44] Secondly, organic waste can be applied to land on which a green cover has been established (e.g. RSA land), provided the manure etc. applied was produced on the producer's own holding (or an agricultural unit of which it forms part). This limited exception is necessary to provide for the disposal of waste produced by normal agricultural activities on the remainder of the holding. The Ministry must, furthermore, be satisfied that it cannot satisfactorily be disposed of elsewhere.[45] Herbicides cannot be applied by general application, but spot treatment is permitted if a type of herbicide absorbed through the leaves and stem is used. Permission can be granted for general applications to control infestation of weeds or pests, or prevent the spread of disease. The minister must be satisfied, however, that the green cover established on the set-aside land will not be damaged or (if this is unavoidable) that it will be satisfactorily replaced.[46] Fungicides and insecticides are prohibited, except (with Ministry consent) where the application is necessary to protect plant health.[47] A green cover must normally be established and maintained throughout the set-aside period.[48] Additional management rules apply, depending upon whether land is put into NRSA or RSA.

Non-rotational set-aside

NRSA offers the greatest potential for long-term environmental gain. Land put into NRSA must be set aside for a period of five years, starting from 15 January in the first year of the set-aside period. The basic environmental controls (see above) on the application of pesticides, herbicides and fertilizer apply throughout this period, and not, as is the case with RSA (below), during only seven months of each year. Some limited agricultural use of NRSA land is, however, permitted. Livestock can be grazed on NRSA land between 1 September and 14 January each year, and hay and silage can be taken annually during this period. The set-aside requirement where NRSA has been chosen was initially set at 18 per cent of the total area on which a producer is claiming arable area payments, i.e. land under crops plus set-aside. The figure was 20 per cent for all other EU Member States except Denmark.

The European legislation[49] prohibits the use of set-aside land 'for any lucrative use incompatible with the growing of an arable crop' and requires

[44] Sched. 2, para.19, ibid.
[45] Sched. 2, para.20, ibid.
[46] Sched. 2, paras.24 and 25, ibid.
[47] Sched. 2, para.23, ibid.
[48] See sched. 2, paras.1–3. There are exceptions allowing, for example, a 2m-wide strip to be left uncovered adjoining land sowed with a seed crop – see sched. 2 para. 4.
[49] Article 3.2, Commission Regulation 762/1994.

its maintenance so as to provide good cropping conditions. It follows that non-agricultural use of the land is not now permissible, whereas it was under the 'pilot' five-year scheme. The detailed management regimes to be applied to NRSA land are left to individual Member States. In the UK NRSA has been implemented by the adoption of four environmental management options overtly aimed at achieving environmental gain − a Grassland option, Natural Regeneration, Wild Bird Cover option and Field Margins option. A management plan can be drawn up for Ministry approval.[50]

The NRSA options offer considerable scope for innovation and specialist environmental management. The Field Margins option, for example, is aimed at creating 'green veins' or corridors of wildlife running through the countryside.[51] Accordingly, it allows for strips of land 20m wide bordering fields to be set-aside. A green cover must be established, and must be cut at least once a year, although an uncut strip of 2m width may be left uncut adjacent to hedges or woodland. The Wild Bird Cover option provides for a green cover to be established by natural regeneration of the previous herbage seed or combinable crop (but not one including maize or legumes).[52] The cover should be replaced at least once every two years. This, also, is a potentially beneficial environmental option. MAFF produces guidance on the application of the management rules, and this stresses the need for farmers to assess agronomic and environmental factors across the whole of their land when weighing the environmental possibilities under the scheme and selecting land to be set aside.[53] Where the Grassland option is chosen, a green cover must be established by sowing a mixture of grass seed and native broadleaved plants not commonly used for agricultural production.[54] This must then be cut short once a year between 15 July and 15 August, although strips up to 2m wide can be left uncut adjacent to woods and hedges, thus creating possible field margins for wildlife habitats. The Natural Regeneration option, finally, offers an alternative under which a green cover can be established by allowing natural regeneration of the previous herbage seed crop or combinable crop (but not one including maize or legumes). The cover must, as with the Grassland option, be cut once a year, but may not otherwise be cultivated − except in the first year, when the farmer can disc or shallow-cultivate the field.

A degree of flexibility is allowed by the management rules, and landowners can submit their own management plans for NRSA land management, e.g. to provide sites for ground-nesting birds. Whether significant

[50] Sched. 2, para.2, SI 1995/1738. And see ibid., paras. 5–8 for the NRSA management options.

[51] MAFF/255/1993.

[52] Sched. 2, para.7(1), SI 1995/1738.

[53] 'Arable Area Payments' (MAFF, 1993), Appendix 3.

[54] Sched. 2, op.cit., paras.5 and 9.

environmental gain ultimately accrues from the new NRSA regime depends in large part, however, upon how popular it proves to be with producers when compared with the RSA option – the other main form of set-aside provided for under the European regulations. The *selection* of management regime to satisfy each producer's set-aside requirement remains entirely voluntary – notwithstanding the introduction of cross-compliance. As we shall see, the flexibility of the RSA management rules, coupled with the lower set-aside requirement (15 per cent, and now 12 per cent for 1995) imposed for RSA, will inevitably result in the bulk of set-aside land going into RSA, and not into the 'environmental' NRSA options outlined above.

Rotational set-aside

Although the layman may think that 'set-aside' would normally involve taking land out of production long-term, he would be mistaken. It is clear from the European regulations that the Commission regard RSA as the norm, and not NRSA or 'mixed' set-aside. Thus, the preamble to Council Regulation (EEC) 1765/92 (emphasis added):

> Whereas in order to benefit from the compensatory payments under the [Arable Area Payments Scheme] producers must set-aside a predetermined percentage of their arable land . . . the *set-aside should normally be organized on the basis of a rotation of areas:* whereas non-rotational fallow *should be permitted*, but at a higher percentage rate which should be determined on the basis of a scientific study of the comparative effectiveness in terms of production restraint of rotational and non-rotational fallow.

Although the preamble to Regulation 1765/92 goes on to talk of 'certain minimum environmental standards' being applied to set-aside land, it is clear that the concept of RSA is determined by agricultural and economic considerations, and not the environmental potential which it offers. This is made explicit in the preamble to Council Regulation 231 of 1994, which states boldly that 'for the sake of *efficiency* set-aside should be on a rotational basis.' To ensure that the system is 'better suited to *agronomic requirements* there should be provision for other forms of set-aside, such as fixed set-aside [and] the combination of rotational and fixed set-aside ("mixed" set-aside)'. The regime applicable to RSA is driven, therefore, by a perceived need to reduce production, while maintaining land in good agricultural condition to increase production if needed in future. More than this, the whole structure of the new set-aside regime, in which RSA is perceived as the norm, is dictated by economic, not environmental considerations. Set-aside is primarily a temporary device of supply-side market management. NRSA, as implemented in the UK, would offer considerable scope for environmental land management. In the overall scheme of things, however, it is clear from the European regulations that even fixed set-aside is justified solely by reference to agronomic considerations – principally the need to introduce flexibility for producers in planning their set-aside requirements and arable cropping. Talk of set-aside offering a 'green dividend' must therefore be viewed with scepticism. The European Commission, and undoubtedly the majority of landowners, regard RSA as the norm. Clearly, the overwhelming popularity of the fallow option under the 'pilot' five-year scheme as the preferred mode of set-aside, would support the view that RSA, and not fixed set-aside, is likely to prove the most popular with producers.[55]

Far from conferring tangible environmental gain, the management regime for RSA is arguably one which not only offers only transient environmental returns, but is in some respects actually damaging – and all at enormous public expense. In theory, RSA can be of benefit in encouraging the growth of rare arable weeds, and can be of benefit to a variety of bird life – particularly seed-eaters (such as finches) and insect-eaters (such as skylarks and game birds).[56] As a consequence of the rotation arrangements, however, any benefit is likely to be transient.

The European rules require land to be set aside for a minimum of seven months commencing on 15 December (at the earliest) and ending on 15 August at the latest.[57] In the UK the set-aside period has been fixed as the period 15 January to 31 August each year – the minimum permitted.[58] The European rules require that land put into RSA cannot be set aside for a subsequent five-year period.[59] Land can therefore be set aside once every six years, in cycle. Unless there were crops in the ground on 1 October prior to the set-aside, the land must have a green cover from the beginning of the set-aside period. Detailed rules governing the establishment and maintenance of a suitable green cover are set out in sched. 1 of the Arable Area Payments Regulations 1995,[60] in an attempt to offset a repeat of the criticism levelled at the negative landscape effects of fallow set-aside under the old five-year scheme.

The very fact that set-aside land is down to plant cover for only seven months before being ploughed up and resown initially gave rise to considerable criticism – not least because of the damage caused to nesting birds

[55] See MAFF statistics cited above, notes 19 and 20.

[56] For researched guidance on management of RSA for these purposes see L. G. Firbank et al., *Managing Set-aside Land for Wildlife* (Institute of Terrestrial Ecology, HMSO, 1993) ch.5.

[57] Commission Regulation 762/94, article 3.4.

[58] SI 1995/1738, Regulation 2.

[59] Commission Regulation 762/94, article 4. Some flexibility is allowed where a farmer has insufficient arable to meet this requirement.

[60] SI 1995/1738.

and other wildlife which may have established itself on the land in the interim. The management rules were, accordingly, amended from 1993/4 onwards to improve the environmental impact of RSA. Cutting of the green cover need not take place until 15 July to 15 August in the year the land is set aside,[61] and exemptions from the requirement to cut green cover will be granted by the ministry where birds are still nesting on the land. It is also intended that more flexible rules allowing for the use of non-residual herbicides will enable weed control to be maintained in a way which will allow producers to delay cutting and cultivation. The new measures, while they go some way to meet environmental criticisms of RSA, are largely permissive, however, and not mandatory. They rely not only on the willingness of farmers to delay cultivation until August, but also on their awareness of the presence of nesting birds or other vulnerable wildlife on the land.[62] The 1995 regulations otherwise permit the cultivation of the set-aside land on or after 1 May to control weeds, and allow for the replacement of the green cover *at any time* to control serious infestations of weeds, or for pollution control reasons approved by the Ministry.[63]

'Mixed' set-aside

Following reforms introduced by Council Regulation 231/1994[64] producers can meet their set-aside requirement by adopting a mixture of NRSA and RSA. In this case the set-aside requirement was fixed initially at 18 per cent of the producer's total arable land plus set-aside.

Non-food crops

Article 7 of Council Regulation 1765/92 permits the use of set-aside land for 'the provision of materials for the manufacture within the community of products not primarily intended for human and animal consumption'. The list of permitted crops which can be grown for non-food processing is long.[65] It includes, for instance, outdoor perennials (such as miscanthus), beans and peas (if not for sowing), seeds such as sunflower and linseed, and short-rotation coppice trees. The attractiveness of the non-food crops option is diminished, however, by the technical requirement it

---

[61] SI 1995/1738, sched. 1, para.9.

[62] 'Earlier weed control is allowed by cultivation in May and even earlier by herbicides and cutting, but the costs to wildlife can be severe. Rare plants will not have set seeds and birds will not have fledged their chicks' (Firbank et al., op.cit., 38, n.53a).

[63] SI 1995/1738, sched. 1, para.13.

[64] OJ L30/2, 3 February 1994.

[65] See Annex 1 to Commission Regulation 334/1993. The detailed rules implementing the non-food crops regime were set out, with considerable complexity, in Commission Regulation 334/1993, OJ No.L300, 7 December 1993.

imposes on producers. Any raw materials grown on set-aside land must be the subject of a contract with a collector or first processor and (in the case of annual crops) this must be signed before the first sowing of the crop.[66] Moreover, if annual crops are to be grown the collector or first processor must lodge security with the Ministry – half within twenty days of signature of the contract, and half within twenty days of receiving the raw materials concerned. The security is intended to guarantee performance of the contract, and the amount which must be put up is 120 per cent of the value of the set-aside payments for each parcel of land covered by the contract.[67] The regulations also require the keeping of detailed records by the processor and/or collectors of all quantities of raw materials bought and sold for processing, names and addresses of onward purchases, or second processors, and of wastage during processing.

Clearly, were many producers to take up this option it would detract from the environmental potential of the other set-aside management options. This is unlikely, however, as the economics of non-food production make it (at least for the time being) an unattractive prospect.[68] Additionally, the administrative requirements imposed by the management rules may act as a further disincentive.

Protecting Environmental Gain: Land Transfers

The imposition of a mandatory set-aside requirement on arable land is likely to cause considerable legal problems where land is transferred. Land can only be used for RSA once every six years. Where land is sold[69] or rented, therefore, the transferee will need to know the detailed history of the land, and may wish to take an indemnity against future loss of set-aside payments should the land prove ineligible for RSA. If the land transferred *is* ineligible, this also has implications for planning the set-aside rotation and cropping on the remainder of the recipient's holding. Where land is let on an agricultural tenancy, on the other hand, the landlord will need to ensure that the tenant keeps detailed records of cropping and areas set aside. If the land is let on a short-term basis it will be important to place restrictions on the area that can be set aside. A short-term tenant could, otherwise, put all of the land rented towards meeting his own set-aside requirement and, in doing so, render it ineligible for set-aside by a future occupier for six years.

[66] Article 6.1 Commission Regulation (EEC) 334/1993.

[67] Article 9.2, ibid.

[68] For a discussion of the economic factors see Neville and Mordaunt, *A Guide to the Reformed Common Agricultural Policy* (1993), pp.44ff.

[69] For a discussion of the potential conveyancing problems, see A Sydenham (1994) 139 Sol.Jo. 1294ff.

Where land has been set aside so as to produce environmental benefits, these may be lost if the holding is sold (or leased) to another producer. New rules governing the transfer of set-aside obligations were introduced by Council Regulation 231/94, and are aimed at 'protecting' environmental gains on set-aside land. The European regulations[70] now provide that a producer can transfer a set-aside requirement to another producer in the same Member State in two situations. He can do so if, under national environmental rules, a producer setting aside arable land is required to reduce his livestock. More importantly, he can do so under a transfer scheme presented to the Commission, providing the Member State submitting it for approval verifies that it does not impair the effectiveness of the set-aside scheme. Transfers under this latter provision will be governed by several basic principles.

(a) A transfer must be restricted to a maximum distance of 20 km or be made *into* an area (further afield than 20 km) for which specific environmental objectives are sought. The 20-km radius is to be calculated as from the place on the exporting holding where the main agricultural equipment is stored. This will be almost impossible of practical implementation in the UK,

(b) Secondly, where a transfer occurs, the set-aside is increased by 3 per cent, i.e. the land set aside plus a further 3 per cent must be set aside by the transferee.

(c) Finally, the set-aside will be subject to the rules applicable to the holding on which the land is actually set aside, i.e. the importing holding. The only exception is set-aside exported to an environmental target area, where the set-aside land 'exported' must be calculated and managed in all cases, as *flexible* set-aside (to which the higher 18 per cent set-aside requirement applies). To discourage landowners from importing 'environmental' set-aside from outside the 20-km transfer limit, and then rotating that land into cropping in the following year, producers who do so will not be allowed to import set-aside under the environmental target area rules for the following three years. This may discourage landowners from rotating imported environmental set-aside, but the sanction lacks rigour.

The economics of the transfer rules are complex. If the importing holding is doing RSA the transferor will have to 'export' 15 per cent plus a further 3 per cent of his eligible arable. If it is doing fixed set-aside –

[70] Article 7.7, Council Regulation 1765/92, introduced by article 10, Council Regulation (EEC) 231/94, OJ No.L30/2, 3 February 1994. And see Article 10 of Commission Regulation (EEC) 762/94. Procedural rules governing transfers and applying the European Scheme safeguards have now been implemented in reg.9 of SI 1995/1738.

under one of the environmental management options (Wild Bird Cover or the Meadowland scheme, for example) – he will have to export 18 per cent plus a further 3 per cent. More than this, however, the set-aside *itself* will be governed by the rules applicable to the importing holding. The set-aside operated by the production unit of the transferee determines the future set-aside status of the land transferred – not any environmentally beneficial use to which the land is currently being put. If the land is in NRSA the transferor will have contracted for five years, and will, therefore, need to indemnify himself against any change in land use which may occur in breach of the set-aside undertakings he has already given. While the new transfer rules are intended to 'protect' environmental gains when land is sold, they are so complex and difficult of application that they may prove of little utility in practice. Further, it now seems that where a transfer takes place, the total area of land set aside on a holding (including the set-aside which has been 'imported ') must not exceed the area of crops for which a subsidy claim is being made. Consequent upon European Commission advice, the MAFF transfer rules now stipulate that no farmer claiming additional 'voluntary' set-aside can import set-aside under the new transfer rules.[71] This, of course, runs counter to the environmental objective of the transfer rules.

The transfer rules are also permissive, not mandatory. Set-aside obligations do not bind the land so as to pass with it – they are contractual, and do not operate *in rem*. Further, the increase in the set-aside requirement where a transfer of obligations *does* take place is driven by agronomic considerations of reducing production, and not by considerations of environmental protection.

A further problem to which land transfers can give rise is the 'dumping' of set-aside requirements, i.e. the purchase or renting of land (perhaps of poor quality) by a producer for the sole purpose of 'dumping' his set-aside requirement on it, without reducing his overall arable production. To prevent this, article 3.4 of Commission Regulation 2293/92 provides that a producer cannot set land aside unless he has farmed it himself during the previous two years. This may prove unduly restrictive, however, and could cause problems where land is transferred by inheritance or under transitional tenancy agreements. The UK has therefore derogated from article 3 by specifying special cases where land *can* be put into set-aside, even if it has not been farmed by the applicant for two years. The special cases cover mostly *bona fide* situations where the requirement would otherwise cause problems. There are, however, several potential

---

[71] *Transfer of Set-aside Obligations Between Producers* (MAFF AR26, 1994), paras.19 and see ibid., paras.52–5 for management of land transferred into 'environmental' target areas.

loopholes which may facilitate 'dumping', contrary to the spirit of the European legislation:

The special cases allowed by the domestic regulations include the following:[72]

(a) Where the land has been acquired by inheritance, or the producer was granted a tenancy by way of succession within the two years prior to the set-aside period.

(b) Where the land has been taken in hand during the last two years by a landlord who has owned it for two years or more.

(c) Where the claimant has acquired[73] an agricultural unit of 60 ha or more, and the land to be set aside is part of that unit. The rationale here would appear to be that no producer would rent or purchase such a large area solely for the purpose of dumping set-aside obligations. There is no requirement for him to *retain* ownership or tenure of the whole 60 ha, however, and one can envisage the use of sub-sales and other associated transactions by which the unscrupulous could use this exception to circumvent the rules.

(d) Where the claimant owns or rents not more than 15 ha of land and, during the last two years, has taken on additional land to be set aside. This is intended to benefit small producers who would otherwise have difficulty meeting their set-aside requirement. It is open to abuse, however, given the complex legal structure of many agricultural enterprises. If a substantial holding is owned by (say) a limited farming company, this exception would be available to an individual member of the enterprise with a small personal land holding – thereby enabling the enterprise to circumvent the restrictions.

(e) Where a claimant landowner let the land for less than two years during the relevant period prior to set-aside – e.g. under a grazing licence or *Gladstone* v. *Bower* tenancy.[74]

(f) Special rules apply where a farmer holds at least 10 per cent of his arable land each year under the share-farming contracts or other forms of short-term arrangement outside the ambit of the Agricultural Holdings Act, 1986. The land can be set aside provided it can be reasonably managed as a single unit with the claimant's other land and is proximate or geographically related to the rest of the unit.

---

[72] Regulation 6 and sched. 1, SI 1995/1738.

[73] By purchase, rent or under a share-farming agreement.

[74] I.e. a fixed term of more than one but less than two years – see *Gladstone* v. *Bower* [1960] 2 QB 384, *EWP Ltd* v. *Moore* [1992] QB 460.

Cross-compliance – the Weaknesses

The mandatory environmental requirements for arable support payments, as we have seen, are very basic. Much of the detailed guidance on environmental management of set-aside, contained in the Ministry literature, remains merely advisory. The scheme adheres, for the most part, to the voluntary principle – notwithstanding the introduction of cross-compliance measures. Further, although the introduction of cross-compliance has been hailed as a major advance, the application of the principle has not been thoroughgoing.

The domestic regulations provide several exemptions from the need to manage set-aside land in accordance with the environmental management rules attached to RSA and NRSA (above). These are set out in Regulation 8 of the Arable Area Payment Regulations 1995. So, for example, a landowner will be exempt if he satisfies the minister that there are good environmental reasons for adopting a different management regime, or if human or animal health and safety are at risk. Curiously, however, the minister can also grant exemption if, at the time when compliance with the environmental management rules is required, 'it is likely that the cost or difficulty of complying ... would be disproportionately high in comparison with the environmental benefit which compliance with that requirement would yield.'[75] The 'disproportionately' high cost of compliance is, therefore, an excusing factor. The required balancing of cost and gain necessitates the measurement of environmental gain in financial terms, and then its evaluation alongside the cost of its achievement. Proportionality involves comparison of like with like – something which is arguably not possible in this context. The agricultural imperative therefore overrides the environmental interest here, even where NRSA is concerned. The rules clearly require a financial valuation to be put on likely environmental gains, without suggesting how this might be achieved. The effectiveness of the environmental conditions could therefore be significantly influenced by the criteria adopted by MAFF to measure likely environmental benefits on set-aside land. Yet no guidance is given in either the legal rules or MAFF's literature on the scheme as to how benefits will be valued or assessed. MAFF are left with complete discretion as to valuation. In some cases, therefore, land could theoretically be taken out of production, but with no tangible environmental gain if the latter were too expensive to put in place.

Further weaknesses are to be found in the sanctions applied for non-compliance with the set-aside management rules. Where a farmer is in breach of the land-management rules applicable to the type of set-aside he is operating, the set-aside compensatory payment is reduced

[75] Regulation 8(3)(f), SI 1995/1738.

by £100 for each hectare of land in respect of which any requirement is breached. If he damages protected features of the site — hedgerows, trees, vernacular buildings or archaeological features — his compensatory payment will be reduced by £100 for each feature which has been damaged or removed.[76] The payment per hectare for set-aside land was fixed at £320 for the 1994/5 marketing year. Cross-'compliance' is arguably a misnomer, therefore, as the concept is not fully applied. A producer can still benefit, even if in breach of environmental conditions in the set-aside management rules. To apply the concept fully, compliance with environmental management requirements would have to be made a condition precedent to the receipt of *all* grant aid, the full amount of which should be forfeited for non-compliance. Here again, public policy seeks to put a limited financial valuation (or 'price tag') on environmental compliance measures, rather than giving them a central role and making them fundamental to the operation of the Arable Area Payments Scheme. Crucially, however, the set-aside rules again fail to indicate *how* the conservation value to be achieved should be measured. This is, of course, a matter of considerable debate among environmentalists and economists, and several potential modes of valuing conservation gains could be applied.[77] The set-aside rules avoid the issue by imposing an arbitrary financial penalty (of £100 for each offence) for environmental damage. While doubtless intended as a deterrent to non-compliance with environmental safeguards, this approach lacks both 'teeth' and logic.

If the environmental management rules lack teeth, they arguably also lack direction. They are not targeted by reference to environmental considerations. No cross-compliance whatever is required for small farms taking advantage of the Simplified Scheme. Neither is cross-compliance applicable to larger holdings with small areas down to arable, provided the requirements for the Simplified Scheme are met. This is the case irrespective of any environmental potential the land might have if set aside. As we have seen, any producer willing to limit his claim for arable support to an area needed to produce 92 tonnes of cereals (the limit set for the Simplified Scheme) can avoid cross-compliance altogether. The very application of the concept is therefore conditioned by agronomic and economic factors, not by its potential as a tool of environmental protection law. Indeed, even where it applies, many farmers will choose their poorest and most unproductive land to satisfy their set-aside requirement — and not necessarily that with the most

---

[76] Regulation 13, ibid.

[77] For an interesting discussion of the possible techniques for measuring environmental benefits in ESAs see Willis and Garrod, 'Measuring the benefits of ESA', in Whitby (ed.), *Incentives for Countryside Management* (1994). Also, generally, *The Cost of Care* (RICS Research Paper, No.15, (1992), esp. s.9, pp.50ff.

environmental potential. They could hardly be blamed for doing so under the current set-aside regime.

Long Term Set-aside: The Habitat Improvement Scheme

One of the schemes provided for under the EC 'Agri-environment' Regulation, and for which community co-financing is available, is 'the long-term set-aside of agricultural land for reasons connected with the environment'.[78] The set-aside must be for a period of twenty years. The European regulations envisage schemes, in particular, for the establishment of biotope reserves, natural parks, or for the protection of 'hydrological systems'.

As a part of the Agri-environment Regulations' implementation in the UK, a new set-aside scheme (known as the Habitat Improvement Scheme) has been established to encourage the long-term set-aside of land in targeted areas, with the intention of creating or improving valuable wildlife habitats. This new scheme is distinct from the Arable Area Payment Scheme (above), and has been structured to adopt a much more targeted approach to possible environmental gain.[79] Unlike the Arable Area Payments Scheme, it applies to both arable and non-arable land.

The European regulation envisages a carefully targeted scheme which only allows for entry into set-aside of land which has clear potential to create or re-create the targeted habitat chosen. With this in mind, the Habitat Improvement Scheme makes grant payments available under the following options, where land is put into set-aside for twenty years.

Saltmarsh

This option is being offered by MAFF as a pilot project on low-lying land in Essex, Kent or Suffolk.[80] If successful, it may be extended. Saltmarshes provide a unique and important wildlife habitat, particularly for birds and invertebrates, and the scheme is intended to re-create this type of habitat on suitable low-lying land which is behind a sea wall and backed by rising ground or a second line of defence against seawater inundation. The establishment of the habitat will require the participation of the coastal defence authorities. Subsequently a grass sward will have to be established, together with a root system to stabilize the substrata and reduce erosion.

---

[78] Council Regulation 2078/92, OJ L215, 30 July 1992, article 1(8).

[79] See generally *Agriculture and England's Environment – Habitat Improvement Scheme, A Consultation Document* (MAFF, 1993) for a general account of the scheme and its rationale in devising the environmental options it offers.

[80] Implemented by the Habitat (Saltmarsh) Regulations 1994, SI 1994/1293.

Water fringe habitats

This option will be available on land situated alongside targeted watercourses.[81] Waterside habitats are in decline generally, and this option will seek to provide a pilot scheme in specific areas to be designated following advice from the Ministry's scientific advisers. Management conditions will prohibit grazing and regulate the introduction of waterside trees, reedbeds, sedges and rushes. A similar option is already available under the Countryside Stewardship Scheme. The Habitat Improvement Scheme will focus more on protecting the watercourse itself, e.g. by prohibiting grazing along water margins.

Existing set-aside land

The new scheme will also apply to land of particular environmental value which is coming out of the old five-year set-aside scheme. Many farmers may have used the opportunity presented by the pilot set-aside scheme – introduced in 1988 – to establish positive environmental management of set-aside land. The Habitat Improvement Scheme aims to consolidate the gains thus made, by allowing the entry of former set-aside land into twenty-year set-aside and the payment of grant aid at £225 per hectare. This will prove useful where land has been managed with a particular environmental aim in view, e.g. to create a buffer zone around an SSSI or a specific wildlife habitat. Applications will have to be supported by one of the environmental agencies e.g. English Nature, Countryside Council for Wales, Countryside Commission, or a recognized conservation organization (e.g. the Royal Society for the Protection of Birds). The regulations implementing this option[82] permit the minister to accept into set-aside land which, in his opinion, 'has been managed in such a way as to establish or protect a habitat which is valuable in terms of the diversity or rarity of wildlife' it sustains. The land must have been in set-aside at some time within the period of thirteen months preceding the date of its entry into the new scheme.

Once the land has been accepted into set-aside, a management plan must be submitted for approval by the Ministry, and then implemented.[83] The management rules prohibit the application of fertilizers, fungicides or herbicides to the land, except for non-residual herbicides used to control non-indigenous weeds and (with Ministry approval) specific infestations. No improvement in land-drainage systems is permitted, and existing trees,

[81] See the Habitat (Water Fringes) Regulations 1994, SI 1994/1291 for the detailed implementation and rules for the scheme.
[82] The Habitat (Former Set-aside) Regulations 1994, SI 1994/1292. See esp. Regulation 2 (definition of 'eligible land').
[83] SI 1994/1292, sched. 2, para.(1).

shrubs and vernacular buildings must be maintained.[84] Written advice must be obtained from the Ministry on the siting and construction of roads or buildings on the land, even where prior notification to the planning authorities is not required under the Town and Country Planning General Development Order 1995.[85] The management rules do not prohibit the grazing of livestock, however, although this may be permitted by MAFF under the terms of the agreed management plan for the holding, provided it does not threaten or damage the habitat which the plan seeks to establish or maintain.

Landlord and tenant

Where land is tenanted, the adoption of long-term set-aside would technically constitute breach of the tenancy agreement. The rules of good husbandry set out in s.11 of the Agriculture Act 1947 require the adoption of optimum cropping techniques and/or stocking levels, so as to maintain efficient agricultural production. The rules are commonly incorporated – expressly – into agricultural leases, and even where this is not done can be enforced by the obtaining of a Certificate of Bad Husbandry from the agricultural lands tribunal. In either case, the rules could ultimately be enforced by notice to quit served by the landlord.[86] The regulations introducing the scheme recognize this problem, and prohibit the minister from accepting an application from a tenant farmer unless he has obtained the written consent of the landlord to the land being entered into twenty-year set-aside.[87] It might be noted that similar provision is *not* made in relation to set-aside under the Arable Area Payments Scheme, where tenancy problems could arise where land is put into NRSA.

Further possibilities: lowland heath and grassland

Two further options have been posited under the Habitat Improvement Scheme – the re-creation of lowland heath, and of damp lowland grassland. Both were held back until the European Community had formally decided to permit land thus entered into set-aside to 'count' against the set-aside requirements under the Arable Area Payments Scheme.[88] Unlike the other

[84] Ibid., sched. 2, paras. (2)–(14) for the detailed management rules applicable under the scheme.

[85] SI 1995/418. For the notification requirements under the General Development Order see *Agricultural Law Tax and Finance,* ed. Lennon and Mackay (Longmans, 1990), sec.E, pp.E.35–E.37.

[86] Under either Case C (certificate of bad husbandry) or Case D (breach of tenancy) in sched. 3 Agricultural Holdings Act 1986. For the problems this causes for set-aside obligations (in the context of the five-year scheme) see further Rodgers, *Agricultural Law* (Butterworths, 1991), pp. 301ff.

[87] See e.g. SI 1994/1292, Regulation 5(2). Similar provision is made in SI 1994/1291 (Water Fringe Habitats) and SI 1994/1293 (Salt Marsh Habitats).

[88] The European Commission have now acceded to the UK request for long-term set-aside to count against a farmer's market set-aside requirement – MAFF/474/94.

habitat improvement scheme options (above) these two management options will only be available on land which is eligible for the Arable Area Payments Scheme. The Lowland Heath option is intended to encourage the establishment of heathland habitats for several declining bird species, such as nightjars, stonechats and linnets. The Damp Lowland Grassland option is intended to establish winter feeding and nesting habitat for geese, waders, swans and ducks. Both options, if adopted, will entail management regimes which prohibit the grazing of livestock or the application of pesticides or fertilizers.

Conclusion

This chapter has sought to assess the environmental potential, and the legal problems, of set-aside – both under the Arable Area Payments Scheme and the Habitat Improvement Scheme. To what extent are these reforms likely to deliver a 'green dividend', and how far do they go in meeting the requirements of both the EU Habitats Directive and the EU's agri-environment programme? The Habitats Directive, as we have seen, recognizes the interdependence of wildlife with the countryside around it. Article 10, in particular, is aimed at facilitating genetic exchange and migration, and ensuring that designated Special Areas of Conservation are not violated. The UK's response[89] does not address article 10 directly. The integration of environmental conditions into the set-aside regime provides a generalized and patchwork response, and one which is not specifically tailored to SACs or genetic exchange in the manner envisaged. The arable set-aside regime, in particular, is underpinned by economic, not environmental, considerations and is likely to be haphazard in its environmental effect. The emphasis which has been placed in some quarters on the 'green dividend' offered by set-aside raises a fundamental question: what *are* the aims of set-aside? The answer must be that its primary function is an economic one – it has been conceived as a temporary technique of market management, operating to reduce market supply and cut production, and to compensate producers (in the interim period) for reductions in cereal prices. Presenting it as a tool of environmental policy arguably confuses the issues, and raises unrealistic expectations of the likely environmental benefits from set-aside. Set-aside is not, of course, a new concept. It has been used in the USA for many years as a soil conservation measure. Studies of the economic effects of successive US Acreage Reduction Programmes and the Soil Conservation Programme have consistently shown, however, that farmers will put the poorest-yielding land into set-aside and intensify production on their remaining arable acres, and that acreage reduction (via set-aside) is an ineffective type of production control

---

[89] Outlined in the Consultation Paper on the Directive (above note 10), esp. at paras.1.5, 1.7 and 4.

mechanism.[90] The end result is 'slippage', over time, in the production-reducing function of set-aside, unless production quotas are also implemented to complement the set-aside (they have not been in the EU). Intensification of production on land *not* set-aside also causes its own environmental problems.

To achieve environmental goals, set-aside needs to be targeted. If it is to have any environmental value, land which is set aside should be taken out of production either permanently or for a long time. There is a clear consensus between conservationists and economists that long-term set-aside is the only form likely to yield significant gains.[91]

The new management rules for set-aside land do not target specific environmental objectives in a 'coherent and complementary way', as has been claimed,[92] with the sole exception of the new Habitat Improvement Scheme for twenty-year set-aside. In financial terms the Habitat Improvement Scheme is very much a Cinderella, however, when compared with the enormous quantity of public finance going into the Arable Area Payments Scheme.[93] Its annual budget has been estimated by the Ministry at £3 million p.a. initially.[94] Any environmental gains are therefore likely to be a purely incidental benefit of a regime conditioned and driven by agronomic and economic considerations.

Cross-compliance, furthermore, fails to provide an effective tool of control to ensure the maintenance of high standards of environmental management. As we have seen, the *application* of the principle in the new set-aside regime is half-hearted and crude. Many environmentalists would argue that the receipt of *all* public subsidy should be conditional on environmental safeguards being adhered to – and not limited to specific subsidies, and part-payments thereon. As a tool of legal control cross-compliance also has conceptual flaws. As a legal technique it relies for its effectiveness on market factors viz. that it is uneconomic to produce arable crops or livestocks without public subsidy. Admittedly, this is the

[90] See e.g. D. E. Ervin 'Some lessons about the political-economic effects of set-aside: the United States experience', pp.3–13 in J. Clarke (ed.), *Set-aside: British Crop Protection Council Monograph No.50* (1992); also D. E. Ervin, 'Cropland diversion in the US: are there lessons for the EEC set-aside discussion?', pp.53–63 in *Removing Land from Agriculture – the Implications for Farming and the Environment*, Baldock and Conder (eds.) (CPRE and IEEP, 1987); C. A. Potter, *Environmental Protection and Agricultural Adjustment: Lessons from the American Experience*, Set-aside Working Paper no.1 (Wye College, University of London, 1986).

[91] See e.g. Bower, pp.5ff. in *Removing Land from Agriculture,* op.cit. (CPRE and IEEP 1987), D. E. Ervin, 'Some lessons about the political-economic effects of set-aside', pp.3–13 in J. Clarke (ed.), *Set Aside,* op. cit. (above, note 90).

[92] Consultation Paper on the Habitats Directive (above note 10) at para.4.1.

[93] Claims for arable area payments were made for a total of 3,184,467 ha in 1993 (MAFF/177/93)

[94] See MAFF release 182/94.

norm within the common organization of most agricultural markets under the CAP, but it need not necessarily always be so. Its conservation effectiveness is also limited, in that it can only be used as a lever to achieve generalized environmental standards through its linkage to standard-rate support payments – it is incapable of delivering specific conservation measures, or of targeting particular environmental problems which may be site-specific.

Whether agricultural reform, and set-aside in particular, delivers a 'green dividend' will await the test of time. Set-aside is unlikely to deliver significant environmental gains in its present form. Its most likely, and lasting, effect may well be to distort the organization of agricultural enterprises – at enormous public expense, and without delivering widespread environmental benefit.

6

Forestry, the Law and the Environment

COLIN T. REID

After many years of stability, the last twenty years have seen dramatic changes in forestry in Great Britain. In that time the environmental benefits of forestry have come to be appreciated as never before, but also the potential for environmental harm if the choices of location, species, design and management are not appropriate. Afforestation and the protection of existing woodland can help to maintain and increase biodiversity, screen land from external pollution and offer great opportunities for recreation while providing a sustainable source of products of many kinds. On the other hand, inappropriate afforestation and forest management can destroy valuable habitats, blight landscapes, trap pollution, adversely change water flow and quality, and exclude visitors from the countryside.

This awareness of the need to consider more carefully the environmental consequences of forestry would by itself have produced changes in the ways in which forestry is promoted and controlled. However changes were also inevitable as a result of political pressures demanding that the private sector, not the state, should be the prime mover in the development of new commercial woodland, and that state enterprises should become more commercial in their outlook. To these factors must be added the promotion of alternative land uses as part of the battle against agricultural surpluses and the extension to forestry of more general developments in environmental law, e.g. environmental impact assessment. As a result of these pressures, the regulation of forestry has been transformed in recent years. However, as trees grow slowly it will take decades before the effects of these changes can be properly assessed, and in making judgements it must always be remembered that the tall forestry plantations which we see today are the product of planting decisions taken well over twenty years ago.[1]

These changes have taken place in an essentially domestic context. The European Community has had an impact by requiring the introduction of environmental assessments for some new planting,[2] and by supporting the promotion of forestry on previously agricultural land,[3] but has not played a significant role in the development of forestry policy as a whole. The Community's involvement also includes a Standing Forestry Committee[4] and initiatives on monitoring the effects of air pollution[5] and on protecting woodlands from fire.[6] It remains to be seen whether the entry of the Nordic countries, to whom forestry is of much greater economic importance, will lead to greater Community activity in this field.

At a broader level, forestry has recently become a major issue in the global environmental debate. However, as the emphasis has largely been on protecting existing natural forests, particularly rain forests, much of the debate has been of little relevance in Britain where, although the preservation of the small area of native woodland which survives is important, the major issue is not the exploitation of existing forests but the development of new ones. Of greater significance has been the broader Statement of Forest Principles which was adopted[7] at the UN Conference on Environment and Development in Rio in 1992. This emphasizes the importance of forests on ecological, economic and other grounds, calls for efforts to maintain and increase forest cover and stresses the need for sustainable forest management.[8] In response to this, and to the General Guidelines for the Sustainable Management of Forests in Europe agreed

---

[1] Two-thirds of the Forestry Commission's woodlands were planted before 1970 (Appendix 2 of the Report of the Comptroller and Auditor General, *Forestry Commission: Timber Harvesting and Marketing* (HC 526 1992–3)). Where no specific source is given for figures they are taken from the Forestry Commission's Annual Reports or from *Our Forests: The Way Ahead* (Cm. 2644, see below).

[2] Directive 85/337 of 27 June 1985 on the assessment of the effects of certain public and private projects on the environment (OJ 85/L 175/40).

[3] Regulation 2080/92 of 30 June 1992 instituting a Community aid scheme for forestry measures in agriculture (OJ 92/L 215/96).

[4] Created by Decision 89/367 of 29 May 1989 (OJ 89/L 165/14).

[5] Regulation 3528/86 of 17 November 1986 on the protection of the Community's forests against atmospheric pollution (OJ 86/L 326/2), as amended *inter alia* by Regulation 2157/92 of 23 July 1992 (OJ 92/L 217/1).

[6] Regulation 2158/92 of 23 July 1992 on protection of the Community's forests against fire (OJ 92/L 217/3).

[7] The statement is described as a 'non-legally binding authoritative statement of principles'; the text can be found at (1992) 31 ILM 882 and in Annex A to *Sustainable Forestry: The UK Programme* (Cm. 2429).

[8] 'Forest resources and forest lands should be sustainably managed to meet the social, economic, ecological, cultural and spiritual needs of present and future generations' (article 2(b)).

in Helsinki in 1993,[9] the British government has produced its own state-ment, *Sustainable Forestry: The UK Programme,*[10] which sets out the policies and actions which the government is pursuing to meet such objec-tives.

This activity at the international level has helped to influence the develop-ment of policies here, and to direct attention to new issues, e.g. concerns about global warming have led to some consideration of the role of forests in Britain as 'carbon sinks'.[11] However such activity is only part of the general awakening to environmental concerns in recent decades, and it is this general process, rather than any specific European or international initiatives, which lies behind many of the changes which have taken place.

General Policy

The background to British forestry policy this century is the devastation in the preceding millennia of our natural forests, which probably once covered about 85 per cent of the land. By the end of the First World War, only 5 per cent of the country was covered with forest and woodland, and the country's dependence on overseas supplies was identified as a serious problem. Initially for strategic reasons, and more recently for economic ones, policy was directed to expanding the area of productive forests, with the Forestry Commission, established in 1919, playing a major part in developing plantations on existing Crown land or on land specifically acquired for this purpose. This policy has been successful in that now 10 per cent of the country is covered by woodland,[12] but it inevitably led to a concentration on quick-growing species planted in a commercially efficient way. Other factors were not wholly ignored, e.g. the opportunities offered for recreation were recognized by the creation of the first Forest Park in 1935, but it was only in the 1970s and 1980s that the desirability of taking a more balanced approach was fully real-ized.

Today, forestry policy is very firmly committed to a multi-purpose approach. The government's main aims are set out in the current *Forestry Policy for Great Britain,* issued in September 1991, as being: 'The sustain-able management of our existing woods and forests. A steady expansion

---

[9] See Annex B to *Sustainable Forestry: The UK Programme* (Cm 2429).

[10] Cm. 2429 (January 1994).

[11] Ibid., para.3.39; growing vegetation traps carbon dioxide and can therefore contribute to reducing the atmospheric concentration of greenhouse gases.

[12] Still well under half the average within the EC; calculated differently, the UK has 40 ha of woodland for every 1,000 head of population compared to an EC average of 170 ha (written answer to House of Commons on 23 June 1993; HC Deb. vol.227 col.203).

of the tree cover to increase the many, diverse benefits that forests provide.'[13] This approach is reiterated in *Our Forests: The Way Ahead: Enterprise, Environment and Access*[14] which sets out the conclusions of the Forestry Review which reported in the summer of 1994. After quoting from the Forest Principles as adopted at the Rio summit,[15] the report states that the twin concepts of multiple purpose management and sustainability in forestry are central to British forestry policy. More detail is added to this as follows:

> Key aspects of the management of existing woods and forests include: promoting the production and supply of quality timber and other forest products; preventing loss of woodlands, and especially ancient semi-natural woodlands; the use of woodlands for public access and recreation; restructuring first-rotation plantations into attractive and more varied woodlands.
>
> The Government are also committed to the continued expansion of the forest area. Grants are targeted to encourage: continued new planting of conifers to meet commercial demand from the wood-processing industry; more planting of broadleaved and mixed woodland on suitable sites; the planting of small woodlands and farm woodlands as a productive alternative use for agricultural land; the extension of semi-natural woodlands, including native pinewoods in Scotland; the creation of woodlands close to areas of population, with benefits for local communities; a general shift of planting 'down the hill' on to land of better quality. All planting schemes are required to meet high standards of design which are in sympathy with the landscape and meet relevant environmental considerations.[16]

Meeting these varied objectives calls for a range of approaches, and during the past decade many aspects of the regulation of forestry have been adjusted to meet the new, broader policy. In formal terms, a significant step was the introduction in 1985 of a duty on the Forestry Commissioners:

> so far as may be consistent with the proper exercise of [their statutory] functions, [to] endeavour to achieve a reasonable balance between
>
> (a) the development of afforestation, the management of forests and the production of timber, and
>
> (b) the conservation and enhancement of natural beauty and the conservation of flora, fauna and geological or physiographical features of special interest.[17]

---

[13] The policy statement is reprinted as Appendix VI to the Forestry Commission's 72nd Annual Report 1991–2 (HC 187 1992–3).

[14] Cm. 2644 (August 1994).

[15] The passage quoted above at note 8.

[16] *Our Forests: The Way Ahead*, paras.1.2, 1.3.

[17] Forestry Act 1967, s.1(3A), as inserted by the Wildlife and Countryside (Amendment) Act 1985, s.4.

In reality, though, this was a recognition of changes which were already taking place rather than a measure to force a shift in attitude.

Of greater practical importance have been the changes to the ways in which financial support is offered to forestry. Until 1988 a major element of this support came through the way in which the tax system could operate for those investing in new plantations. It was possible to set the costs of planting against income from other sources, thereby greatly reducing the liability to tax in that year, while at a later stage escaping tax on the income received when the trees were harvested or sold.[18] This possibility was thought to lead to plantations being created for short-term financial purposes, without proper consideration of environmental factors or even their long-term value. Accordingly the system was changed so that tax relief, which had been available without consideration of the details of the particular project, was removed[19] and the financial support directed wholly through the grant schemes, under which grants are paid only to projects which have been individually scrutinized and found to comply with general policy.

The grant schemes themselves have been transformed to reflect the changes in forestry policy. The Forestry Grant Scheme which operated from 1981 to 1988 required that timber production be the primary objective of any project. Today, however, the Woodland Grant Scheme reflects the multiple objectives of the government's policy. Timber production is no longer the primary objective, but takes its place alongside improving the landscape, providing wildlife habitats, offering opportunities for recreation and sport, improving the economy of rural areas and providing a use for land instead of agriculture. The scheme also offers a higher rate of grant for the planting of broadleaved species, reflecting both the higher costs of such planting (including the longer wait for any financial return) and the greater environmental benefits which broadleaved trees bring in most parts of the country. All projects must comply with the Forestry Commission's guidance on landscape and environmental protection, and in some cases an environmental assessment may be required.[20]

The basic grant scheme is now supplemented with further schemes to encourage particular forms of forestry. Support is available for the exten-

---

[18] For a full description see T. D. Lynch, *Taxation of Woodlands in the UK* (W. Green & Son, Edinburgh, 1989).

[19] Finance Act 1988, s.65 and sched. 6; commercial woodlands now operate outwith the income-tax system, with no tax due on the income but no relief on the expense of establishing young trees – see T. D. Lynch, *Taxation: The End of an Era?*, 1990 SLT (News) 297.

[20] The best source of information on the various grant schemes and procedures is the range of helpful publications produced by the Forestry Commission; I must also record my gratitude to the staff at the Commission and in the Scottish Office who have been most helpful in responding to my queries.

sion of native pinewoods in Scotland, there are grants to assist the management of trees once they are established, and further supplements to promote community woodlands near towns and cities, where informal recreation will be encouraged, and to encourage planting on agricultural land. The range of grants available enables the government to target aid and thus to influence the sorts of forest which are being developed.

These new initiatives have been successful in altering the types of planting which are taking place. e.g. the proportion of broadleaved trees planted has increased greatly.[21] However, although the incentives have led to a considerable amount of agricultural land being planted, overall the area of new planting in recent years has fallen well short of the government's aim of 33,000 ha each year.[22] Indeed the Forestry Review in 1994 reveals concern that not enough conifers are being planted to guarantee long-term supplies to the wood-processing industry, and accordingly the value of the grants for conifers has been increased. Similarly changes have been made to the required density of planting in order to encourage high-quality timber, but with lower densities being approved for new semi-natural woodlands, small-scale projects and amenity woodland.[23]

The commitment to multi-purpose forestry does, of course, bring difficulties at times in setting priorities and ensuring that an appropriate balance is in fact struck. One particular way in which this issue has been highlighted is in relation to Forest Enterprise, the branch of the Forestry Commission responsible for managing forests in state hands. The difficulty here is largely one of quantifying the non-tangible benefits of particular management decisions in order to check that appropriate priorities are being adopted.[24] It has been suggested that there is a need for better models in order to measure the full costs involved, and for more careful monitoring to ensure that commensurate benefits are in fact produced; the report of the Forestry Review in 1994 suggests that these criticisms have been accepted.[25]

Decisions which are taken for environmental or amenity purposes may

---

[21] In 1993–4 broadleaved planting accounted for 60 per cent of all new planting; even in Scotland where broadleaves are not always appropriate, between 1982 and 1992 the proportion of broadleaved planting increased from 0 to 22 per cent (written answer to the House of Commons on 12 February 1993, HC Deb., vol.218, col.850).

[22] Announced in a written answer to the House of Commons on 9 February 1987 (HC Deb. vol.110, col.39).

[23] *Our Forests: The Way Ahead*, paras.2.7–9.

[24] This issue has been raised both by the House of Commons Select Committee on the Environment in its report on Forestry and the Environment (First Report 1992–3, HC 257, at para.129) and by the National Audit Office in the Comptroller and Auditor General's Report, *Forestry Commission: Timber Harvesting and Marketing* (HC 526 1992–3, at paras.8–9).

[25] *Our Forests: The Way Ahead*, paras.3.11–17.

entail direct costs, but there may often be a greater element of notional profit forgone, e.g. harvesting a single-age plantation over several years may bring environmental benefits but may cost more and may mean that some trees are felled before or after their commercial prime. Moreover, in relation to forestry the usual difficulties in and arguments over quantifying amenity and environmental benefits are exacerbated by the long time-scale involved; it is likely to take twenty years at least before it is possible to assess properly whether today's amenity planting really is producing worthwhile benefits. Whatever one's view on the methods which should be adopted to check whether the balance in any particular case is appropriate, the task will not be easy.

A forestry policy which embraces a range of objectives, objectives which may at times be incompatible, will not by itself be able to determine exactly what should occur in every case. It is therefore important to examine the mechanisms through which these policy aims of expanding tree cover and securing sustainable and multi-purpose forest management are carried into practice.

Institutional Structure

Since 1980, two major changes have taken place in the way in which the forestry industry is organized. In the first place, it has been increasingly through the private sector, not the state, that the goal of expanding the forests has been pursued. Secondly, the internal structure of the Forestry Commission has changed markedly. In both cases the driving force has been the political ideologies of the Conservative government, committed to rolling back the extent of state involvement in many activities and to ensuring that such state enterprises as remain are run in a more commercial way.

The private sector has always had a major role in the development of forestry, and since the formation of the Forestry Commission the development of forests on land owned, purchased or leased by the state has been matched by encouragements to private landowners. The decision to place even more reliance on the private sector for the expansion of our forests has, however, had two main consequences. In the first place, it bestows greater significance on the mechanisms for regulating private forestry and on the grant schemes (and previously tax provisions) which offer incentives to forestry. The sort of woodlands which have been planted during the last ten years, and will be in future, are increasingly shaped not by the direct actions of a public body, but by the success of these mechanisms in encouraging private landowners to plant trees and to do so in ways compatible with the multiple objectives of the government's policy.

A second consequence, and the one which has attracted more controversy, has been the sale of land by the Forestry Commission. Both existing plantations and bare land for new planting have been sold in order to make available to the private sector the basic resource required for forestry development. This has been a cause of considerable public debate and disquiet, particularly in relation to public access to the land, as it is feared that private owners will be unwilling to continue the Forestry Commission's policy of allowing free access and indeed encouraging many recreational uses of its land. Measures have been adopted to address this issue, but it remains controversial (see below).

The effect of this policy has been significant. The Forestry Commission still holds marginally under 1,110,000 ha of land, but more than 185,000 ha have been sold since 1981[26] and less than 3,500 ha of the land retained is forestry land which has not yet been planted. A target for sales of a further 100,000 ha by the end of the century was announced in 1989.[27] Similarly, the area of land planted annually by the Commission has fallen by a third during the last ten years, and increasingly the planting is the restocking of plantations that have been harvested, not the planting of bare land.[28] It has however, been realized that there is an important role to be played by the Commission in support of the special initiatives for new forests in certain parts of the country (e.g. central Scotland, the new National Forest – see below) and land is being acquired and planted as a 'pump-priming' exercise in such areas.[29]

The restructuring of the Forestry Commission has taken place in several stages, with the most recent moves being announced as a result of the Forestry Review in 1994. The changes reflect the government's wish for state enterprises to be subjected to market disciplines and the general policy within the public sector of separating those responsible for regulating an activity from those actually engaged in it.[30] The Forestry Commission has the legal status of and functions as a government department and has its duties, functions and powers set out in legislation, primarily the Forestry Act 1967. The Commissioners are Crown appointments, in large part drawn from those with knowledge or experience of the industry,[31] and they report to the Forestry Ministers, viz. the Secretary of State for Scotland (who is the lead minister), the Secretary of State for Wales and

---

[26] A reduction from over 50 per cent to under 40 per cent of the total forests in Britain.

[27] See the Forestry Commission's 70th Annual Report 1989–90 (HC 75 1990–1), Appendix VI.

[28] In 1984 over 15,000 ha were planted, only two-fifths of this being restocking, whereas in 1993 under 11,000 ha were planted, four-fifths by way of restocking (Forestry Commission's 73rd Annual Report 1992–3 (HC 151 1993–4), 100).

[29] Forestry Commission's 73rd Annual Report 1992–3 (HC 151 1993–4), paras.176–9.

[30] Cf. the changes in the water industry and in the control of waste disposal.

[31] Forestry Act 1967, s.2.

the Minister of Agriculture, Fisheries and Food (on all issues, administratively separate but essentially parallel arrangements apply in Northern Ireland – throughout this chapter it is the position in Great Britain which is described). Policy for the Commission is generally announced by ministers in Parliament, orally or in the form of written answers.

Since 1992 the Forestry Commission has operated as two distinct entities, the Department of Forestry and Forest Enterprise. The first of these is itself divided into two. The Policy and Resources Group serves to support and advise ministers and is responsible for policy development and finance. The Forest Authority is the body responsible for actually implementing policy, in particular through the operation of the grant schemes and felling controls by means of which private forestry is regulated. Its aims include encouraging good forestry practice, in particular safeguarding woods of special environmental importance, and ensuring that the expansion of the forest area will bring 'sustainable economic, environmental and social benefits, while protecting the natural and cultural heritage'.[32]

Forest Enterprise is the body responsible for managing the Commission's forests. This separation from the policy and regulatory branch of the Commission was intended partly to promote financial efficiency, and Forest Enterprise has been set the target of becoming self-financing by 1995–6.[33] However, the strategic objectives which have been adopted reflect not only the aim of increasing the wood-producing capacity of the forest estate and the net value of the body's commercial enterprises, but also the multiple-purpose objectives of the government's forestry policy, so that increasing the attractiveness and conservation value of the forests and increasing opportunities for public recreation are also included.[34] It is now proposed that Forest Enterprise be replaced with a 'Next Steps Agency', still within the public sector but operating at arm's length from the Forestry Authority and monitored by it in the same way as the private sector.[35] Already, the Forest Authority has to approve Forest Enterprise's operations through a system of forest-design plans.[36] Political debate continues on whether such moves will eventually lead to privatization.

Taken together, the increased involvement of the private sector and the restructuring of the Forestry Commission mean that the role of the Commission is being transformed. Increasingly the Commission's role is that of regulator, and its impact on forestry in this country will be felt not through its own direct management of large areas of forest, but through the various controls which it exercises over the activities of others who

[32] Forestry Commission's 72nd Annual Report 1991–2 (HC 187 1992–3), para.117.
[33] By 1993–4 the net call on public funds had already been reduced to £1.4million.
[34] Forestry Commission's 72nd Annual Report 1991–2 (HC 187 1992–3), para.56.
[35] *Our Forests: The Way Ahead*, paras.3.18–20.
[36] Forestry Commission's Annual Report 1993–4 (HC 661 1993–4), 20, 32.

own and manage the plantations and woodlands throughout the country. These controls must now be considered.

Controls on Planting and Felling

There are two main stages at which it is possible to control forestry: planting and felling. In Britain these are dealt with in very different ways.[37] Felling is the subject of a formal licensing system, whereas there are generally no legal controls on planting. Instead, control is exerted by means of a grant system which operates in a context where no significant planting is economically viable without grant support, with the result that all planting will in fact fall to be officially considered and will proceed only if approved. One possible means of imposing control which is not used is the town and country planning system. It is expressly provided that the use of land for forestry is not 'development' and therefore does not require planning permission,[38] an exception which can extend to activities some distance from the forest land itself.[39]

Part II of the Forestry Act 1967 lays down the powers of the Forestry Commission to control felling. The felling of trees is a criminal offence, unless a licence has been obtained from the Forestry Authority or one of the exceptions apply. No licence is required for topping or lopping, felling trees in gardens, orchards, churchyards or public open spaces, felling trees smaller than 8 cm in diameter or felling necessary to abate a nuisance. The occupier of land is further permitted to fell no more than 5 cubic metres in any calendar quarter, provided that no more than 2 cubic metres are sold, or trees smaller than 10 cm in diameter as thinnings.[40] There is a right of appeal against the refusal of a licence or imposition of conditions, with the final decision being taken by the minister after a hearing before a special reference committee. If unlicensed felling takes place or if a replanting condition in a licence is not fulfilled, an order to restock the land can be sought from a court, ultimately authorizing the Forestry Commission to carry out the planting itself and recover the costs from the landowner.

In keeping with the policy of retaining and expanding the area of trees in the country, licences will normally be granted subject to a restocking condition, and where broadleaves are felled the restocking requirement will specify broadleaves. Any felling application relating to an ancient and semi-natural woodland will be very carefully scrutinized and is likely

[37] See generally, C. T. Reid, *Nature Conservation Law* (W. Green, Edinburgh, 1994), ch.6.3 and paras.6.4.20–3.

[38] Town and Country Planning (Scotland) Act 1972, s.19(2); Town and Country Planning Act 1990, s.55(2).

[39] *Farleyer Estate* v. *Secretary of State for Scotland* 1992 SLT 476.

[40] Forestry Act 1967, s.9.

to be approved only if part of a broader management plan aimed at conserving the woodland. The Forestry Authority will investigate allegations of unlawful felling, and between 1991 and 1994 over 200 cases were investigated, leading to sixty-two successful prosecutions (and formal warning letters in other less serious cases) which in turn led to restocking notices in thirty-nine cases.

The felling of trees can also be regulated by the use of Tree Preservation Orders made by planning authorities under the town and country planning legislation. Under detailed and complex legislative provisions,[41] orders affecting individual trees or areas of woodland can be made in the interests of amenity, and the permission of the authority must thereafter be sought if the affected trees are to be cut, lopped, topped, felled or destroyed. This system may be important for some small areas of woodland, but it is not really suited for dealing with larger areas. There is an untidy overlap with the system of felling licences, exacerbated by the difference in compensation rules; when a felling licence is refused there is no entitlement to compensation for any loss arising from the fact that the land cannot be cleared and put to more profitable uses, but such compensation may be available if consent to fell trees protected by a Tree Preservation Order is refused.[42] Practical arrangements have been made so that the matter is dealt with initially as a forestry one, but with full weight being given to amenity considerations, and only if a felling licence would be granted (which will normally occur only if replanting is intended) is the matter considered by the planning authority.[43]

Planting is controlled in a very different way. There are no legal controls on afforestation or on the replanting of land after harvesting. Landowners are free to plant as many trees of whatever sort they wish without having to seek any form of official approval. In practice, however, all significant planting is scrutinized by the Forestry Authority as it is only with support from the various grant schemes that forestry is economically viable at present. Although the procedures are not directly regulated by statute, it has been held that the process may be subject to judicial review.[44]

The success of this approach to regulation does, of course, depend on all proposals in fact being presented for grant support. At present it is estimated that in each year only about 200 ha (comprised of many small

---

[41] Town and Country Planning (Scotland) Act 1972, ss.57–60, 98–9C, and Town and Country Planning Act 1990, ss.198–214D, each with associated Statutory Instruments; see Reid, *Nature Conservation Law*, ch.6.4.

[42] Forestry Act 1967, ss.10(4), 11; Town and Country Planning (Scotland) Act 1972, s.163; Town and Country Planning Act 1990, s.203; see *Bell* v. *Canterbury City Council* (1988) 56 P and CR 211.

[43] Reid, *Nature Conservation Law*, paras.6.4.20–3.

[44] *Kincardine and Deeside District Council* v. *Forestry Commissioners* 1992 SLT 1180.

areas) are planted without grant-aid, but this rests on the current economics of forestry and the continued willingness of government to provide
substantial financial incentives (in 1993–4 grants worth £29,800,000 were
paid). The desire to ensure that all planting fell to be considered by the
grant-approval process was the major factor in the decision in 1988 to
direct all financial support for planting through the grant scheme. It was
feared that the opportunities for tax relief might themselves be sufficient
to encourage planting without grant support, and hence without the details
of the proposals being officially considered and approved. Despite increases
in the value of the grants to make up for the loss in tax relief, that decision, coupled with the recession, led to a dramatic reduction in the area
of new planting.[45] This suggests a need to refine the system if the target
of a significant expansion of the forest area is to be achieved, but also
demonstrates the power of these economic mechanisms as a control strategy.

Applications for grants are initially scrutinized by the Forest Authority
in order to ensure that they are acceptable on silvicultural and environmental
grounds. There are guidelines on the design of plantations, the mix of
species, etc., and it is very unlikely that approval would be given today
to any proposal for rectangular blocks of densely packed alien conifers
of the kind planted in the past and now so visible as maturing plantations. Consultations are held with a number of public bodies in accordance with agreed criteria; the bodies include local authorities, the
agriculture departments, the conservancy councils, the Countryside Commission in England and the Red Deer Commission in Scotland. Some
streamlining of the consultation procedures is likely, but the government
has emphasized their importance in ensuring that the environmental and
other consequences of a proposal are properly considered.[46]

Consideration of the proposal will also be guided by the Indicative
Forestry Strategy prepared by the relevant strategic planning authority.
These strategies, which should form part of the structure or unified development plan, are intended to indicate preferred areas where geographical
and other considerations are suitable for forestry, potential areas where
the ground is suitable but there are some constraining interests, and sensitive areas where there are serious constraints on forestry developments.
The preparation of these strategies offers the opportunity for some public
participation in the decision-making process, the absence of which was a
justified criticism of the procedures in the past. Public involvement is
also made possible through the fact that applications which include new
planting (as opposed to restocking) are included in a public register and

---

[45] Over 25,000 ha of new planting was carried out in 1988–9, compared to an average
of just over 15,000 ha in the following four years.

[46] Government response (Cm.2259, January 1993) to the report of the House of Commons Select Committee on the Environment: *Forestry and the Environment* (HC 257-I
1992–3), commenting on para.65 of the Committee's report.

members of the public are able to make representations before a decision is made.

If there are objections to a proposal, the aim of the Forestry Authority is to produce a final plan which is acceptable to all concerned. If the objections cannot be resolved, it is possible for the matter to be referred to a Regional Advisory Committee. The membership of these committees has recently been extended[47] to enable those members statutorily drawn from the forestry and timber industry to be balanced by members with interests and experience in environmental and recreational matters. The aim of the committees is again one of seeking consensus, and to encourage this they meet in private, although the proposals to be considered are advertised, members of the public are invited to make representations and can be individually invited to attend, and the reports of the committees (which may not be unanimous) are published. Again, this opening of the process to a degree of public scrutiny is a fairly new development.[48] The final say on whether a grant will be paid lies with the minister.

The one legal control on new planting comes through the formal requirement in some circumstances for an environmental assessment to be carried out. This requirement stems from the EC's directive on environmental assessment[49] which includes 'initial afforestation where this may lead to adverse ecological effects' among the projects which must be subject to an environmental assessment before being approved in circumstances where there is 'likely to be a significant effect on the environment'. The directive has been implemented by the Environmental Assessment (Afforestation) Regulations 1988,[50] which echo these somewhat vague definitions of when an assessment is required. The implementation, as well as being slightly late,[51] is not technically correct, as the assessment is linked to the award of a grant, not to any formal approval for the planting of trees; as noted above, in practice this will mean that all significant projects are covered, but it remains legally possible for planting to take place without grant support, thereby evading the assessment requirements.

It is the Forestry Authority which decides if an assessment is required, and its opinion can be sought before an application is made. If the issue is disputed, the minister can be called on to give a ruling on whether the assessment is necessary. The most likely projects to be caught by this

[47] Forestry Act 1991, s.16, amending Forestry Act 1967, s.38(3).

[48] C. T. Reid, *Publicity for Forestry Applications* (1993) 39 SPEL 34 (1993), 5 ELM 97.

[49] Directive 85/337 of 27 June 1985 on the assessment of the effects of certain public and private projects on the environment (OJ 85/L 175/40).

[50] SI 1988 No.1207.

[51] See *Kincardine and Deeside District Council v. Forestry Commissioners* 1992 SLT 1180.

procedure are those which affect areas designated for their conservation or landscape value, e.g. Sites of Special Scientific Interest. If an assessment is required, the applicant must provide an environmental statement setting out the likely impacts of the planting, the appropriate conservancy council must be consulted and the statement must be made available for public consultation before the decision is made.

The grant schemes have a major influence on the sort of forestry which is carried out and their power as a form of regulation is becoming obvious. As noted above, the grant schemes have been significantly altered in recent years to reflect the multiple objectives of today's forestry policy. The higher grants for broadleaved planting have led to a huge increase in the area of these trees planted, and the supplement for native pinewoods in Scotland has attracted planting and regeneration covering 4,200 ha. Indeed the success of the grant schemes in promoting such forms of environmentally sensitive forestry can be shown by the fact that in the Forestry Review it is noted that so much of the new planting has been carried out under the various schemes furthering environmental and amenity objectives that there is a need to increase the level of support for primarily commercial planting in order to ensure long-term supplies.

The grant schemes allow for some regulation not only of the initial planting but also of the care of the trees subsequently. Planting grants have been paid on the basis of 70 per cent when planting is finished, 20 per cent after five years and 10 per cent after ten.[52] This provides a means of ensuring that the trees are in fact properly established, and payments will be withheld if their management is unsatisfactory. The Forestry Review proposes that there be only two payments, with all of the withheld sums being paid after five years, but the Forestry Commission would retain the right to carry out inspections and claim repayments for the full ten years.[53] Additionally, grants are now available to support the management of existing woodlands, but their take-up has been slow and it is proposed that this grant be targeted at woodlands of special environmental or amenity value and that there be a system of discretionary grants for one-off measures to improve existing woodlands.[54]

It is apparent from the above that the law plays a fairly insignificant part in determining what is happening in our forests. The Forestry Commission operates within a statutory framework and exercises statutory powers, but legal disputes have not been a feature of the regulatory system. Other than through the initial legal authorization to pay grants,[55] the grant

[52] For natural regeneration the payments are 50 per cent when the work to encourage regeneration is carried out, 30 per cent when adequate stocking is achieved and 20 per cent five years later.

[53] *Our Forests: The Way Ahead*, para.2.11.

[54] Ibid., paras.2.16–17.

[55] Forestry Act 1979, s.1.

schemes and procedures which in effect control new planting generally operate on a non-statutory basis,[56] seeking consensus when conflicts arise, not formal adjudication. Even the more legalistic regime for controlling felling licences appears not to have engendered much work for the courts, other than in relation to prosecutions for unlicensed felling, and even here recourse to the higher courts is rare.[57] As part of the much more legalistic planning system, Tree Preservation Orders have been the subject of more litigation, and questions relating to land tenure may also reach the courts,[58] but generally forestry has attracted comparatively little legal activity.

The control of forestry offers an interesting case-study of how different approaches to regulation can work. The experience of recent years has shown the power of economic incentives in shaping behaviour, and it will be interesting to observe whether the continuing adjustment of the schemes will eventually produce an enduring structure or whether refinements will always be necessary to adjust to changing circumstances. The contrast between the absence of formal controls on planting and the formalized licensing of felling is very marked and only time will tell whether the revised procedures for grants, with indicative strategies and greater openness, can provide a wholly acceptable form of regulation, despite the continuing potential for the whole structure to be bypassed by anyone prepared to forgo grant aid.

What has been described are the control mechanisms for forestry on private land, not that held by the Forestry Commission. On such land the regulation of what is done has been essentially a matter for the internal management controls of Forest Enterprise. This body is committed to ensuring that all of its work lives up to the environmental and other standards expected of others, and the introduction of forest design plans to be approved by the Forestry Authority is a move towards an assimilation of the regulatory structures for private and public forestry.

Conservation

Environmental concerns are now reflected in all aspects of forestry, and are central to the policy of sustainable and multi-purpose forestry. Indeed the expansion of the area under trees is by itself seen as being environmentally desirable, provided that certain standards are met. Protection of the forest

[56] Although it is subject to judicial review; see *Kincardine and Deeside District Council* v. *Forestry Commissioners* 1992 SLT 1180.

[57] One example is *Campbell* v. *Webster* 1992 SCCR 167, an appeal against the level of fine imposed for unlicensed felling.

[58] Especially whether the landowner is entitled to resume for afforestation land which is held by a tenant as part of a croft (e.g. *Shaw* v. *Cummins* 1987 SLCR 157, *Dunbeath Estate* v. *Gunn* 1988 SLCR 52) or agricultural holding (e.g. *Fotheringham* v. *Fotheringham* 1987 SLT (Land Ct.) 10, *Thomson* v. *Murray* 1990 SLT (Land Ct.) 45).

environment, and steps to maintain and enhance the environmental benefits which forests can bring are consistent themes in the Forest Principles agreed at Rio,[59] and the Helsinki Guidelines call not only for sustainable and environmentally sound management but expressly state that 'the conservation and appropriate enhancement of biodiversity should be an essential operational element in sustainable forest management and should be adequately addressed . . . in forestry policies and legislation.'[60]

In Britain these concerns are reflected in both the Forestry Policy for Great Britain[61] and the UK Programme for Sustainable Forestry[62] and are carried into effect in many ways, primarily through the activities of the Forestry Commission in both of its capacities as regulator and occupier of large areas of woodland. The Commission is now under a duty to seek a balance between timber production and environmental protection,[63] but environmental awareness was already developing rapidly before this duty was imposed.

As the management of its own forests is concerned, one of the strategic objectives of Forest Enterprise is 'to increase the attractiveness and conservation value of our forests and woodlands'.[64] This is being put into practice in many ways, from the formation of policy to the training of staff and establishment of forest nature reserves. At a general level the opportunity is being taken as older plantations reach maturity to enhance their conservation and landscape value by phasing the felling period over an extended time-scale in order to avoid even-age plantations, and when replanting to increase the diversity of species and to ensure that the landscape, conservation and recreation are taken into account as well as timber production.[65] More specifically, it is planned to create a regeneration zone of 3,000 ha for native pine in Scotland, doubling the area of remanent pinewoods currently managed by Forest Enterprise.[66] The conservation value of such measures can be illustrated by the fact that nearly 1,000 ha of woodland at Haldon Forest in Somerset have been designated an SSSI, the significance being that this is a man-made woodland and much of the potential wildlife has arisen through careful design and management.[67]

In the year to March 1993 the net expenditure of Forest Enterprise on

[59] See above note 7.
[60] Resolution 2, article 1; see *Sustainable Forestry: The UK Programme*, Annex B, above n.9.
[61] September 1991; see above note 13.
[62] See above note 10.
[63] Forestry Act 1967, s.1(3A), as added by Wildlife and Countryside (Amendment) Act 1985, s.4.
[64] Forestry Commission's 72nd Annual Report 1991–2 (HC 187 1992–3), para.56.
[65] Forestry Commission's 73rd Annual Report 1992–3 (HC 151 1993–4), para.143.
[66] Ibid., para.164.
[67] Ibid., para.166. There are about 400 SSSIs on land held by Forest Enterprise, covering c.64,000 ha.

recreation, conservation and heritage amounted to £13.4million,[68] to which can be added the estimate of £5.8million of notional income forgone as a result of departures for environmental and amenity reasons from the optimum harvesting plans.[69] As Forest Enterprise strives to meet its target of becoming self-financing, or is converted into a 'Next Steps Agency', it is obviously important that there are measures in place to ensure that the drive for commercial profitability does not squeeze this very significant environmental role.

The position of Forest Enterprise as occupier of large areas of land (1,099,530 ha throughout Great Britain) means that its impact is not restricted to the immediate management of its trees. Considerable benefits can arise from, or damage be caused by, the way in which a whole range of issues on this land are approached. Important matters will include decisions on pest-control measures, on the granting of game rights and permission to hunt, on the construction of roads, and on the exploitation of minerals.[70] It is therefore important for all aspects of its activities to be undertaken with conservation in mind.

In the private forests, conservation aims are being furthered by the design of the grant schemes and the standards which are imposed before grants are awarded or felling licences issued. Grants will only be awarded if the design of planting, the mix of species and the management plan all meet the Forestry Authority's guidelines, which have increasingly given weight to conservation requirements, and in some cases an environmental assessment will be required. The enhanced environmental representation on the Regional Advisory Committee and the increased openness of the decision-making procedures should also help to ensure that conservation issues are properly taken into account.

The most obvious changes have been to the grant schemes themselves, which now expressly promote conservation, not merely timber production. Broadleaved forests in Britain generally offer greater benefits for wildlife than conifers,[71] and the increased levels of support within the basic Woodland Grant Scheme for broadleaved trees has led to a marked increase in the number of such trees being planted. Broadleaves accounted for more than 60 per cent of all new planting in the year to

---

[68] Ibid., p.62.

[69] Report of the Comptroller and Auditor General: *Forestry Commission: Timber Harvesting and Marketing* (HC 526 1992–3), para.8.

[70] In 1992–3, almost 25,000 deer were culled, 149 km of new roads were built and 160 km upgraded; £5million has been raised from mineral extraction in the ten years to 1993.

[71] But see 'Conifer forests are not the "deserts" they seem', *New Scientist,* 17 September 1994 (No.1943), p.16. The native Caledonian forest in Scotland is an important exception to the general position.

March 1994,[72] and in particular planting under the schemes to promote farm woodland has been predominantly of broadleaves. Attempts have also been made through the availability of management grants to encourage the care of existing woodlands. In Scotland special attention has been paid to native pines with supplements being available for their planting or regeneration, requiring not only that native trees be established, but that trees from local stock be used. This scheme too has led to increasing areas being planted or regenerated in this way.

The Forestry Review has proposed further adjustments to the grant schemes which should promote conservation by exempting from the increased density requirement new native woodlands on appropriate sites, by making available to farmers a premium for excluding livestock from existing native woodland where grazing pressure is preventing regeneration, by concentrating the management grants on woodlands of special environmental value and by introducing discretionary grants for one-off environmental improvement measures. Other projects, such as the birchwood initiative which is studying the growth, management and utilization of birchwoods in upland areas, also contribute to the goal of sustainable and environmentally sensitive forestry. Ancient and semi-natural woodlands may also qualify for certain exemptions from inheritance tax.[73]

In all these ways, conservation has come to lie at the heart of modern forestry regulation. How effective all of these measures are will only become truly apparent once the trees being planted today have grown into mature woodland and can be compared with the geometrically designed, single-age, single-species plantations of foreign conifers which were the norm decades ago and which now provide the most obvious forestry features in the landscape.

Access to Woodlands and Recreation

Encouraging the use of forests for recreation is one of the other strong themes in promoting multi-purpose forestry. Again this is reflected in many ways for woodlands in the public and private sectors, and by initiatives for developing new woodlands which seek to involve a wide range of bodies. The disposal of land to the private sector, however, has raised serious concerns about whether access and recreational opportunities will be maintained, concern which perhaps reflects a general satisfaction with the performance of the Forestry Commission on its own land.

Encouraging recreational use of the forests is nothing new for the Forestry Commission, whose first Forest Park was established in 1935. In recent years a new designation of Woodland Parks has been created, for smaller

---

[72] Nearly 50,000 ha of new broadleaved woodland have been planted since 1985.
[73] Inheritance Tax Act (*né* Capital Transfer Tax Act) 1984, s.26.

areas of woodland which are of particular value to local communities for recreation and which are managed primarily for that purpose.[74] These formal designations are supported by further measures to encourage recreational use, e.g. Forest Enterprise operates twenty-nine interpretation centres on its land, twenty-nine camping and caravan sites and four cabin sites. Miles of forestry roads are made available for recreational use, e.g. in 1991–2, 200 miles were made available as cycle tracks in Dumfries and Galloway alone, and local arrangements allow land to be used for a whole variety of sports, from motor rallying to water sports and orienteering.

Perhaps more important, though, is the general policy of allowing the public the 'freedom to roam' throughout the woodlands managed by Forest Enterprise, except where safety requirements prevent this. The fact that so much land is available for informal recreation in this way is of great significance, and it is estimated that there are about 50 million visits to Forest Enterprise land each year. One constraint on such access is that where land is held under lease[75] the terms may preclude public access, but it is now the policy to endeavour to purchase the freehold of such land where significant access and recreational benefits may accrue.[76] On land which it holds, the activities of visitors is controlled, not only by the power of Forest Enterprise as occupier to decide who is permitted access and on what terms, but also through by-laws.[77]

For private woodland, there have been measures to encourage owners to allow wider access. The provision of opportunities for recreation and sport is one of the aims of the basic Woodland Grant Scheme, and there is a Community Woodland Supplement for the planting near towns and cities of new woodlands which can be used for informal recreation.[78] Improving recreation was one of the specific objectives of the management grants, which are now targeted more closely on proposals to increase environmental and recreational benefits. The Forestry Commission and private owners' groups are also trying to demonstrate from their experience that the problems which owners fear will arise from allowing public access are more imagined than real.

These measures have been supported by the development of a range of initiatives to encourage new woodlands where they will be of particular amenity value. There are specific schemes for central Scotland, the Welsh Valleys, Sherwood Forest and a new National Forest in the Midlands,

---

[74] Forestry Commission's 72nd Annual Report 1991–2 (HC 187 1992–3), para.83, and 73rd Annual Report 1992–3 (HC 151 1993–4), para.174.

[75] Such land accounts for 25 per cent of Forest Enterprise land in England and Wales, much of it in lowland England.

[76] *Our Forests: The Way Ahead*, para.4.14.

[77] Forestry Commission By-laws 1982, SI 1982 No.648.

[78] Over 300 ha were planted within this scheme in 1992–3.

frequently involving partnerships with local authorities and development bodies, and a more general plan to develop a number of community woodlands. This plan, worked out initially with the Countryside Commission, and the more specific initiatives call for an integrated approach to be taken by local authorities, the Forestry Commission, other public bodies and private landowners, working in close contact with local community groups, to create new and diverse woodlands near to towns, which will be designed from the start as places for people to enjoy.

A number of such projects are being developed, and in all such areas, private landowners are encouraged to take advantage of the various grants available for establishing woodland. It has also been realized that there is a greater need than initially envisaged for the Forestry Commission itself to play a more significant 'pump-priming' role and to this end land has been purchased in a number of locations to enable the Commission to create woodlands itself. As with so many forest initiatives, it will take a long time to assess whether they are a success; even the 'ideal' timetable in the *Advice Manual for the Preparation of a Community Forest Plan*[79] says that it will take ten years for the basic framework of a community forest to be designed and established, and thirty years before the main structure is established and operating.

All of these measures to improve access and recreation, and to encourage private landowners to make their woodlands available to the public have been overshadowed by the debate on the consequences of the Forestry Commission selling land to the private sector. There is a real concern that private owners will not continue the Forestry Commission's policy of allowing a 'freedom to roam' and of encouraging recreational use, and that consequently large areas of countryside may become closed to the public. This issue has been addressed in several ways, but so far without producing any satisfactory guarantee that access will be protected. The operation of any such arrangements may be complicated by the existence of third-party rights (e.g. shooting rights, mineral rights, limitations on private rights of way) or by obligations to offer land back to the original vendor when no longer required by the Commission.

The guidelines for the selection of areas for disposal include the use of forests for public access and recreation among the factors to be taken into account when the land to be sold is being identified,[80] and the Forestry Review in 1994 has proposed that a more rigorous and consistent classification be introduced. Land which is not accessible from public roads, but can be reached on public rights of way will now be regarded as

---

[79] Countryside Commission, 1991.

[80] Forestry Commission's 62nd Annual Report 1981–2 (HC 363 1982–3) Appendix V; that these guidelines are still relevant is reiterated in the Revised Statement of Policy and Practice on the Disposal of Property Managed by the Forestry Commissioners, Forestry Commission's 70th Annual Report 1989–90 (HC 75 1990–1), Appendix IX.

generally available for access. There is to be a general presumption against the sale of woodlands with a high level of access, unless access agreements are in place or the purchaser is able to guarantee continued public access (e.g. if the land is bought by a local authority or the Woodlands Trust). If access arrangements cannot be made, the case will be referred to the minister before a sale can proceed.[81]

The public interest can also be protected by sales to certain bodies without the land reaching the open market. Where sizeable areas are identified for sale, or where there is a known conservation, recreation or amenity interest, this fact is publicized, and a body expressing a firm interest, e.g. a local authority or conservation trust, may be given preference if it can obtain sponsorship from the relevant government department or agency. This sponsorship entails an unequivocal statement from the department or agency that the acquisition of the property by the body concerned to the exclusion of other potential purchasers would be particularly in the public interest. Terms of sale are then negotiated privately, with the price being assessed by the district valuer at the open market value. This procedure for sponsorship sales enables land to pass without the risk of competitive bidding to bodies which will continue to hold it in the public interest while the Forestry Commission is able to secure a fair price, in keeping with the commercial purposes which underlie such sales.

Where land is being sold, special arrangements were introduced in 1991. Under these, before offering woodlands for sale on the market, the Forestry Commission will offer to enter into a management agreement with the appropriate local authority to secure continuing access. Such agreements will provide for continuing public access for informal quiet enjoyment and run with the land, so that any purchaser from the Commission will be bound by the terms of any such agreement.[82] The main provisions of a model agreement are set out in the detailed statement of these arrangements.[83] In order to encourage the making of such agreements, it is now proposed that local authorities should be given greater flexibility in adjusting these terms, that the Forestry Commission should meet the authority's reasonable legal expenses in drawing up an agreement and that stronger links be established with Scottish Natural Heritage, the Countryside Council for Wales and the Countryside Commission to

---

[81] *Our Forests: The Way Ahead*, paras.4.5–10.

[82] The chosen mechanism is a management agreement under the Wildlife and Countryside Act 1981, s.39, or the Countryside (Scotland) Act 1967, s.49A (as added by Countryside (Scotland) Act 1981) rather than an access agreement which local authorities are empowered to enter under the National Parks and Access to the Countryside Act 1949, s.64, and the Countryside (Scotland) Act 1967, s.13.

[83] This statement has not been formally published; for the general position see the Forestry Commission's 71st Annual Report 1990–1 (HC 36 1991–2), Appendix VII.

ensure that expert advice is readily available to authorities.[84] So far agreements have been made in only a few cases,[85] and these arrangements have not been able to calm fears that the selling of Forestry Commission land entails a significant threat to continued public access.

Conclusion

The aims of forestry policy in Great Britain are those of expanding the area of forests and of securing the range of benefits which come from a sustainable management of woodlands, benefits which include environmental improvements and recreational opportunities. These aims are reflected at all levels of the arrangements for forestry in this country. They appear in the ministerial statements of policy and in the objectives of the various branches of the Forestry Commission. They are put into practice in Forest Enterprise's management of its own estates and through the grant schemes which support private owners, the advice and guidance made available to them, the criteria applied in issuing felling licences and the special initiatives to promote community forests and other projects where timber production is not the sole, or even the primary, purpose of a particular woodland.

This position has been reached through a whole range of adjustments to the arrangements for forestry in this country. The basic structure has remained unaltered, with publicly managed estates still accounting for a very significant proportion of the woodlands in the country while private forestry is controlled through a combination of legal regulation to control felling and financial incentives to encourage planting of the appropriate sorts in the the appropriate places. Yet the altered priorities of the grant schemes, the movement of all incentives from the undiscriminating tax system to the more careful grant system, the increased openness of the procedures and the greater role for environmental considerations add together to amount to a wholesale transformation of the way in which forestry is regulated and carried out in practice.

This transformation has been accompanied by massive restructuring within the Forestry Commission and a commitment to reducing the area of woodland in public hands. In the long term, this change will fundamentally alter the ways in which forestry policy is applied, as the main feature will no longer be one of what the Forestry Commission is doing on its

---

[84] *Our Forests: The Way Ahead*, paras. 4.11–13.

[85] By April 1993, five agreements had been made, with a further twenty-seven under negotiation (Forestry Commission's 73rd Annual Report 1992–3 (HC 151 1993–4), para.182.); by April 1994, the sale of eight more woodlands (123 ha) had been completed with access agreements, seventeen further agreements had been reached and in one case land had been sold directly to a local authority (Forestry Commission's Annual Report 1993–4 (HC 661 1993–4), 42).

own land, but of how it is able to regulate the private sector, especially if, as some argue, the change of Forest Enterprise into a 'Next Steps Agency' opens the possibility of ultimate privatization.

In this changed picture, it is difficult to predict whether the existing arrangements will in fact prove to be a satisfactory way of regulating a form of land use which can have immense environmental consequences. The recent Forestry Review already suggests that there is a need for improved mechanisms to seek an appropriate balance between the multiple objectives which can be pursued in our woodlands, and that the long-term reliance on the informal controls on new planting offered by a grant scheme may prove inadequate. At present, though, it is too early to judge the overall effect of all of the recent changes. We look out today on plantations reflecting priorities decades ago which we now consider were too narrow; only when the woodlands planted today have reached maturity will it be really possible to judge whether we have done better.

7

Public Access to the Scottish Countryside

JEREMY ROWAN-ROBINSON

Despite occasional suggestions to the contrary, the law of trespass is alive but perhaps not in the best of health in Scotland. It provides a logical starting point for any discussion of public rights of access to the Scottish countryside.

As in England and Wales, one of the substantive rights of ownership is the right to the exclusive use of land.[1] If a person has no right or permission to be on land, the owner, because of this substantive right, may act to exclude that person. However, unlike England and Wales, trespass in Scotland is not a wrong for which damages may be sought in the absence of proof of damage.[2] None the less, the owner may direct a person who has no right or permission to be on the land to leave, either by the most direct or by an alternative route; and there is some authority for suggesting that such force as may reasonably be necessary may be employed where a person resists ejection.[3] However, direct action as a remedy has its limitations. An owner of a large Highland estate would have to employ an army of wardens to ensure that unauthorized people do not enter or are required to leave the land.

Apart from directing a person to leave the land, an owner may also be in a position to seek interdict, the Scottish equivalent of an injunction. However, the award of an interdict is discretionary; it must be against a

---

[1] W. M. Gordon, *Scottish Land Law* (The Scottish Universities Law Institute, 1989), para 13-06.

[2] Ibid., para. 13-10.

[3] *Wood* v. *North British Railway Co.* (1989) 2F 1; *Bell* v. *Shand* (1879) 7 SLR 267; *Aitchison* v. *Thornburn* (1970) 7 SLR 347.

named person and the owner must show reasonable anxiety that the trespass will be repeated.[4] Only through repetition is the owner's right to exclusive use infringed. The requirements to name the trespasser and to show reasonable anxiety of repetition present severe practical problems for the owner. The result is that interdict is rarely employed.

Exceptionally, a trespass, or the activities associated with a trespass, may constitute a criminal offence. In particular, under the Trespass (Scotland) Act 1865 it is an offence to camp on private land without the consent and permission of the owner or legal occupier of the land. This legislation seems rarely to be invoked. And at the time of writing considerable concern is being expressed on behalf of those seeking access to the countryside about the provisions of the Criminal Justice and Public Order Act 1994 directed at 'travellers' and hunt saboteurs which extend the categories of criminal trespass.

Although the owner has the right to exclusive use, invoking the remedies can, as suggested, present quite serious practical difficulties. It is for this reason that the law of trespass in Scotland is described as not in the best of health, and this poor health has consequences for public access to the countryside, and in particular for the development of 'permissive' access which is discussed below.

A person who has a right or permission to be on the land is not, of course, a trespasser. Access to the Scottish countryside is quite often taken by right or permission of the owner. The term 'owner' is used in this chapter to include not just the proprietor of the *dominium utile* but everyone who is in a position to permit or to grant a right to the public to have access over land. In certain circumstances this may be the occupier, where the land is tenanted, rather than the owner of land. It is appropriate, therefore, to consider the circumstances in which such right or permission may arise.

Public Access to the Countryside by Right

This chapter is concerned with access by the public to the Scottish countryside. No consideration, therefore is given to the circumstances in which private rights of access, such as a servitude right of way across a neighbour's land corresponding to an easement south of the border, might arise.

The principal rights of public access to the countryside arise through public rights of way, public-path-creation agreements, access and management agreements and access orders. These are discussed in turn.

[4] Gordon, op. cit., para. 13-10.

Public rights of way

The law relating to public rights of way in Scotland is complex, and in some respects, unsatisfactory.[5] Although a public right of way may be created by specific grant by the owner, in practice most such rights of way arise by prescription. The Prescription and Limitation (Scotland) Act 1973 provides in s.3 that:

> If a public right of way over land has been possessed by the public for a continuous period of twenty years openly, peaceably and without judicial interruption, then, as from the expiration of that period, the existence of the right of way as so possessed shall be exempt from challenge.

To establish a public right of way it is necessary to show that there is a public place at either end of the route, that the route has been used openly and peaceably by members of the public to get from one public place to the other continuously for twenty years, that the use has been as of right and not by permission, and that the route is sufficiently clear.[6] The nature of a right of way in Scotland is defined essentially by the use made of it. There are not rigid categories such as exist south of the border. The common kinds are footpaths, bridleways for horse traffic, drove roads for cattle and carriage roads for vehicles. A carriage road encompasses the other uses and a bridleway encompasses use as a footpath.

'Public place' is a term that gives rise to some difficulty. It includes a public road, a village, a public harbour, a church and so on. It does not necessarily include beauty spots, picnic areas or mountain tops which the public make a practice of visiting. The public must have a right to be in the place. Popular tracks to mountain tops may not, therefore, be public rights of way, even though used continuously for more than twenty years, if the mountain top is not a public place. And the public do not acquire a right to be on the top simply because they have been going there for twenty years. The Scottish Rights of Way Society have recommended that the term 'place of public resort' should be substituted for 'public place' as a requirement for establishing a public right of way.[7]

An owner may interrupt the use by the public so as to stop a prescriptive right being acquired. This may be done physically by placing an

---

[5] For a general discussion of the law relating to rights of way in Scotland see Gordon, op. cit., ch.24; J. Rowan-Robinson, W. M. Gordon and C. T. Reid, *Public Access to the Countryside: A Guide to the Law, Practice and Procedure in Scotland* (Scottish Natural Heritage and COSLA, 1993); Scottish Rights of Way Society Ltd, *Rights of Way: A Guide to the Law Scotland* (1989).

[6] J. Rowan-Robinson et al., op. cit., para. 4.1.8ff.

[7] Scottish Rights of Way Society Ltd, 'Proposals for the Reform of the Law Relating to Public Rights of Ways in Scotland' (1990).

effective barrier across the route[8] or judicially by commencing proceedings to establish that the route is not a public right of way. It is doubtful whether a sign which says 'private road' would be regarded as an effective barrier if it is commonly ignored by the public.

Any person may take steps to assert that the requirements outlined above are satisfied with regard to a particular route. However, in the event of disagreement with the owner, the position can only finally be established by an application for a decree of declarator in the Sheriff Court or in the Court of Session. The Scottish Rights of Way Society follow up a considerable number of queries about the status of routes every year and have from time to time initiated court action. However, such action is expensive and, not surprisingly, queries about the status of a route will generally be referred to the appropriate planning authority, which has important duties in this respect.

S.46 of the Countryside (Scotland) Act 1967 requires planning authorities to assert, keep open and free from obstruction any public right of way. Of course, as the duty only arises in connection with routes that are public rights of way, an authority may decline to act where the status of a route is uncertain. Furthermore, the meaning of the word 'assert' in s.46 has given rise to difficulty.[9] Some authorities believe that it refers to the process of obtaining a decree of declarator as to a route's status from the court. Others consider that it is sufficient simply to declare formally and publicly that a route is a public right of way. It is probable that the former interpretation is correct because if the owner disputes the status of a route, the dispute can only finally be determined by reference to a court.

There is no definitive map of public rights of way in Scotland; nor are planning authorities under any obligation to maintain any form of record of such routes, although some do.[10] The difficulty with such records is that the status of a route can be unclear and the public may not know whether access is being taken as a right or as of grace. This can only be determined with finality if the owner agrees or accepts that it is a public right of way or if a court has determined that it is.

The uncertainty is aggravated by the fact that a route which has been identified as a public right of way may cease to be so in Scotland if it is not used for twenty years.[11] In other words, there is no finality about the

---

[8] Where the route obstructed is a public right of way, a member of the public may take direct action to remove the obstruction provided he or she acts quickly. However, if the status of the route is uncertain, it would be advisable to establish first of all that it is a public right of way.

[9] See. J. Rowan-Robinson, *Review of Rights of Way Procedures* (Scottish Natural Heritage, 1994), paras. 3.1.1ff.

[10] Ibid., paras. 3.1.23ff.

[11] Gordon, op. cit., para. 24-149.

status of a route. This is in contrast to the position in England and Wales where a public right of way can only cease to exist by way of a formal order procedure.

Because of the difficulty of establishing the status of a route and because there is no finality about the status, the Ordnance Survey do not show public rights of way on their maps of Scotland.

The consequence of this uncertainty has been a steady erosion of the network of routes over the years as a result of changing land use. Owners, developers and those undertaking schemes of public works have no easy way of establishing what public rights of way stand in the way of their plans and may have little incentive to inquire too closely. The public and planning authorities do not have the resources or cannot collect the evidence to safeguard routes. It is likely that a substantial part of the heritage of routes has been lost to the public because of afforestation, hydro-electric schemes, agricultural intensification, changing estate management practices, major road schemes and the electrification of railways.[12]

To halt this erosion, the Scottish Rights of Way Society and others have proposed the setting up of an 'Index' of routes.[13] An administrative process for establishing the status of a route would be introduced modelled on the planning application procedure with a right of appeal to a suitably qualified person appointed by the Secretary of State. Entry on the index would be conclusive evidence of the existence and character of the right. This and other suggestions for reform of the law relating to public rights of way are currently under consideration as part of the Access Review by Scottish Natural Heritage (SNH). In their policy paper *Enjoying the Outdoors: A Programme for Action* (1994), SNH accept that the present arrangements for the protection of rights of way are too weak and conclude that the prime need is for a simplified administrative system for asserting rights of way.

Public-path-creation agreements and orders

One of the difficulties with the network of public rights of way is that it may not meet modern requirements. There is a demand for circular and interconnecting routes. Public rights of way established to meet the social and economic requirements of earlier generations may not satisfy the recreational requirements of today.

The provision for securing linear access incorporated into the Countryside (Scotland) Act 1967, as amended, are intended to enable planning authorities to help to meet these requirements by updating old routes and creating new ones.

[12] Scottish Rights of Way Society Ltd, op. cit.
[13] Ibid.

A planning authority may seek an agreement with an owner of land whereby the latter agrees to the creation of a public path along a specified route. A public path is a term which can be applied to both footpaths and bridleways. The incentive for an owner to enter into such an agreement will vary but may include a desire to regulate or manage existing pressure for access, a desire to open up opportunities for public access, and the prospect of securing a money payment.[14] The effect of such an agreement is that a member of the public making use of the path is not to be regarded as a trespasser[15] but the precise extent of the right of access conferred on the public will be determined by the wording of the agreement.

Failing agreement, a planning authority may act unilaterally. The Countryside (Scotland) Act 1967 confers power to make a public-path-creation order against the wishes of an owner.[16] Such an order may be made where the authority have identified a need for a path and they consider it expedient to create one, bearing in mind both the benefits of a path for the convenience of local residents or the convenience or enjoyment of a substantial section of the public; the order requires confirmation by the Secretary of State. An owner is entitled to compensation for any depreciation or damage resulting from such an order.

A questionnaire survey of planning authorities undertaken by the Countryside Commission for Scotland in 1990 showed that fifty-six public-path-creation agreements had been entered into since the power was introduced and three orders had been made.[17] The Commission's annual reports during the 1970s show a very slow take-up of these statutory provisions. Although there has been some activity since then, much of it (for example, fifty of the fifty-six public-path-creation agreements) has been linked with the programme of long-distance routes.[18] This programme has clearly been helpful in opening up opportunities for public access to the countryside; but it seems that the powers conferred in the 1967 Act for creating public paths are playing no more than a very limited role in rationalizing and extending the existing network of public rights of way. The reasons for the low take-up are considered below in the discussion of access agreements.

Access and management agreements and access orders

While the provisions for creating public paths in the 1967 Act offer an opportunity for planning authorities to rationalize arrangements for linear

---

[14] Rowan-Robinson et al., op. cit., paras. 4.2.6ff.

[15] Ibid., para. 4.2.13.

[16] S.14.

[17] Rowan-Robinson, op. cit., paras. 3.2ff.

[18] Ibid.

access, a different concept, more akin to the 'freedom to roam' (below), was introduced by the provisions in the 1967 Act relating to area access.[19] The aim of the provisions is to open up whole areas to the public for the purposes of open-air recreation. The provisions apply to areas of 'open country', which is defined as being land consisting predominantly of mountain, moor, heath, hill, woodland, cliff or foreshore, and any waterway.[20]

Area access may be secured by an access agreement entered into by a planning authority or SNH with an owner. An agreement will define the boundaries of the area in question and state its duration. Limitations may be imposed on the right of access which is conferred; some areas are defined as 'excepted land' and remain closed to the public. Provision may be made for sums to be paid to meet the expenses incurred by the owner consequent on, and in consideration of, the making of the agreement.[21] As with a public-path agreement, the effect of an access agreement is that a member of the public is not to be regarded as a trespasser if he or she enters the land for the purpose of open-air recreation; but it will be necessary to refer to the terms of the agreement to establish the precise extent of the right of access conferred. The access entitlement does not, however, extend to a list of prohibited activities, which include the driving of vehicles on the land and wilfully causing damage to the land or anything on it.[22] A person misbehaving on the land in one of these ways reverts to being a trespasser. The right of access is thus 'very much a right to enter land for peaceful and harmless recreation, such as walking, mountaineering, bird-watching, cross-country skiing and canoeing, without disturbing the environment or the lawful uses being carried out on the land'.[23]

If a planning authority or SNH believe that it is impracticable to secure an agreement with an owner, they may act unilaterally to secure public access by making an access order.[24] An access order will have no effect unless and until it is confirmed by the Secretary of State. Where the value of a person's interest in land is depreciated by such an order or where their enjoyment of land is disturbed, they are entitled to compensation.[25]

The questionnaire survey conducted by the Countryside Commission for Scotland in 1990 showed that sixty-three access agreements had been entered into since the provisions were introduced. No access orders had

[19] Part II.
[20] S.10(2).
[21] S.13(2).
[22] Defined in s.11(4) and sched. 2 to the 1967 Act.
[23] Rowan-Robinson et al., op. cit., para. 8.4.20.
[24] 1967 Act, s.14.
[25] 1967 Act, s.20.

been made. This is hardly surprising. The practical difficulties of securing and managing public access to land against the express wishes of the owner are likely to be considerable and such an approach would seem to be the antithesis of the sort of partnership approach which underlies the access provisions in the 1967 Act. This comment applies equally to public-path-creation orders.

As with public path agreements, there was a slow take-up of access agreements during the 1970s but rather more activity during the 1980s. And, again, as with public-path agreements, nineteen of the access agreements were actually directed not at securing area access but linear access, the linear-access arrangements at that time being unsatisfactory. Several access agreements were used to support the provision of country parks. Generally, however, the use of access agreements to promote 'peaceful and harmless recreation' has been limited and the former Countryside Commission for Scotland in successive Annual Reports expressed disappointment about the low take-up of the use of powers.

Research conducted for the Commission during 1991[26] suggests that there are three reasons for the low take-up of the power to negotiate access agreements, and that these reasons apply also to the public-path provisions (above). First of all, owners consider that the advantages of agreements are outweighed by their disadvantages. In particular, a statutory agreement involves loss of control by the owner over public access. This loss overrides the advantages of payment and the prospect of the support of a ranger service. In the event, the payment, based as it is on the loss to the landowner rather than the gain to the public, is generally regarded as inadequate.

Secondly, planning authorities are concerned about the extent of the continuing obligation imposed on them by such agreements in terms of maintenance, repairs and ranger support at a time of severe restraint on public expenditure. They are also aware that the negotiation of such agreements can be resource-intensive. The Countryside Commission for Scotland's Annual Report for 1979, for example, indicates that the time taken to negotiate and complete such agreements varies from six to eighteen months, with some taking several years to settle.

Thirdly, there is a discernible feeling amongst some planning officers that agreements 'operate to restrict and regulate rather than extend access for the public and they see no reason why the authority should pay for something which hitherto has been enjoyed by tradition'.[27] This view is also held by some public-interest groups such as the Mountaineering Council for Scotland and the Scottish Council of the Ramblers' Association.

[26] Rowan-Robinson, op. cit., para. 3.2.5.
[27] Ibid.

There is some preliminary indication, and it is no more than that at present, that management agreements are being perceived in a more favourable light, at least by owners. S.49A of the Countryside (Scotland) Act 1967[28] enables planning authorities and SNH to enter into a management agreement with an owner. For planning authorities, the purpose of such agreements is to do, or to secure the doing of, whatever in the opinion of the parties may be necessary to preserve or enhance the natural beauty of the countryside or to promote the enjoyment of the countryside by the public. For SNH, the purpose of such agreements is to do, or secure the doing of, whatever in the opinion of the parties may be necessary to secure the conservation and enhancement or foster the understanding and enjoyment of the natural heritage of Scotland. Management agreements may contain financial provisions.

Only limited use has been made of the provision to date but the indications are that some planning authorities and owners are beginning to see management agreements as a more effective way of providing access to the countryside than access agreements.[29] This interest mirrors the debate about management agreements that took place south of the border some years ago.[30] At first sight, the legislation seems to offer greater flexibility than the provisions relating to access agreements. It seems that the terminology is also important. The term 'access agreement' has an emphasis that discourages owners; 'management agreement' suggests the prospect of a continuing partnership between owner and public authority. However, it is too early to say whether the take-up of this provision will be more encouraging than has been the case with access agreements.

Before leaving management agreements, it should be noted that the Forestry Commission has indicated that, where feasible, it will offer to enter into a management agreement under s.49A with the appropriate planning authority to safeguard public access opportunities prior to the disposal of woodland. Government policy since 1980 has been to dispose of a proportion of the Commission's estate and in June 1989, the Secretary of State for Scotland announced that the Commission had been asked to proceed with the further disposal of 100,000 ha of forestry land, much of it in Scotland. 'Guidelines on continued public access to Forestry Commission woodlands after sale' were produced under which advance notice of sale would be given to planning authorities to allow time for an agreement to be negotiated. It is not intended that compensation should be paid for the agreement but the planning authority would, of course, assume a continuing maintenance obligation. Preliminary research indicates

[28] Inserted by the Countryside (Scotland) Act 1981, s.9 and subsequently amended by the Natural Heritage (Scotland) Act 1991.
[29] J. Rowan-Robinson, op. cit., paras 3.2.7–3.2.9.
[30] M. J. Feist, *A Study of Management Agreements* (Countryside Commission, 1978).

that, notwithstanding the continuing disposal of forestry land, only one such agreement has been concluded in Scotland.[31] The principal reason for the very limited use of agreements seems to be the severe constraint on local authority resources.

Public Access to the Countryside by Permission

In the introduction to this chapter, it is stated that a person who has a right or permission to take access to land is not a trespasser. Having considered the circumstances in which a right of public access might arise, it is now appropriate to look at the circumstances in which permission might be given. A permission does not create a right in land; it is a contractual arrangement between the parties and may be enforced as such. It is convenient to look, first of all, at the position regarding linear access and, secondly, at area access.

Permission to take linear access

Because of the problems in Scotland with establishing that a route is a public right of way (above), and because of the limited take-up of the public-path-creation agreement provisions, reliance is increasingly being alaced on the permission of the owner as a way of securing linear access for the public.[32]

If an owner and a planning authority, for whatever reason, prefer to avoid the formality of a public-path-creation agreement but the owner is willing to permit public access along a defined route, the arrangement will be concluded informally and the route becomes what is generally referred to as a 'permissive path'. Permissive paths are also being created as a response to a request from an owner for the diversion of a route.[33] The planning authority may be uncertain about the status of the route and the applicability of formal diversion procedures; alternatively, they may simply prefer to avoid the formality of a diversion order. Either way, the resulting diversion is a permissive path. There may or may not be an exchange of correspondence governing such arrangements for access. If there is, it will be necessary to refer to the correspondence for the duration of the arrangement and the terms of the permission.

Sometimes this sort of management is negotiated by a particular user group. The British Horse Society, for example, because of the relatively limited number of bridle paths and bridleways in Scotland, have negotiated a number of permissions for access for their members.

---

[31] C. Mitchel, 'Safeguarding Public Access to Former Forestry Commission Land', (dissertation submitted for the degree of BLE, Department of Land Economy, Aberdeen University, 1994).

[32] J. Rowan-Robinson, op. cit., paras 3.3.1–3.3.5.

[33] Ibid., para 3.1.53.

Increasingly, however, it seems that permissive paths are being created where a planning authority has responded to a complaint by a member of the public about the obstruction of a route but the status of the route is unclear.[34] It seems that the authority's primary objective in such cases is not to assert a right but, by discussion with the owner, to safeguard public access. The result is a 'voluntary' access arrangement. Such a way forward is attractive because it is neither time-consuming nor expensive. The outcome of the discussion may or may not be reflected in correspondence.

The disadvantage of this response is that the public's position is precarious. It relies on the continuing good will of the owner and, subject to the terms of any correspondence, it may be terminated at any time. There is, however, little evidence of this happening in practice. Continuing public access may also be subjected to conditions such as a prohibition on publicity for the route.

The freedom to roam

For many people, the most important opportunity for access to the Scottish countryside is not the network of public rights of way, nor the specific statutory or voluntary arrangements. It is the 'tradition' that, subject to responsible behaviour, people may roam the countryside at will. This tradition is extensively exercised in practice, in particular in the upland areas. The question addressed here is the extent to which this practice is carried on by permission of the owner.

It should be made clear, first of all, that no right to roam at will can arise at common law. Access to the hills taken over a long period of years will not create a prescriptive right to roam.

Nor is there any statutory right to roam, apart from the access provisions of the Countryside (Scotland) Act 1967 which have already been described. There have, however, been a number of attempts over the years to create a right by placing the freedom to roam on a statutory footing. The first was in 1884 when James Bryce MP promoted the Access to Mountains (Scotland) Bill. Although the Bill was unsuccessful, the House of Commons in 1892 resolved that:

> in the opinion of this House, legislation is needed for the purpose of securing the right of the public to enjoy free access to uncultivated mountains and moorlands, especially in Scotland, subject to proper provisions for preventing any abuse of such right.[35]

Nothing came of this resolution. Subsequently, the mass trespass on Kinder Scout in 1932 in what is now the Peak District National Park

[34] Ibid., para 4.4.1.
[35] Hansard, 4 March 1892, col. 128.

brought the issue to the fore again. The Second World War intervened but in 1947 the Hobhouse Committee recommended that the public should have the right to wander in England and Wales over uncultivated mountain, moor, heath, down, cliff, shore and lakeside. This recommendation was not implemented. Instead, the provisions for access agreements and orders were introduced.

More recently, the Labour Party in its policy document 'Out in the Country' (1990) proposed that the public should have a right of access to uncultivated land. And in the same year there was a further unsuccessful attempt during the passage of the Scottish Natural Heritage Bill to give statutory effect to the freedom to roam. Sixty years after the mass trespass on Kinder Scout, the Ramblers' Association in 1991 organized further mass trespasses to draw attention to the desirability of extending rights of access. And in 1994, Margaret Ewing MP followed in the footsteps of James Bryce by introducing a Bill on Access to the Countryside in an attempt to achieve the same end. Notwithstanding wide support, Mrs Ewing was no more successful than her predecessor.

In the mean time SNH have inherited a review of the access arrangements in Scotland from the Countryside Commission for Scotland. During the consultation exercise which formed part of the review, a number of influential respondents urged the case for placing the freedom to roam on a firmer footing. The Scottish Council of the Ramblers' Association, for example, in a paper entitled 'Head for the hills' (1990) commented:

At present, far too many people believe, or are resigned to accept that land should be closed to the public unless a special case for allowing access can be proved. We must turn these assumptions right round. There should instead be a presumption that public access to open uncultivated countryside should be allowed as a right.

On the other hand, bodies such as the Scottish Landowners' Federation firmly resist such arguments. In the policy paper 'Access: a review by the Scottish Landowners' Federation' (1990) the Federation commented:

There is pressure from the Ramblers and other groups for legislation to be introduced to enshrine the 'Right to Roam'. This should be resisted . . . The present flexible situation may have its drawbacks and these may well increase, but we believe it would be far preferable to work to achieve goodwill and responsibility rather than to impose an inflexible system of law which will bring rigidity and ill will on all sides.

It is difficult to see how such opposing views can be reconciled. In their policy paper *Enjoying the Outdoors: A Programme for Action* (1994)

SNH attempt to square this circle by advocating that a person taking access for peaceful open-air recreation over open country should not be regarded in law as a trespasser unless required to leave by a proprietor or someone acting with his or her authority. Whether legislation will follow remains to be seen.

In the introduction to this chapter it was pointed out that, if a person has no right or permission to be on land, he or she will be a trespasser. It will be clear from what has been said so far that there is at present no right, derived from common law or conferred by statute, to roam at will in the Scottish countryside. None the less, the freedom to roam is widely exercised in practice. The question arises whether this practice relies on permission or whether widespread trespass is taking place.

Permission may be express or implied. 'Permission to be on land', says Gordon,[36] 'may be construed as a licence to be there. But a licence has no technical meaning in Scots law. The terms will be a matter of contract between the parties.' As a contract, the arrangement may be brought to an end according to the terms of the permission, or failing that, at the will of the owner. Some owners expressly permit the public, or a particular user group, to roam at will on their land. The permission may be withdrawn or restricted at certain times of the year, for example, when deer culling is going on.

For the most part, however, there is no express permission. The question is whether, if an owner fails to take such measures as effectually to stop trespass, a person can claim an implied permission. In *Dumbreck* v. *Addie*[37] Viscount Dunedin in the House of Lords, while acknowledging dicta to that effect in earlier case law, rejected the proposition. A failure by an owner to fence land, he observed, was not to be construed as a permission to enter. He went on to acknowledge, however, that there will be circumstances when the response of an owner might be construed as an implied permission:

Of course a proprietor may do nothing at all to prevent people coming over his lands, and they may come so often that permission will be held to be implied, or he may do something, but that something so half-heartedly as to be equivalent to doing nothing. For instance, a mere putting up of a notice 'No Trespassers Allowed' or 'Strictly Private' followed, when people often come, by no further steps, would I think leave it open for a judge or jury to hold implied permission.

It would seem that whether or not there may be said to be an implied permission will be very much a matter of fact and degree. However, as Viscount Dunedin went on to stress, 'it is permission that must be proved,

[36] W. M. Gordon, op. cit., para. 19–24.
[37] 1929 SC(HL) 51.

not tolerance, though tolerance in some circumstances may be so pronounced as to lead to a conclusion that it was really tantamount to permission.'

Whether in the light of this it may be argued that the public roam at will in Scotland with the implied permission of owners is unclear. There will be cases where an owner is genuinely willing to allow the public on land providing they act responsibly. The Scottish Landowners' Federation, for example, was reflecting the attitude of many of its members when it went on record in its access policy paper (1990) as recognizing the principle of responsible access to the countryside by the public. There will, however, be other cases where an owner is simply making the best of a bad job. The owner does not want the public on the land but knows that, short of a very substantial commitment of expenditure, in practical terms there are no effective steps that can be taken to exclude them. It is uncertain whether an implied permission would arise in such a case.

However, even where it can be shown that permission may be implied, the public's position is precarious. The permission may be withdrawn at any time by the owner. A member of the public could be asked to leave the land and if he or she fails to do so they become a trespasser. At that point there is no doubt that they are on the land without right or permission.

Access and Conservation

So far in this chapter no mention has been made of the conservation implications of public access to the countryside. There is, of course, a coincidence between areas of landscape importance and the demand for public access. People are often seeking access to the best viewpoints, the areas of particular beauty and the popular mountain tops. There is also some coincidence between areas of landscape importance and areas of scientific interest. The impact of public access is felt not simply in terms of wear and tear on the countryside but also in terms of an affliction of car parks, picnic areas and toilets. Public access will sometimes be inimical to conservation objectives.

The impact of public access on the Scottish countryside is nowhere near as great as in the popular areas of England. None the less the problem has been recognized. The question is how far conservation objectives are a consideration in access arrangements. The answer is, hardly at all.

With common law rights of way, conservation considerations are largely irrelevant. They cannot stand in the way of an assertion of the right; nor can the public be excluded simply because access harms the countryside. However, planning authorities may attempt to limit harm through the exercise of their power to maintain and repair a route. This might take the form of supporting a route so as to encourage the public to follow a defined line.

Conservation considerations also carry little weight with statutory access arrangements under the 1967 Act. However, it may be noted that certain nature reserves will be closed to public access even if they fall within an access area. And it is fair to suggest that the whole ethos of access agreements is to provide an opportunity for peaceful and harmless recreation which is, in general terms, in tune with conservation objectives. However, the sheer number of people seeking access may militate against these objectives at times.

Exceptionally, management agreements under s.49A of the 1967 Act may have specific conservation objectives while at the same time promoting public access. Experience with them has been very limited but it has been suggested that they might be used to enhance the access experience, linear or area, by providing for environmental improvements. Access and conservation objectives may also be linked under other statutory provisions such as those providing for environmentally-sensitive-area agreements, for agreements with the Capital Taxes Office to secure inheritance tax relief, and for grant-aid for the planning of community woodlands.

Opportunities for public access governed by an express permission from the landowner may contain such restrictions or impose such obligations to safeguard conservation interests as the landowner may determine. This is a matter for negotiation between the parties. However, conservation considerations have no role to play where access is taken by implied permission. In such cases observance of the countryside code provides some safeguard.

Conclusion

What is clear from this chapter is the unsatisfactory state of the arrangements by which the public take access to the Scottish countryside. The law relating to public rights of way has been shown to be inadequate to protect the network, and many routes have been lost to the public over the last fifty years; with the exception of the long-distance routes, the statutory provisions for securing public access are proving to be of limited use; and the freedom to roam relies at best on an implied permission and is thus precarious and at worst has no basis in law.

There are steps that can be taken to improve the position. Suggestions have been made to SNH during the access review for improvements to the law governing public rights of way; some of these have been outlined above and some have been picked up by SNH in their 1994 policy paper. Of the statutory provisions, management agreements appear to have sufficient flexibility to offer attractions both to planning authorities and to owners. Greater use of such agreements will, however, require a greater commitment of public resources and it would seem unrealistic to expect this at the present time.

However, the focus of attention is on the freedom to roam and the outcome of the access review with regard to this is awaited with interest. There is no obvious reform which would reconcile the conflicting viewpoints. It remains to be seen how close to doing so SNH have come with their suggestion that a person taking access for peaceful open-air recreation over open country should not be regarded in law as a trespasser unless required to leave by the proprietor.

8

Nature Conservation and Access to the Countryside

ANGELA SYDENHAM

Introduction

A glance at the index of a standard textbook on public rights of way or highway law reveals that conservation does not feature. This is hardly surprising as highway law is of ancient origin[1] whilst conservation and environmental concerns are a comparatively recent development. Nevertheless many public rights of way are part of our heritage and their routes often follow old historic tracks. They give the public access to the countryside and have a conservation and environmental importance in their own right.

In contrast to public rights of way, access arrangements involving local authorities, statutory agencies and central government are often integrated with measures for protecting the environment.[2]

Public Rights of Way

Public rights of way are highways. This is a difficult concept to accept. The word highway conjures up a vision of a metalled trunk road or motorway, not a dusty, unsurfaced footpath through a cornfield. Although

The author acknowledges, with thanks, the help of Dr Alan Woods in making comments on this chapter. Many of the ideas in the last section are based on papers produced for the Country Landowners' Association by Dr Woods.

[1] See, however, s.105A Highways Act 1980: Environmental Assessment of certain highway projects.

[2] For a discussion of the wider issues see the symposium papers from the conference on Public Access and Conservation, Wednesday 7 April 1993, organized by the Byways and Bridleways Trust.

many landowners consider that they own public rights of way this is true only as far as the sub-soil is concerned. Where the path is maintainable at public expense the surface is vested for a determinable fee simple[3] in the Highway Authority, not the landowner.

It is not always a simple matter to discover whether or not a highway is maintainable at public expense. Some are; others are maintainable by the landowner; others still are not maintainable by anyone at all. S.36(6) of the Highways Act 1980 provides that highway authorities shall make and keep up to date a list of the streets within their area which are highways maintainable at public expense. Street is defined by S.329 to include 'any highway and any road, lane, footpath, square, court, alley or passage, whether a thoroughfare or not, and includes any part of a street'.

Theoretically, therefore the list should include public rights of way in rural areas. The lists vary in the highways they cover and in the accuracy of their recordings.

Colin Sydenham, in the *Rights of Way Law Review*,[4] has set out the history concerning highways maintainable at public expense. He states:

(a) At common law all highways were maintainable by the inhabitants at large of the parish, unless some other person could be shown to be liable by reason of tenure, inclosure or prescription.

(b) This presumption was changed by Section 23 of the Highways Act 1835, which provided that future highways should not be maintainable by the inhabitants of the parish unless a procedure corresponding to the modern adoption was carried out. This Section however did not apply to footpaths[5] or bridleways (except bridleways which had been set out under an Inclosure Act), so that new highways in these categories continued to be maintainable by the inhabitants at large.

(c) This anomaly was removed by the National Parks and Access to the Countryside Act 1949, which subsumed public footpaths and bridleways under the expression 'Public Paths'.[6] This Act set up a new machinery for the adoption of public paths,[7] and provided that Section 23 of the 1835 Act should apply to any public path dedicated after the commencement of the [1949] Act,[8] unless the new machinery was used.[9] Thus public paths created after that

[3] Highways Act 1980 s.263(i); *Tithe Redemption Commission* v. *Runcorn Urban District Council* [1954] 1 Ch.383.

[4] Greater rights over minor highways, *Rights of Way Law Review* (June 1993), s.3.3.

[5] *Robinson* v. *Richmond (Surrey) BC* [1955] IQB 401.

[6] National Parks and Access to the Countryside Act 1949 s.27(6).

[7] By 'public path agreements', s.39 ibid.

[8] 16 December 1949.

[9] National Parks and Access to the Countryside Act 1949 s.49.

date could not become maintainable by the public at large except by operation of one of the formal statutory procedures.

(d) The Highways Act 1959 consolidated the law affecting all highways including public paths. It abolished the maintenance duties of the inhabitants at large,[10] and substituted the concept of maintenance 'at the public expense'.[11] All existing highways which were subject to the old duty became subject to the new concept.[12] It repealed the National Parks and Access to the Countryside Act 1949, but re-enacted similar provisions. Public footpaths and bridleways could still be created by formal procedures such as [dedication and] adoption,[13] and only if those formal procedures were followed would they be maintainable at public expense.[14]

(e) The modern consolidating statute is the Highways Act 1980, which again re-enacts similar provisions. There are formal procedures for the creation of public footpaths and bridleways,[15] and unless they are followed a newly created public way will not be maintainable at public expense.

To sum up the rules: if the path is created formally or adopted by operation of the appropriate statutory procedures, then it will be maintainable at public expense. If it has been created informally (see below), then if informal creation took place before December 1949 the way will be maintainable at public expense. If created after that date it will not be.

The importance of discovering whether or not the surface is vested in the highway authority or the landowner may arise when the landowner wants to metal the surface. He may need to do this because he also has a right to use it for his own purposes and an unsurfaced road is not suitable for his farm vehicles. On the other hand, it may be in the interests of the environment that the surface should not be metalled. If the road or path is publicly maintainable then that is the end of the matter. The Highway Authority can prevent any interference with its own property. However, even where this is not so the Highway Authority may have sufficient powers to prevent the metalling of the surface. In order to do the necessary work the route will have to be obstructed for a certain period of time. This might amount to a public

[10] Highways Act 1959 s.38(i).
[11] S.38(2) ibid.
[12] S.38(2) (a) ibid.
[13] S.27 ibid.
[14] S.38(2) (e) ibid.
[15] Highways Act 1980, sub-sections 25, 26.

nuisance. A number of offences may also be committed under Part IX of the Highways Act 1980.[16]

Whoever owns the surface of the right of way, the public has the right to pass and repass. If the highway is a footpath then the right is limited to walking. A bridleway may be used for riding or leading a horse (a horse is defined to include a donkey or mule). Bicycles are also allowed on bridleways, provided that they give way to other lawful users.[17] A byway open to all traffic may be used by all kinds of vehicles.[18] A road used as a public path has at least bridleway status.[19] Besides passing along the route the public have ancillary rights such as taking a rest or eating a picnic. Exceeding these rights will amount to a trespass.[20]

Sometimes an unsurfaced track will be described as a green lane. Such a term has no legal meaning. It may or may not carry public rights of way. Where there are public rights the green lane could be a footpath, bridleway or carriageway. Often the lanes are of historic importance with ancient hedgerows.

The Countryside Commission in their booklets covering public rights of way instruct users to follow the Country Code.[21] This code emphasizes the importance of respecting the countryside, including farming activities, not causing a nuisance by noise, litter or water pollution, and protecting wildlife, plants and trees.

The Wildlife and Countryside Act 1981 – the definitive map

The National Parks and Access to the Countryside Act 1949 imposed a duty on Surveying Authorities to record the public rights of way in their area. The law is now contained in the Wildlife and Countryside Act 1981.[22]

Rights of way are recorded on the definitive map and statement. Some maps and statements are better than others. Many are incomplete and inaccurate. Before 1981 there was no obligation on the Surveying Authority to inform the landowner direct that rights of way were being recorded across his land. Landowners claim that many private estate roads and

---

[16] See sub-sections S131 (i)(b) (removing soil or turf), 137(i) (wilful obstruction), 148 (c) (depositing anything on highway resulting in interruption), 161(i) (depositing resulting in injury or danger to user).

[17] Countryside Act 1968 s.30.

[18] Highways Act 1980 s.329. Some bridleways also have public driveway rights – the right to drive animals of any description along the highway.

[19] Wildlife and Countryside Act 1981 s.56.

[20] See *Harrison v. Duke of Rutland* [1893] 1QB 142 (Harrison used a public carriageway for the purpose of disrupting a shoot), *Hickman v. Massey* [1900] 1QB 752 (journalist walked back and forth studying and taking notes of the form of the racehorses).

[21] E.g. the three separate Countryside Commission publications, *Out in the Countryside, A Guide to Definitive Map Procedures, A Guide to Procedures for Public Path Orders.*

[22] Wildlife and Countryside Act 1981, s.53.

other tracks were recorded as public rights of way. User groups, on the other hand, claim that numerous rights of way were missed off the map, and that others have been lost through subsequent cultivation and development.

The statements which accompany the maps may, in addition to defining the position of the route, record the width of the right of way, or certain limitations or conditions attached to the public rights.

The effect of s.56 of the Wildlife and Countryside Act 1981 is that the entry of public rights of way on the map and statement is conclusive evidence of their existence. Unfortunately the converse is not true. There may be perfectly valid rights of way which are not recorded on the map. Or those recorded may have a higher status than those shown.

S.53 (3) (c) (ii) and (iii) of the Wildlife and Countryside Act 1981 make provision for the amendment of the definitive map and statement. Modification orders may be made (a) to delete a right of way from the definitive map and statement because it was included in error, (b) to show a bridleway or road used as a public path or a footpath, or a byway as a bridleway or footpath, where the status has been incorrectly recorded[23] or, (c) to correct an error in the map or statement without changing the status of the right of way. Modification orders can also be made to show additional rights of way, or those of higher status, on the map and statement. Such orders will be made following a legal event, such as a public-path order (see below), or where there is evidence that existing rights of way are not properly recorded. It is the recording of existing rights of way for the first time on definitive maps which causes the most misunderstanding and controversy.

Additions to the definitive map

Public rights of way can be created by orders or agreements under the Highways Act 1980 or other statutes or by being set out in an Inclosure Award. Sometimes a landowner will have expressly dedicated a public right of way. More usually a landowner will have informally dedicated a public right of way. Dedication may be presumed from evidence of use by the public for a number of years or from the construction of historical documents. Examples of the latter are old maps, estate documents or records such as tithe maps or increment-value duty records under the Finance Act 1909–10.

The most usual form of claiming a highway is under the deemed dedication provisions of s.31 of the Highways Act 1980. The claimant must show that there has been uninterrupted use by the public over a period of at least twenty years. The use must be as of right, that is without force,

---

[23] See *R* v. *Secretary of State for the Environment ex parte Burrows and Simms* [1990] 3 All ER 490.

secrecy or permission. It must also be by members of the public, not employees of the landowner. The period of twenty years is counted back from the date on which the public right was first brought into question, however long ago. This might involve putting up a notice indicating the path was a private right of way only or erecting a physical barrier. Evidence of use, or of interruption of use, since that date is not relevant.

Dedication may also be implied at common law. Twenty years' use is not needed. Indeed in one case eighteen months was held to be sufficient.[24] However, unlike the presumed dedication under the Highways Act 1980, the burden of proof is on the applicant.

The presumption of dedication can be rebutted by producing evidence to show that the landowner had no intention to dedicate. A landowner's frame of mind is not sufficient. It used to be said that a landowner must make it obvious to members of the public that he had no such intention. However in a recent unreported case *Jaques* v. *Secretary of State for the Environment* (27 May 1995) Mr Justice Laws stated: 'It is plain that the landowner must disapprove an intention to dedicate by overt acts directed to members of the public in question, but equally plain that they need not actually bring home to the public that there is no right to use the way.' The landowner can disprove his intention by lodging with the highway authority a statement and declaration under s.31(6) of the Highways Act 1980. In addition, or alternatively, the route could be physically closed one day a year, but to make sure the public are aware that the path will be closed, and the reason for closing it, a notice to that effect should be erected. Or if the landowner does not want the path used at all he should put up a notice stating 'Private path, no unauthorized access' or 'Private: no public right of way'. Signs such as 'Trespassers will be prosecuted' are both inaccurate, as trespass is a civil wrong and not a crime, and ineffective. It should be stressed that any measures rebutting dedication apply only to the future. They do not have retrospective effect so as to take away existing rights.

It has been suggested[25] that notification, as of an area as a Site of Special Scientific Interest, might prevent a successful claim for subsequent deemed dedication. Certainly if access were prohibited it would be a criminal offence for a landowner to dedicate a right of way. There can be no claim to a private right arising by long use where such use is illegal.[26] The same reasoning must apply to the acquisition of a public right. Evidence that users have been turned back and not allowed to use the route will also be relevant.

---

[24] *North London Ry* v. *Vestry of St Mary's, Islington* (1872) 27 LT 672.

[25] J. D. C. Harte, *Rights of Way Law Review*, s.3.1, pp. 1–9.

[26] *Cargill* v. *Gotts* [1981] 1 WLR 441, *Hanning* v. *Top Deck Travel Group Ltd*, (1994) 68 P. & C.R, (1993) EGCS 84.

If there are objections to an order to modify the definitive map, then it has to be referred to the Secretary of State. Usually, before making a decision whether or not to confirm an order, he will hold a public inquiry. This inquiry will be concerned with evidence as to use, any relevant documentary evidence and any acts by the landowner to rebut an intention to dedicate.

It is extremely difficult to convince those not well versed in the law that the procedure for modifying definitive maps is not concerned with *creating* new rights of way but with recording *existing* rights. The effect may be that rights of way which are not apparent on the ground will nevertheless be held to have legal status. There is a legal adage 'once a highway, always a highway'. Unless that highway has been closed or diverted by following the proper statutory procedures it will still exist in law. There is no implied abandonment as there is for a private right of way.

It follows from this that arguments based on security, amenity, conservation or the environment are totally irrelevant when it comes to amending the definitive map. Notwithstanding this it has been recently held that irrelevant objections to a definitive map order are still objections duly made.[27] These objections cannot simply be dismissed by the Surveying Authority. The order still has to be referred to the Secretary of State for a decision as to whether the map should be amended.

Reclassification of roads used as public paths (RUPPs)

The National Parks and Access to the Countryside Act 1949 introduced a category of 'roads used as public paths'. These were defined as highways other than public paths used by the public mainly for the purpose for which footpaths and bridleways are also used. A highway recorded on the definitive map as an RUPP has at least bridleway status.[28] It may also carry vehicular rights but these would have to be proved.

The Countryside Act 1968 provided that RUPPs should be reclassified either as a byway open to all traffic or as a bridleway or as a footpath. On a reclassification consideration had to be given to whether any vehicular rights existed, whether the route was suitable for vehicles having regard to its position and width, its condition and state of repair, and the nature of the soil. If it had been used by vehicular traffic in the past, consideration also had to be given to whether the extinguishment of vehicular rights would cause undue hardship. In other words reclassification was not based only on legal status. The definition itself and the reclassification tests set out in the 1968 Act, not to mention circulars produced by the Ministry of

---

[27] *Lasham Parish Meeting* v. *Hampshire CC and Secretary of State for the Environment* [1993] JPEL 841.
[28] Wildlife and Countryside Act 1981 s.56.

Housing and Local Government and the Department of the Environment and Welsh Office produced endless confusion.[29]

S.54 of the Wildlife and Countryside Act 1981 therefore amended the test. This Section provides that an RUPP must be reclassified as a bridleway unless vehicular rights are proved to exist, in which case it will be reclassified as a byway open to all traffic. If bridleway rights are proved not to exist then it must be reclassified as a footpath. There is no longer any test of suitability of the route nor are any environmental conditions taken into account.

Vehicles in the countryside, especially four-wheel drive vehicles, are of great concern to many landowners, walkers and riders.[30] Some have pleaded that the amenity and suitability test of the 1968 Act should be reintroduced. Others have suggested that there should be a legal distinction between a horse and cart and the petrol engine, even though case law has established that the mode of propulsion is immaterial.[31] Moreover the difficulty of amending the law is that most highways, not just byways open to all traffic, were originally used by horse and cart and so highway law generally does not distinguish between different types of vehicle.

Whatever the emotive issues it is difficult to justify treating one group of people with legitimate rights more stringently than others unless there are very good reasons for doing so. Where the use of byways open to all traffic presents a real or perceived problem then such use can be regulated by traffic orders made under the Road Traffic Regulation Act 1984. S.1 of this Act gives Highway Authorities power to make traffic regulation orders

  for avoiding danger to persons or traffic;
  for preventing damage to the road;
  for facilitating the passage on the road of any class of traffic including
    pedestrians;
  for preventing the use of the road by unsuitable vehicular traffic in
    relation to the characteristics of the road;
  for preserving the character of the road in a case where it is especially
    suitable for use by persons on horseback or on foot;
  for protecting the amenity of the area through which the road runs.

These wide powers are supplemented by s.22 which enables a traffic regulation order to be made in designated special areas of countryside

[29] See para. 10, sched. 3, Countryside Act 1968, *R* v. *Secretary of State for the Environment ex parte Hood* [1975] 3 WLR 172 (without new evidence RUPP could not be reclassified as a footpath), para. 76, Circular 44/68 of Minister of Housing and Local Government, DoE and Welsh Office Circular DoE 123/77.

[30] See the report of the Byways Working Party to the Rights of Way Review Committee, 3 June 1991.

[31] *Lock* v. *Abercester* [1939] Ch. 861, *Kain* v. *Norfolk* [1949] Ch.163.

for the additional purpose of conserving or enhancing the natural beauty of the area or of affording better opportunities for the public to enjoy the amenities of the area or recreation or the study of nature in the area. In other words an order can be made as a precautionary measure before the damage occurs.

The cost of the traffic regulation orders means that they are very infrequently used. A simple suggestion outlined in the journal of the Byways and Bridleways Trust[32] is that byways should be legally redefined so that they have a weight restriction and a mandatory speed limit of 20 miles per hour. This would discourage four-wheel-drive vehicles. The weight limit would have to include exceptions for farm vehicles and those with private access rights.

Although an RUPP may be reclassified as a byway open to all traffic, this does not oblige a Highway Authority to provide a metalled carriageway or a carriageway which is by any other means provided with a surface suitable for the passage of vehicles.[33] Nevertheless there is concern amongst Highway Authorities that where byways open to all traffic are out of repair, possibly due to the action of four-wheel-drive vehicles, then proceedings may be taken against them under s.56 of the Highways Act 1980. Where there is such a threat then the simplest engineering option might be to metal the surface of the path. Such repair or improvement work could destroy the special character of many of these ancient tracks.

Highways Act 1980, Town and Country Planning Act 1990, Public Path Orders and Agreements

Public paths can be created, extinguished and diverted under the Highways Act 1980. The orders can be made only if the tests laid down in the particular section are satisfied. Even then the local authority, which has the order-making power, has discretion whether or not to make the order. In making its decision the authority will take into account the conflicting views of those who want, and oppose, the order. Conservation and the environmental issues are relevant. There are no statutory grounds on which objections may be made.

New footpaths or bridleways can be created by order under s.26 of the Highways Act 1980. The authority has to be satisfied that there is a need for the new path and that it is expedient to create one, having regard to the extent to which it would add to the convenience or enjoyment of a substantial section of the public or of local residents, and the effect that the creation would have on the rights of those with an interest in the

---

[32] No.5 1994, by Simon Best.
[33] Wildlife and Countryside Act 1981, s.54 (7).

land, taking into account the provisions for compensation. There is a duty to have due regard to the needs of agriculture and forestry.[34]

New public footpaths and bridleways can also be created by agreements with the local authority under s.25. The authority must consult with any other local authority in the area but does not have to consult the parish council or the public. It must, however, have regard to the needs of agriculture and forestry. The new path may be made subject to limitations and conditions.

A parish council may also enter into an agreement for the creation of new footpaths and bridleways under s.30. It has to be satisfied that the path would be beneficial to the inhabitants of all or part of the parish, and it can only agree a path over land in its own parish or in an adjoining one.

Footpaths and bridleways can be extinguished under s.118 of the Highways Act 1980. Before an order is made it must appear to the authority that it is expedient to stop up the path on the grounds that it is not needed for public use. Before confirming the order the authority or the Secretary of State must be satisfied that it is expedient to confirm the order having regard to the extent to which the path is likely to be used and the effect which closure would have on the land served by it, taking into account the provisions for compensation under s.28. In making and confirming the order the local authority and Secretary of State must disregard any temporary circumstances preventing the use of the path by the public.

It is almost impossible to obtain an extinguishment order unless it is made in association with a creation order. There are nearly always objections on the ground that the path is still needed for public use.

S.119 provides for the diversion of bridleways and footpaths. Before making the order the authority must be satisfied that it is expedient to divert the path in the interests of the public or of the owner, lessor or occupier of the land crossed by the path. The Countryside Commission's 'Guide to procedures for public path orders' makes clear that conservation matters are relevant:

> Path users might want a change that gives them access to a new area, or one that gives them more interesting views, a more direct route or a better surface to walk or ride on. A farmer might want a change to reduce interference with agricultural operations. A landowner might want a change to increase privacy. A developer might want a change so that the path fits in better with development proposals. The Highway Authority might want a change because of difficult maintenance problems such as permanently boggy ground or natural erosion, to improve the amenities in the area, or increase path users' safety and enjoyment by avoiding the need to walk or ride on roads.

However, the power to make diversions is circumscribed by s.119.

[34] Highways Act 1980, s.29.

The authority has to be satisfied that the diversion order does not alter any point of termination of the path, other than to another point on the same path, or another highway connected with it, which is substantially as convenient to the public. Nor can the termination be altered where it does not lead to another highway. Before confirming an order the authority or the Secretary of State must be satisfied that the diversion is expedient in the interests of the persons stated in the order and that the path will not be substantially less convenient to the public as a consequence of the diversion. It must also be expedient to confirm the order having regard to the effect it will have on public enjoyment of the path as a whole, on other lands served by the existing path and on land affected by any proposed new path, taking into account the provisions for compensation.

If the applicant wants to divert or close a byway open to all traffic then he or she will have to persuade the local authority to apply to the magistrates' court under s.116 of the Highways Act 1980. The parish council must consent to the application and so can effectively veto any proposals. S.116 also covers diversion and extinguishments of bridleways and footpaths. This procedure is usually followed where orders are being made in respect of vehicular rights of way at the same time as bridleways and footpaths. The Secretary of State has advised authorities that they should not use these powers in respect of footpaths and bridleways unless there are good reasons for doing so.

Diversions and extinguishment orders can also be made to enable development to take place over a public right of way under s.257 of the Town and Country Planning Act 1990. Before making or confirming an order the authority or Secretary of State must be satisfied that it is necessary to do so to enable the development to be carried out in accordance with the planning permission that has been granted. Alternatively the development must be permitted development under a general or special development order or development by a government department. Conservation or environmental factors are not therefore taken into account in deciding whether to make the order though they may have been for the purpose of deciding whether to grant the planning permission itself.

The orders must be sought in parallel with the request for planning permission. Obtaining planning permission for the development does not remove the need to secure any necessary change to a public right of way through a Town and Country Planning Act order. This point is sometimes ignored by developers. Once a building has been constructed over a public right of way it is too late to obtain an order under the Town and Country Planning Act. The building will have to be demolished or a public-path order obtained under the provisions of Highways Act 1980.

The Right to Roam

There is no general right to roam[35] although in uncultivated areas there may be *de facto* access. Members of the public do not have a general right of access to land in England except on highways. Access can be provided to areas of land rather than defined routes only as a result of specific Acts of Parliament, by the granting of rights by landowners, or by agreement with landowners. The courts have also accepted that residents of an area, but not the general public, can acquire the right to use village greens for 'lawful sports and pastimes', where there is a tradition of such use.

Common land

There is considerable confusion about public rights over 'common land'. Many people wrongly believe that common land implies public owner-ship and they have a right to wander over it at will. In fact, most com-mon land is private land over which commoners have specific rights of use, e.g. to graze sheep or cattle, to collect firewood or to fish. These rights are in addition to those of the owner of the common. Some com-mon land is land which is, or was,[36] 'waste land of the manor, not subject to rights of common'.

The public have access on public rights of way over common land just as they do on rights of way over auy other land. Otherwise there is no general right of public access unless granted by statute or by the landowner.

S.193 of the Law of Property Act 1925 gives the public a right of access for air and exercise over metropolitan and urban commons (i.e. those commons which were within the areas covered by the former urban district councils). The same section provides that the landowner can declare by revocable or irrevocable deed that the provisions shall apply to any of his land which is subject to rights of common.

The public may also enjoy a right of access over certain rural com-mons by orders made under the Commons Act 1876, or over commons subject to a management scheme under the Commons Act 1899, or over commons subject to special Local Acts. The Dartmoor Commons Act 1985 provides a right of access for the purpose of open-air recreation to commons registered under the Commons Registrations Act 1965 which are situated within specified districts. Unusually this right includes ac-cess on horseback as well as on foot. The Report of the Common Land Forum[37] recommended that, subject to certain restrictions, there should

---

[35] *Attorney General* v. *Antrobus* [1905] 2 Ch.188. But note the much-criticized case of *R* v. *Doncaster Metropolitan Borough Council ex parte Braim* (1987) 85 LGR 233.

[36] *Hampshire County Council* v. *Milburn* [1990] 2 All ER 257.

[37] The Report of the Common Land Forum, Countryside Commission, CCP 215.

be a right of access to persons on foot for the purpose of quiet enjoyment.

The Public Health and Open Spaces Act 1906 enables local authorities to purchase any land as an open space. The National Trust is obliged by the National Trust Act 1907 to keep its commons unenclosed and unbuilt upon as open spaces for the recreation and enjoyment of the public.

Most of the Acts relating to commons have specific provisions for the conservation and improvement of the commons. The National Trust has a national policy of preservation of the environment. It has to be said, though, that existing legislation does not provide a basis for comprehensive management of common land for the purposes of agriculture and forestry, management of game, conservation of landscape and wildlife, or provision of public access and recreation.

The Common Land Forum considered that further legislation was necessary if commons were to be more effectively managed in the interests of owners, commoners and the general public. The Forum was particularly concerned to provide mechanisms for resolving conflicts between different interests and activities on the commons.

A key element in any new legislation would be provision to establish commons management associations to bring together owners, commoners and the public (through local authorities). The associations should be able to take account of all interests and resolve conflicts.

Town and village greens

Town and village greens are areas of land, registered under the Commons Registration Act 1965, which come within the following definition:

(a) Land which has been allotted by or under any Act for the exercise or recreation of the inhabitants of the locality;

(b) Land on which the inhabitants of any locality have a customary right to indulge in local sports and pastimes;

(c) Land on which the inhabitants of any locality have indulged in such sports and pastimes as of right for not less than twenty years.

The phrase 'lawful sports and pastimes' has never been defined. It has been accepted as including such activities as the village cricket match,[38] maypole dancing[39] and practising archery.[40]

Two Acts were passed in the nineteenth century which provide protection for village greens. S.12 of the Inclosure Act 1857 makes it an offence to damage or encroach upon a village green. The section covers

---

[38] *Fitch* v. *Rawling* (1795) 2 H.Bl 393.
[39] *Hall* v. *Nottingham* (1875) 1 Ex D 1.
[40] *New Windsor Corporation* v. *Mellow* [1975] 1 Ch.380.

any act which injures the green or interrupts its use as a place for exercise and recreation. S.29 of the Commons Act 1876 makes 'encroachment on or inclosure of a town or village green, also any erection thereon or disturbance or interference with or occupation of the soil thereof which is made otherwise than with a view to the better enjoyment of such town or village greens' an offence.

Access by agreement

There are various schemes under which landowners and farmers can provide public access to areas of land in return for payments. These are operated by government departments (e.g. the Countryside Access Scheme for set-aside land operated by the Ministry of Agriculture, Fisheries and Food), statutory agencies (e.g. the Countryside Stewardship Scheme operated by the Countryside Commission) and local authorities (e.g. access agreements under s.64 of the National Parks and Access to the Countryside Act 1949 or management agreements (which may incorporate access) under s.30 of the Wildlife and Countryside Act 1981). Informal arrangements can also be made without payment.

Access agreements may specify restrictions on public use, for example access must be on foot only, entry must be via certain access points, dogs must be kept on leads, camping is not permitted and so on. Access may be suspended temporarily, for example to reduce the risk of fire during very dry weather, or to prevent the spread of a livestock disease. By-laws may also be made to control public behaviour.

Access agreements may place certain obligations on the owner; for example, to keep all rights of way open, to notify the relevant authority before carrying out certain types of work on the agreement land or to farm the land following a specified management regime. Access agreements will usually be publicized, on site through notices at access points or nearby parking areas, and sometimes on maps available to the public.

The Countryside Commission published a discussion paper in 1994 entitled 'Access payment schemes'. This stated:

15. Existing payment schemes have been closely linked to conservation objectives. By targeting certain land types or geographical areas, they have concentrated largely on parts of the countryside where improved management has the greatest potential to enhance landscape, wildlife and/or archaeological interest.

16. Within the targeted areas or land types the growing number of schemes also seek, where this extra investment is judged to represent good value for money, to provide better public access, both for its own sake and so that the public can experience at first hand the conservation benefits achieved by agreements.

However, the Commission went on to state:

59. Payment schemes should be flexible enough to target conservation benefits and access benefits either jointly or separately. Many agreements successfully provide both at the same time, either by buying both conservation and access 'products' directly under the contract, or by buying one of these in such a way as to benefit the other. Some agreements, for example, enhance the natural beauty or habitat management of sites that the public already uses, or of field margins that have public rights of way over them.

60. However joint benefits do not always flow from agreements, and should not be seen as necessary in every case. Not all land that merits a conservation management agreement justifies the payment of an access incentive, and there may be situations where the wildlife strategy is to exclude or minimise public access. Equally, landscape or wildlife interest and enhancement should not be seen as prerequisites for using payments schemes to improve public access.

Ministry of Agriculture schemes[41]

Two schemes have been established by the Ministry of Agriculture, Fisheries and Food: the Countryside Access Scheme, applicable to suitable non-rotational set-aside land; and the Access Tier, applicable to suitable land under agreements in designated Environmentally Sensitive Areas.

The Countryside Access Scheme is a voluntary scheme open to farmers who have land in non-rotational set-aside under the Arable Area Payments Scheme. Its objective is to provide new opportunities for public access to suitable set-aside land for walking and other forms of quiet recreation.

The scheme targets only land which is particularly suited for new or increased public access (e.g. land providing access to a vantage point or attractive landscape feature or linking two or more existing ways). Farmers entering land into the scheme are required to manage the land in accordance with the set-aside rules, and also to observe a range of other conditions, including maintaining free passage over the land, providing and maintaining adequate means of entry, and keeping the land free of litter and other refuse. The access opportunities have to be publicized.

The Access Tier is a voluntary management option for farmers managing land under agreements in Environmentally Sensitive Areas (ESAs). These are parts of the countryside which have been designated as being of particular environmental importance. The objective is to provide new opportunities for public access for walking and other quiet recreation. The Tier is again targeted on land which is particularly suitable for new or significantly increased access. Land accepted into the Tier remains

---

[41] Agriculture Act 1986 section 18; Agricultural Environmental Regulations 1994; Council Regulation (EEC) No.2078/92 of 30 June 1992 on agricultural production methods compatible with the requirements of the protection of the environment and the maintenance of the countryside; Official Journal of the European Communities L215/85–90.

subject to the environmental management conditions of the ESA in question and farmers also have to maintain free passage over the land, provide and maintain adequate means of entry, keep the land free of litter and other refuse and respect other conditions designed to ensure that access is compatible with environmental objectives.

The Countryside Stewardship scheme[42]

Countryside Stewardship is a pilot scheme operated by the Countryside Commission in partnership with the Department of the Environment, English Nature and English Heritage and designed to protect, maintain, enhance or re-create certain traditional English landscapes (e.g. chalk downland, heathland, enclosed moorland, coastal land, water meadows, historic landscapes and parklands). After 31 March 1996 responsibility for the scheme will pass to the Ministry of Agriculture, Fisheries and Food.

Public access is an important element in the scheme. Although it is not required in all cases, the targeting arrangements favour land which is already used by the public, or to which the applicant is prepared to allow new access in return for an additional premium.

Payments for access are not available in respect of rights of way or other rights of access or where there is an established tradition of access (e.g. de facto access). Access under the scheme is permitted and no new rights of way will be created (although there is scope to agree permanent new rights under special arrangements). Agreements under the scheme last for ten years.

Access is publicized by the Countryside Commission to ensure that people know what land is available and to encourage use suited to the size and nature of the site. A county register of access land is being compiled. Agreement holders are required to notify their local parish councils of the availability of access.

The Countryside Council for Wales has introduced a similar pilot scheme, Tir Cymen (which can be translated from the Welsh as 'a well-crafted landscape') in three districts in Wales. This also makes provision for access.[43]

Other agency schemes

The Forestry Authority[44] offers a one-off Community Woodland Supplement under its Woodland Grant Scheme to encourage new woodlands to be planted and made available for public access close to towns and cities. The Forestry Authority also offers special payments under the Woodland Grant Scheme for the management of woods to which the public have access.

---

[42] Countryside Act 1968 s.4.
[43] Environmental Protection Act 1990 s.130.
[44] Forestry Act 1979 s.1 (1).

English Heritage[45] may provide grant-aid to encourage the presentation of scheduled ancient monuments and important archaeological sites to the public, where public access is appropriate.

Local authority agreements

The largest areas with negotiated access arrangements are those areas of 'open country' covered by agreements under s.64 of the National Parks and Access to the Countryside Act 1949. Such agreements provide for payments and the application of by-laws and ranger services to the land involved.

'Open country' is defined for the purposes of such agreements as land consisting wholly or predominantly of mountain, moor, heath and down, cliff or foreshore, woodlands, rivers, canals, expanses of water through which rivers flow, and land adjacent to them.

Local authorities also have powers under s.39 of the Wildlife and Countryside Act 1981 to enter into management agreements 'for the purposes of conserving or enhancing the natural beauty or amenity of the countryside or promoting its enjoyment by the public'. Such agreements have advantages in that they can apply to any type of rural land, not simply open country. They can also link public enjoyment with land management in a positive way.

Co-ordinating Access Schemes

The number and varying conditions of the statutory schemes is confusing. Ideally the approach to payment schemes involving public funds should be consistent whether the funding body is a government department, statutory agency or local authority. Given the increasing range of payment schemes, it is also important that attempts are made to co-ordinate their implementation at both national and local levels. An important principle must be that access should be considered alongside other uses of land, not elevated above them by being given overriding priority. This means that the rights of owners and occupiers, and the present and future needs of farming, forestry, game management, wildlife, the landscape, our historic heritage, the local communities and other users (i.e. those who are not the prime focus of any new provision for access) must all be taken into account. There should be proper arrangements for management to deal with the inevitable conflicts of interest which will arise from time to time.

Conclusion

There is a potential conflict between conservation and access. However, perceived problems may not be based on fact. A recent report, *The*

---

[45] Historic Buildings and Ancient Monuments Act 1953 s.3A.

Environmental Impact of Leisure Activities, by the Environmental Committee of the House of Commons[46] published on 12 July 1995, made the following finding:

> We note that according to the balance of evidence we received, compared to other activities, leisure and tourism do not cause significant widespread ecological damage to the countryside. However there is no need for complacency. We believe that there are important issues to address, involving transport, rural culture and leisure management, as well as conflicts in specific areas. (para.32)
>
> We also note that the cultural conflicts are just as real as, and sometimes more important than, the physical problems. Indeed they are often the root cause of the various tensions and dissatisfactions that are redefined as threats to the environment. (para.33)

The Committee stressed the importance of management and voluntary access agreements.

> We feel that access agreements can contribute to resolving the conflicting interests of walkers, farmers and landowners. We urge the National Park Authorities, local authorities and the Ministry of Agriculture, Fisheries and Food to pursue access agreements with vigour. We believe that access should be significantly increased by the year 2000. (para.62)

They also emphasized the importance of sensitive repair of footpaths.

> We believe that footpath work should be subject to a consistent code of practice. We endorse the Code produced by a Joint Working Group of the Lake District National Park Authority, English Nature and the National Trust: 'The repair and maintenance of paths in open country will be subject to the following considerations:
>
> (a) That the repairs are necessary to prevent or ameliorate visual intrusion and environmental damage;
> (b) Works should be of a high standard of design and implementation using indigenous materials, sympathetic in colour and texture to the immediate surrounding area. Uniformity of construction should be avoided, e.g. steps;
> (c) Techniques used should protect existing vegetation and, normally, only locally occurring plant species should be used in restoration. Non-local species will be acceptable only where necessary as a 'nurse crop', and where natural succession will rapidly result in their disappearance;
> (d) The more remote the path, the more stringently the criteria for path repairs should be applied. This will be a matter of judgement but, in general, the more remote or wild the location the less acceptable an obviously engineered path will be;

[46] House of Commons Session 1994–5, Environment Committee, Fourth Report, *The Environmental Impact of Leisure Activities*, I (HMSO).

(e) Repaired paths should be suitable to the routes used and constructed on a scale appropriate for the intended use as a footpath, bridleway or byway; and

(f) Before any repair work is agreed, the question should be asked "is there a better solution?" '

The use of waymarks, cairns or other intrusive features, other than those traditionally established on summits and path junctions, will be discouraged.

A sustained commitment of resources to path management will be sought, so that small scale continuous maintenance can replace infrequent major repairs as the normal method of path management. (para.117)

A sensible way to ensure the desired protection of the environment would be for the Countryside Commission to initiate a review of statute law and by-laws governing unlawful, irresponsible and inconsiderate behaviour in the countryside. One product of such a review would be a comprehensive set of model by-laws which could be applied to all land to which the public have access, either as of right or under an agreement. In each case, the by-laws selected from the model should be tailored to particular situations. They should be enforced by, and at the expense of, the relevant local authority, statutory agency or government department. This would provide a legal framework for resolving and reconciling conflicts and tension between public access, conservation, land-use interests and the environment regardless of whether the public access depended on ancient highway law or modern access agreements.

9

Legal Issues of Alternative Land Use

MICHAEL CARDWELL

Introduction

For some years farmers have received encouragement to seek alternatives to traditional forms of agriculture. The effects of such encouragement may be gauged by the government's estimate that nearly 80,000 persons whose work is based upon farms are reliant upon non-farming activities.[1] Indeed, it has been suggested that diversification in England and Wales has given rise to the equivalent of 31,000 posts in full-time paid employment.[2] Such developments have been supported by a host of initiatives, for example the Farm Diversification Grant Scheme, the Farm and Business Non-capital Grant Scheme and the Farm and Conservation Grant Scheme.[3] There are arguments that in practical terms the scope for

[1] Ministry of Agriculture, Fisheries and Food (MAFF) News Release 160/94.
[2] J. McInerney and M. Turner, *Patterns, Performance and Prospects in Farm Diversification* (University of Exeter, 1991), 30.
[3] The Farm Diversification Grant Scheme 1987 SI 1987 No.1949, later amended by the Farm Diversification Grant (Variation) Scheme 1988 SI 1988 No.1398, the Farm Diversification Grant (Variation) Scheme 1991 SI 1991 No.2, and the Farm Diversification Grant (Variation) (No.2) Scheme 1991 SI 1991 No.1339; the Farm Business Non-capital Grant Scheme 1988 SI 1988 No.1125, later amended by the Farm Business Non-capital Grant (Variation) Scheme 1991 SI 1991 No.1406, and the Farm Business Non-capital Grant (Amendment) Scheme 1992 SI 1992 No.3175; and the Farm and Conservation Grant Scheme 1989 SI 1989 No.128, later amended by the Farm and Conservation Grant (Variation) Scheme 1990 SI 1990 No.1126, the Farm and Conservation Grant (Variation) Scheme 1991 SI 1991 No.1338, the Farm and Conservation Grant (Variation) Scheme 1993 SI 1993 No.2901, the Farm and Conservation Grant (Variation) Scheme 1994 SI 1994 No.1302, the Farm and Conservation Grant (Variation) (No.2) Scheme 1994 SI 1994 No.3002, and the Farm and Conservation Grant (Variation) Scheme 1995 SI 1995 No.890.

further diversification is now reduced; and, correspondingly, the availability of grants has been curtailed.[4] Nonetheless, the adoption of alternative land uses would seem to remain an objective of government policy, with fresh impetus being provided by the recent reforms effected by the Agricultural Tenancies Act 1995 ('the 1995 Act') and, to a lesser extent, by change in planning guidance.[5] This trend would seem likely to continue in the light of the 1995 *White Paper on Rural England*, which shifts emphasis to reform of the planning system. The need for diversification is reiterated and the place of the local planning authorities in achieving that objective is highlighted. Moreover, a new Rural Business Use Class may be introduced; and PPG 7 on 'The Countryside and the Rural Economy' is to be revised.

At the same time, the 1992 reforms to the Common Agricultural Policy have entrenched the central role of set-aside as a means of reducing the Community's structural surplus in the arable sector. The original Five Year Scheme, introduced in 1988, would appear to have had only a marginal effect. Indeed, it is estimated that in the three years to 1991 a mere 3.5 per cent of United Kingdom arable land was taken out of production.[6] However, following the 1992 reforms, the Arable Area Payments Scheme would appear to have rendered set-aside in effect compulsory for the vast majority of farmers in this sector. With the level of intervention support reduced, financial viability would seem dependent upon the receipt of arable area payments, the receipt of such payments in turn generally being dependent upon placing land into set-aside.[7] Although under the

---

[4] See, in particular, MAFF News Releases 354/92, 417/92 and 432/95. The payment of grants has been increasingly directed to environmental matters rather than the promotion of alternative business structures. However, McInerney and Turner have found evidence that farmers saw opportunities for further growth in leisure-based activities, op. cit., 41.

[5] The reform of agricultural tenure effected by the 1995 Act will be considered below. As regards changes to planning guidance, see e.g. the changes to Planning Policy Guidance Note (PPG) 2 relating to development in the Green Belt, heralded by DoE News Release 108/94.

[6] MAFF News Release 225/91.

[7] In the case of the Five Year Scheme, for the European Community legislation see, in particular, the consolidating Council Regulation (EEC) 2328/91 OJ 1991, L218/1; and for the United Kingdom implementing regulations, see the Set-aside Regulations 1988 SI 1988 No.1352, as amended by the Set-aside (Amendment) Regulations 1989 SI 1989 No.1042, the Set-aside (Amendment) Regulations 1990 SI 1990 No.1716, and the Set-aside (Amendment) Regulations 1991 SI 1991 No.1993. In the case of the Arable Area Payments Scheme, there has been a plethora of European Community legislation. See, in particular, Council Regulation (EEC) 1765/92 OJ 1992, L181/12, Commission Regulation (EEC) 2293/92 OJ 1992, L221/19 (now repealed as from the 1994/5 marketing year), and Commission Regulation (EC) 762/94 OJ 1994, L90/8. For the original United Kingdom implementing regulations, see the Arable Area Payments Regulations 1994 SI 1994 No.947, later amended by the Arable Area Payments (Amendment) Regulations 1994 SI 1994 No.2287. For the current regulations, see the Arable Area Payments Regulations 1995 SI 1995 No.1738, as amended by the Arable Area Payments (Amendment) Regulations 1995 SI 1995 No. 2780. For works on the Arable Area Payments Scheme, generally, see note 51.

Arable Area Payments Scheme the various set-aside obligations are less 'active' than, for example, the forms of alternative land use which were promoted under the Farm Diversification Grant Scheme, they none the less give rise to complex issues relating to agricultural tenure, many of which await clear resolution.[8]

Problems flowing from such alternative land use are not confined to the landlord-and-tenant relationship. For example, there can be little doubt that the owner-occupier as much as the tenant will need to take into account the tax consequences of diversifying into a new trade; and the enhanced emphasis on environmental matters may even create difficult questions for trustees in relation to their investment powers.[9] Further, matters of planning law will have broad impact. That having been said, the tenant farmer is exposed to a further tier of hazards as a result of his more limited interest in the land. This may not be surprising in that such alternative land use is liable to run counter to a landlord-and-tenant system based until recently upon the need to promote agricultural output.[10]

Consideration may first be given to the position of tenants protected by the Agricultural Holdings Act 1986 ('the 1986 Act'). Although it is now provided that in the case of tenancies granted on or after 1 September 1995 the protection of the 1986 Act may only be obtained in certain limited circumstances, for some time there must inevitably be a considerable number of tenants who remain subject to its provisions.[11] Under this head four aspects may be highlighted. First, in an extreme case alternative land use may cause the tenant to lose altogether the protection of the 1986 Act – at the same time forfeiting, for example, any succession rights. Secondly, as previously mentioned, planning law has not at all times proved conducive to diversification into new business enterprises. While certain difficulties affect landlord and tenant alike, the tenant also faces additional hurdles as a consequence of the 1986 Act. Thirdly, alternative land use may lead the tenant to breach the rules of good husbandry, again with potentially severe consequences under the 1986 Act. Fourthly, non-farming activities may be included

---

[8] It may be noted that the non-agricultural use and forestry options available under the original Five Year Scheme have not been carried through into the Arable Area Payments Scheme.

[9] A. MacCulloch and C. T. Reid, 'Obstacles to environmentally sensitive land management' (1993) *Environmental Law and Management*, 5, (6), 202–4.

[10] See e.g. C. P. Rodgers, 'Agricultural tenure, land use and conservation in the United Kingdom', in M. R. Grossman and W. Brussaard (eds.), *Agrarian Land Law in the Western World* (CAB International, Wallingford, 1992), 148–70, at 151.

[11] For the circumstances in which a tenancy granted on or after 1 September 1995 still falls under the 1986 Act, see s.4 of the 1995 Act.

as a relevant factor on rent review.[12] Having considered the position of tenants protected by the 1986 Act, the effect of the reforms implemented by the 1995 Act may be addressed, with particular reference to the extent to which scope for alternative land use has been improved.

At the same time there are strong arguments that the tenant concerned by the dangers of alternative land use should look to the United Kingdom Parliament rather than the European Community for the enactment of measures in his or her favour. As the European Court stated in the case of *R* v. *MAFF ex parte Bostock*, 'legal relations between lessees and lessors, in particular on the expiry of a lease, are, as Community law now stands, still governed by the law of the Member State in question'.[13] That case may have concerned milk quotas; but there is good reason to believe that a like approach would be adopted to Community legislation implementing the Arable Area Payments Scheme – and, indeed, more general legislation promoting environmental considerations.

Tenants Protected by the 1986 Act

Loss of statutory protection

Tenants protected by the 1986 Act who adopt alternative land uses may derive some comfort from the statutory definition of an 'agricultural holding'. In particular, s.1(1) does contemplate some non-agricultural use, an 'agricultural holding' meaning the aggregate of the land in a contract for an agricultural tenancy, 'whether agricultural land or not'.[14] This in turn is reinforced by the definition of a 'contract for an agricultural tenancy', the definition being satisfied if 'having regard to – (a) the terms of the

---

[12] On these aspects, generally, see e.g. H. Hargreave, 'Diversification: problems for the tenant farmer' (1990) 134 *Sol. J.* 1032–3; M. Gregory, 'The implementation of agricultural diversification', in W. Howarth and C. P. Rodgers (eds.), *Agriculture, Conservation and Land Use* (University of Wales Press, Cardiff, 1992), 8–31, at 22–7; A. A. Lennon, 'Set-aside of agricultural land: policy, practice and problems', in Howarth and Rodgers, op. cit., 32–50, at 40–3; M. N. Cardwell, 'Set-aside schemes and alternative land use: some problems for the tenant farmer' [1992] *Conveyancer*, 180–94; C. P. Rodgers, 'Agricultural tenure, land use and conservation in the United Kingdom', in Grossman and Brussaard, op. cit., 148–70, at 160–2; A. A. Lennon and R. E. O. Mackay (eds.), *Agricultural Law, Tax and Finance* (Longmans, London, looseleaf, Release 10), at G4.13; M. Gregory, *Conservation Law in the Countryside* (Tolley, Croydon, 1994), 71–2; and C. T. Reid, *Nature Conservation Law* (W. Green/Sweet and Maxwell, Edinburgh, 1994), 298–9.

[13] Case 2/92, [1994] ECR I-955, at I-985.

[14] Cf. s.1 of the Agricultural Holdings Act 1948 ('the 1948 Act'), which referred to 'the aggregate of the agricultural land'.

tenancy,[15] (b) the actual or contemplated use of the land at the time of the conclusion of the contract and subsequently, and (c) any other relevant circumstances, the whole of the land comprised in the contract, subject to such exceptions only as do not substantially affect the character of the tenancy, is let for use as agricultural land' – s.1(2) of the 1986 Act. In such wording may be found echoes of the 'substantial user' test, derived from earlier case law on the 1948 Act and perhaps most clearly stated by Jenkins LJ in *Howkins* v. *Jardine*: 'the substance of the matter must be looked at to see whether as a matter of substance the land comprised in the tenancy, taken as a whole, is an agricultural holding. If it is, then the whole of it is entitled to the protection of the Act. If it is not, then none of it is so entitled.'[16] Accordingly, no severance was permissible.[17]

Another key factor is the limitation of 'agricultural land' to land used for agriculture for the purposes of a trade or business (or, a far less likely alternative, land so designated by the Minister).[18] In addition, 'agriculture' itself is somewhat traditionally defined so as to include 'horticulture, fruit growing, seed growing, dairy farming and livestock breeding and keeping, the use of land as grazing land, meadow land, osier land, market gardens and nursery grounds, and the use of land for woodlands where that use is ancillary to the farming of land for other agricultural purposes'.[19]

Recent authority on what constitutes an 'agricultural holding' may be found in the case of *Gold* v. *Jacques Amand Ltd.*[20] In particular, the court was required to consider whether there was use as 'agricultural land'. On the facts there was no clear and express provision as to user.

---

[15] The importance of an express user covenant has for some time been central when seeking to establish which statutory code applies to a property *ab initio* – see e.g. *Wolfe* v. *Hogan* [1949] 2 KB 194; *Whitty* v. *Scott-Russell* [1950] 2 KB 32; *Court* v. *Robinson* [1951] 2 KB 60; and *Russell* v. *Booker* (1982) 263 EG 513. Furthermore, breach of such an express user covenant may entitle a landlord to serve a notice to quit.

[16] [1951] 1 All ER 320, at 329. The wording now consolidated in s.1(2) of the 1986 Act was first introduced by para.1 of sched. 1 to the Agricultural Holdings Act 1984. On the 'substantial user test', generally, see J. Muir Watt, *Agricultural Holdings* (13th edn, Sweet and Maxwell, London, 1987), 3–7; M. Slatter and W. Barr, *Farm Tenancies* (BSP Professional Books, Oxford, 1987), 7–9; H. A. C. Densham, *Scammell and Densham's Law of Agricultural Holdings* (7th edn, Butterworths, London, 1989), 24–7; and C. P. Rodgers, *Agricultural Law* (Butterworths, London, 1991), 16–25.

[17] In this Jenkins LJ followed the Agricultural Holdings Act 1908 decision of *Re Lancaster and Macnamara* [1918] 2 KB 472. Cf. s.33(1) of the Agricultural Holdings Act 1923, which allowed claims in respect of compensation for agricultural improvements and disturbance even where the tenancy as a whole did not qualify as an 'agricultural holding' (a provision not re-enacted in the 1948 Act). See also *Dunn* v. *Fidoe* [1950] 2 All ER 685.

[18] S.1(4) of the 1986 Act. Such designation may occur under s.109(1) of the Agriculture Act 1947.

[19] S.96(1) of the 1986 Act.

[20] (1992) 63 P. and C.R. 1.

However, a substantial part of the business consisted of buying in and selling on bulbs as a wholesaler. Indeed, there was evidence to the effect that only some 15–20 per cent of the trade consisted of sales of plants grown on the 6 acres subject to dispute. None the less, the court held that the property was used as 'agricultural land'; and in this it would seem to have been influenced by both the intentions of the parties and the fact that the only permitted planning use was use as agricultural land.

However, even if the property does satisfy the definition of an 'agricultural holding' *ab initio*, changes in land use may trigger the loss of that statutory protection. The dangers are magnified in that it is possible for the adoption of non-agricultural business activities to render the 1986 Act inapplicable – and yet fail to attract the protection of the business tenancy regime under Part II of the Landlord and Tenant Act 1954 ('the 1954 Act'). It would seem that a new contract to that effect is required with the landlord.[21]

An early example of such risks consequent upon diversification may be found in the case of *Monson* v. *Bound*.[22] The property had been let expressly for the purpose of horticulture. None the less, over a period of time 65 per cent of the turnover came to be derived from the sale of cut flowers, pot plants, shrubs and wreaths; and only one-sixth of those items were grown on the premises. The court held that on the facts the protection of the agricultural holdings legislation was no longer available. By contrast, a less strict approach was adopted in the later decision of *Wetherall* v. *Smith*, also heard under the 1948 Act. In particular, it was stated that the protection of statute would only be lost where, during the period leading up to service of the notice to quit, agricultural use 'had been wholly or substantially abandoned'.[23] Since the introduction of the 1986 Act definition, the courts would seem to have followed the more generous approach taken in *Wetherall* v. *Smith*. Thus, in *Short* v. *Greeves* the tenant retained his statutory protection, notwithstanding that some 60 per cent of the turnover appeared to

---

[21] See e.g. *Russell* v. *Booker* (1982) 263 EG 513 (where the tenant ceased to be protected by the agricultural holdings legislation without acquiring the protection of the Rent Act 1977). Such new contract may be express or implied. However, for the court to imply a new contract, it would seem that the tenant must show that the landlord had full knowledge of and accepted that change of user: ibid., at 516. Furthermore, mere receipt of rent in the knowledge of the change of use is insufficient: there must be affirmative assent – *Wolfe* v. *Hogan* [1949] 2 KB 194. See also e.g. *Court* v. *Robinson* [1951] 2 KB 60; *South West Water Authority* v. *Palmer* (1983) 268 EG 357; and, for perhaps a less strict view, *Re Summerson, Downie* v. *Summerson* [1900] 1 Ch.112. On this aspect, generally, see e.g. Rodgers, op. cit., 23–4.

[22] [1954] 1 WLR 1321. 'Horticulture' fell within the definition of 'agriculture' for the purposes of the 1948 Act: see now s.96(1) of the 1986 Act (set out above).

[23] [1980] 2 All ER 530, at 538, *per* Sir David Cairns.

originate from non-agricultural items as a result of the successful expansion of a garden centre.[24]

A matter of some importance would seem to be the ability to produce evidence of land use over the relevant period prior to the notice to quit.[25] Examination of 'day-to-day conduct' is required – although this need not be minute examination.[26] As pointed out in *Short* v. *Greeves*, evidence may be difficult to collate. Much may depend on the respective turnover derived from home-grown and bought-in produce; yet few tenants would keep accounts differentiating the two categories of receipt.[27]

Accordingly, under the 1986 Act there would seem to be good grounds for believing that a diversifying tenant farmer will receive a sympathetic ear from the courts. Moreover, the approach adopted would seem consistent with a long-standing and general willingness to ensure the effectiveness of statutory protection.[28] That having been said, this area has been perceived to be in need of reform, leading to the introduction of the farm business tenancy regime under the 1995 Act.

Planning

As noted, planning law constraints apply to freehold owners and tenants alike. However, it is arguable that the heavier constraints fall upon tenants; and although in *Gold* v. *Jacques Amand Ltd* the permitted planning user came to the assistance of the tenant, in general the provisions of the town and country planning legislation may prove a more effective brake on diversification than those relating to tenure.

The statutory definition of 'agriculture' for the purposes of both sets of legislation is very similar.[29] Yet, while the cases under both the 1948 Act and the 1986 Act have allowed the tenant considerable scope for diversification, as a rule it would seem that planning permission will be

[24] [1988] 08 EG 109; and see H. W. Wilkinson, 'Mixed holdings of agricultural land', (1988) 138 N.L.J. 329–30; and C. P. Rodgers, 'Agriculture as business, business as agriculture: selecting the code of tenancy protection', [1988] *Conveyancer*, 430–6. There was some doubt as to whether the 1948 Act definition or that now found in the 1986 Act applied; but Dillon L. J. felt that it would not make 'any real difference in substance to the outcome'.

[25] In *Wetherall* v. *Smith* [1980] 2 All ER 530 the court suggested that it would be necessary to consider the land use over the two years or so prior to service of the notice to quit. See also *Bradshaw* v. *Smith* (1980) 255 EG 699 (a case concerning 'agricultural land' for the purposes of ss.6 and 26 of the Rent Act 1977, by reference to the definition contained in s.26(3) of the General Rate Act 1967), where the court was prepared to treat the 'relevant date' as either the date of the application or the date of the hearing.

[26] *Wetherall* v. *Smith* [1980] 2 All ER 530, at 538.

[27] [1988] 08 EG 109, at 111.

[28] The general policy in this regard is well stated in *Johnson* v. *Moreton* [1980] AC 37.

[29] S.96(1) of the 1986 Act (set out above); and s.336(1) of the Town and Country Planning Act 1990.

required for relatively small departures from agricultural use.[30] This can be illustrated by reference to some of the decisions regarding farm shops – enterprises which have been a favoured form of diversification.[31]

In this context identification of the appropriate planning unit may frequently be a preliminary issue. More specifically, where the diversification affects but a small part of a farm, there may be difficulties in ascertaining whether there is one or more planning unit. The consequences may be important: for example, activities insufficient to amount to a change of use over the farm taken as a whole could easily amount to a change of use on a particular site if deemed a separate planning unit.[32] The position may be complicated where the farmer's operations are spread over different blocks of land which are not contiguous.[33]

As a general rule, planning law seems to take a firm stance regarding farm shops. PPG 7 states that it is

> normally assumed that use of a farm shop only for the sale of goods produced on that farm is a use which is ancillary to the use as a farm and therefore does not require specific planning permission, whereas use as a farm shop selling a significant amount of 'imported' produce is a separate use and therefore subject to full planning control.[34]

The case law may be seen at times as even more restrictive. As a general rule it would seem that sales of imported produce over a *de*

---

[30] See, generally, e.g. A. J. Scrase, 'Agriculture – 1980s industry and 1947 definition', [1988] JPL 447–60; J. D. C. Harte, 'Land development: the role of planning law', in Howarth and Rodgers, op. cit., 108–38, at 117–19; and Lennon and Mackay, op. cit., at E2.1–2.7.

[31] See e.g. sched. 2 to the Farm and Conservation Grant Regulations 1991 SI 1991 No.1630, and McInerney and Turner, op. cit., at 9–10 and Appendix II. For the employment implications, see P. M. L. Glover, 'Farm shop workers: employed in agriculture?', (1992) 136 *Sol.J.* 728–9. Similar considerations apply to numerous other activities, such as lairage (*Warnock* v. *Secretary of State for the Environment and Dover D.C.* [1980] JPL 590) and bottling spring water ([1990] JPL 714). For the practical rather than more narrowly legal implications, see e.g. M. Haines and R. Davies, *Diversifying the Farm Business* (BSP Professional Books, Oxford, 1987), 225–48.

[32] See, in particular, the principles set out in *Burdle* v. *Secretary of State for the Environment* [1972] 3 All ER 240; and *R. W. Ramsay and Ramsey Sports Ltd* v. *Secretary of State for the Environment and Suffolk Coastal D.C.* [1991] JPL 1148.

[33] See e.g. *Fuller* v. *Secretary of State for the Environment* [1988] 01 EG 55.

[34] At Annex B2. However, for recognition of the importance of non-local produce in farm shops, see e.g. Written Answer, Hansard (HC) 26 May 1994, vol.244, cols.240–1: local planning authorities should, *inter alia*, take account of 'the desirability for the farmer to provide a service throughout the year, which may require him to bring in non-local produce to overcome the problems of seasonality and provide continuity of employment and to ensure that a sufficiently wide selection of produce can be offered'. In this context 'non-local' means 'produce originating from beyond the farm holding and its environs'. As mentioned, above, the *White Paper on Rural England* proposes that PPG 7 be revised; see *Rural England – A Nation Committed to a Living Countryside* (1995) CM. 3016 at pp.34–35.

minimis level will give rise to a material change of use from agriculture for which planning permission is required. For example, in *Williams* v. *Minister of Housing and Local Government* the court held that there was a material change of use when the owner of a nursery garden commenced the sale of imported fruit, notwithstanding that the imported element amounted to only some 10 per cent of turnover[35] – an approach in marked contrast to that taken in *Short* v. *Greeves* and *Gold* v. *Jacques Amand Ltd.*[36] Certain aspects of the decision may be highlighted. First, it was accepted that use for agriculture necessarily includes the selling of the products. Secondly, while the quantitative change had been small, a change in the 'character of the use' had occurred. Thirdly, addressing directly the problem of identifying the relevant planning unit, the court held that on the facts it should look at the farm as a whole rather than the shop in isolation.

Subsequently a similar line was followed in many cases, including *Allen* v. *Secretary of State for the Environment and Reigate and Banstead Borough Council*[37] and *Brill* v. *Secretary of State for the Environment and Chiltern District Council.*[38] In *Allen* the court affirmed the importance of the distinction between the sale of home-grown and imported produce. Indeed, the Deputy Judge felt bound by precedent to accept that even significant sale of home-grown produce would not amount to a change from agricultural use – although it could be argued that such would be more likely to change the 'character' of the property than the sale of small quantities of imported produce.[39] In *Brill* some 25 per cent of the total annual turnover was derived from imported produce; and it was accepted that this, exceeding the *de minimis* level, constituted a material change of use. Accordingly, the question was whether or not planning permission should be granted. In the circumstances planning permission was refused, a key factor being the location of the property within the Green Belt. Arguments had been put forward to the effect that the imported

---

[35] (1967) 65 LGR 495. In the Ministerial planning decision reported at [1992] JPL 1199–1203 concern was expressed as to the correct measure for distinguishing between home-produced and imported items.

[36] For a comparison with the leniency adopted by the court in *Gold* v. *Jacques Amand Ltd* under the 1986 Act, see the planning decision of *Jacques Amand Ltd* v. *Secretary of State for the Environment* [1993] EGCS 123.

[37] [1990] JPL 340.

[38] [1993] JPL 253.

[39] In the Ministerial planning decision reported at [1992] JPL 1199–1203 significant emphasis was placed on the effect of the sales on the character of the property. The percentage of imported produce was considered but one element in the overall assessment; and, for example, the likelihood that the operation would have very much the character of a farm shop at the height of the 'pick-your-own' season contributed to the decision that a material change of use arose. It was also felt of some importance that the site was located within the Green Belt.

produce was essential to maintain the viability of the enterprise. These were rejected on the facts, without being ruled out altogether.[40]

One approach adopted to overcome such difficulties has been the grant of planning permission subject to a condition limiting the sale of goods not produced on the farm, as, for example, in *Bromsgrove District Council v. Secretary of State for the Environment and Harrison*.[41] Further, on occasion it would seem that government policy guidance in favour of diversification may be a key factor determining the grant of planning permission even where the sales of imported produce are very significant. As stated in PPG 7, 'The increasing efficiency of agricultural producers and changes in agricultural policy mean that retaining as much land as possible in agricultural use no longer has the same priority. The priority now is to promote diversification of the rural economy so as to provide wide and varied employment opportunities for rural people, including those formerly employed in agriculture and related sectors.'[42] Consistent with this emphasis, in a somewhat unusual case planning permission was granted for a farm shop within the Green Belt selling as much as 80 per cent 'bought-in' produce. The decision emphasized the special circumstances, which included not only the government guidance already mentioned (which was said in any event not to be conclusive), but also the fact that the proposal made use of an existing vernacular building and that the adopted local plan encouraged the provision of local shops.[43] None the less, such a decision may become more frequent following amendment of planning guidance so as to facilitate diversification within the Green Belt.

However, while the grant of planning permission in such circumstances may suit the requirements of an owner-occupier, the fact that planning permission is required at all may lead to serious problems for a tenant farmer. In particular, a programme of limited diversification adopted by a tenant may be insufficient to take the farm outside the 1986 Act, yet sufficient to trigger the need for planning consent; and that planning consent may provide an effective ground for the landlord to serve a notice to quit under the 1986 Act. Such a notice to quit could be served pursuant to a

---

[40] See also *Powell v. Secretary of State for the Environment* [1992] EGCS 155; and *Bromley L.B.C. v. Secretary of State for the Environment* [1994] EGCS 3 (in the latter case the court held that, while it might be appropriate to sanction change of use for a redundant farm building in the Green Belt, the same latitude did not extend to open land).

[41] [1988] JPL 834. See also [1993] JPL 187–91 (the proportion in value of retail sales of imported plants, trees and shrubs was restricted in any calendar year to 5 per cent of total retail sales; and imported produce was not to include manufactured goods other than essential containers for natural produce).

[42] Para.2.3.

[43] [1993] JPL 388–9. For another, earlier, example of the influence of such planning guidance, see [1988] JPL 435–6.

contractual provision in the tenancy agreement or under Case B.[44] Even if the planning permission relates to only a part of the holding, the position of the tenant is still precarious. The landlord may be able to circumvent the general rule that a notice to quit should extend to all the tenanted land through either a contractual provision permitting him to resume possession of part;[45] or, alternatively, by severance of the reversion. In the latter circumstances the freehold land in respect of which planning permission has been granted is transferred into new ownership, the transferee subsequently serving an effective notice to quit.

Accordingly, the dangers for the tenant are considerable. The need for planning consent may arise even where the extent of diversification is relatively insignificant; and there may be little opportunity to resist any ensuing notice to quit. Most notably, if Case B is available to the landlord, the tenant's remedy is confined to disputing the reasons stated in the notice. It may be that the notice to quit covers only a fraction of the holding; but even the loss of a small area could have a severe and disproportionate effect upon operations over the remainder. An additional factor in this context is that it is open for the landlord as well as the tenant to seek planning permission for diversification, leaving the tenant at risk even where he himself is content to continue with traditional agriculture.

An illustration of such difficulties may be found in two cases, *Fowler* v. *Secretary of State for the Environment and North Wiltshire District Council*[46] and *John* v. *George*.[47] In the former the tenant of Battlelake Farm, Purton, Wiltshire, objected to the landlord's application to develop the farm as an equestrian centre. The objection was based on the personal and major hardship which would arise if planning permission were granted. A key factor was that the landlord could serve an effective Case B notice to quit; and the tenant would be obliged to leave the holding and family home – and also other land adjacent, which could not be efficiently farmed by itself, not least since the buildings were sited upon Battlelake Farm. The inspector's decision to grant planning permission was upheld on appeal. An aspect of the court's judgement which deserves close attention

---

[44] I.e. Case B in sched. 3 to the 1986 Act, as amended by the Agricultural Holdings (Amendment) Act 1990. Further, should the diversification proceed without the landlord's consent, it may well constitute a breach of a term of the tenancy restricting use to agricultural use only.

[45] S.25(2)(b) of the 1986 Act. It is vital that any such contractual provision should permit the tenant sufficient time to make any claims for statutory compensation – see e.g. *Coates* v. *Diment* [1951] 1 All ER 890; and *Parry* v. *Million Pigs Ltd* (1980) 260 EG 281. The landlord must also ensure that he accurately identifies the land for which planning permission has been granted – although it seems that the court will allow some latitude: *Omnivale Ltd* v. *Boldan* [1994] EGCS 63.

[46] [1993] JPL 365.

[47] [1995] 22 EG 146.

is the denial of any special treatment to agricultural tenants under the planning legislation: Parliament had provided under the 1986 Act that the grant of planning permission may lead to the service of an effective notice to quit and there was no reason why, as a matter of law or reasonableness, the person responsible for granting planning permission for non-agricultural development of an agricultural holding should still attach more importance to that consequence than to any other personal consideration.

In the latter case the plaintiff held an agricultural tenancy of a 130-acre farm. Foilowing extensive storm damage in 1990, he entered into discussions as to future action with Mr Charles George, who was at that point landlord together with Mrs George. These discussions led to the plaintiff agreeing in principle that investigations should be pursued into a plan to sell the farmhouse and existing farm buildings (the latter with the benefit of planning permission for conversion to residential use); and to use the sale proceeds to construct new farm buildings and a bungalow. However, no contract to such effect was ever concluded. Subsequently, with the plaintiff's support, planning permission was granted for the conversion of the existing farm buildings and for the erection of the new farm buildings; but planning permission for the bungalow was refused. Relations between the parties then broke down. On 5 November 1991 Mr and Mrs George conveyed the freehold of the farm buildings to the defendants on trust for their infant daughter when she reached eighteen or finished full-time education; and on 30 January 1992 the defendants served a notice to quit in respect of the farm buildings relying on Case B. The court ruled in favour of the defendants. Argument based on estoppel failed. In particular, there had been no promise in conduct or words not to serve notice to quit based on the planning permission; and there had been no alteration by the plaintiff of his position in reliance upon any promise. Besides, there was no estoppel by convention. Additional argument that the severance of the reversion was ineffective also failed. The court held the transaction to be *bona fide*, distinguishing the case of *Persey* v. *Bazley*, where the conveyance had been merely to nominees.[48] The motive for the transaction did not alter its legal consequences; and, *inter alia*, on the facts the trustees were bound to have regard to the daughter's interest as from the date of the conveyance.[49]

Thus, by virtue of the planning legislation taken together with the 1986 Act, the fact that the diversification has been insufficient to take the property outside the 1986 Act altogether may still leave the tenant farmer in a position where his interest is inadequately protected. If the proposals contained

---

[48] (1983) 47 P. and C.R. 37.

[49] It was noted that, pending the vesting of their daughter's interest, Mr and Mrs George might themselves enjoy an entitlement; but such did not prevent the court holding the conveyance valid.

in the *White Paper on Rural England* are implemented, this danger should at least be reduced.

Rules of good husbandry

At times the traditional landlord-and-tenant relationship also seems ill suited to the more passive forms of alternative land use, as promoted by both the set-aside schemes and other initiatives directed specifically at environmental concerns. In this context emphasis may be placed on the set-aside obligations under the Arable Area Payments Scheme, it being of such widespread application.[50] The original provisions governing the management of set-aside land under the scheme were set out in sched. 2 to the Arable Area Payments Regulations 1994 and provided for both rotational and non-rotational set-aside.[51] In the former case the establishment and maintenance of a green cover was the primary requirement, while in the latter case it was possible to adopt the Grassland Option, the Natural Regeneration Option, the Wild Bird Cover Option or the Field Margins Option. In any event farmers were not to damage, destroy or remove, *inter alia*, existing hedges, ponds, vernacular buildings or stone walls. Accordingly, as from inception the protection of the environment constituted a significant objective of the management obligations, the European Community legislation in terms directing Member States to apply 'appropriate environmental measures'.[52] These original provisions have now been amended to afford greater flexibility; but again the same concerns are found. For example, Commission Regulation (EC) 762/94 lays down the framework for 'guaranteed' set-aside, where the farmer undertakes to set-aside land for five years, the purpose of this amendment being expressly to 'implement environmental measures on the non-rotational fallow'.[53]

  This emphasis is reinforced under the more specifically environmental

---

[50] The permanent and rotational fallow options under the Five Year Scheme give rise to similar considerations.

[51] SI 1994 No.947. On the Arable Area Payments Scheme, generally, see e.g. D. J. Ansell and R. B. Tranter, *Set-aside: In Theory and in Practice* (University of Reading, 1992); Lennon and Mackay, op. cit., at G4.5–4.7; and C P. Rodgers, 'Set Aside land management – the Arable Area Payments Scheme' (1994) *Bulletin of the Agricultural Law Association*, 13, 2–8.

[52] E.g. article 7(3) of Council Regulation (EEC) 1765/92 OJ 1992, L181/12. It may also be noted that similar criteria affect other areas of the reformed Common Agricultural Policy. For instance, under the Sheep Annual Premium Scheme and the Suckler Cow Premium Scheme legislation has been introduced to prevent overgrazing.

[53] OJ 1994, L90/8, preamble. For the current United Kingdom regulations, see the Arable Area Payments Regulations 1995 SI 1995 No.1738, as amended by the Arable Area Payments (Amendment) Regulations 1995 SI 1995 No. 2780 (the management requirements being set out in sched. 2, including special conditions for guaranteed set-aside land). And see Rodgers, above, Chapter 5, at pp.117ff.

schemes. Early illustrations are provided by Environmentally Sensitive Areas (ESAs) and Nitrate Sensitive Areas (NSAs).[54] The former, designated under s.18 of the Agriculture Act 1986, have been hailed as the government's flagship;[55] and both continue to receive strong support. Indeed, following the increase of the number of ESAs in England by six to twenty-two, it is calculated that they now cover over 10 per cent of English agricultural land; and related annual expenditure is planned to rise to £63 million by 1996/7.[56] With regard to NSAs, the original ten contained in the pilot scheme were augmented in 1994 by a further twenty-two designations.[57]

In this context a central feature is the expanding number of measures to comply with the European Community 'Agri-environment Regulation', Council Regulation (EEC) 2078/92.[58] Not least, the policy objectives set out in its preamble highlight the extent to which agricultural production has ceased to form the overriding consideration. Accordingly, it can be recited, *inter alia*, that 'because of the scale of the problems such schemes should be applicable to all farmers in the Community who undertake to use farming methods which will protect, maintain or improve the environment and the countryside and to refrain from further intensification of agricultural production'. At a national level later developments with regard to both ESAs and NSAs are encompassed within the programme to implement the Community regulation; and new initiatives include

[54] On ESAs, NSAs and other forms of management agreement, see e.g. Rodgers, op. cit., 276–93; C. P. Rodgers, 'Agricultural tenure, land law and conservation in the United Kingdom', in Grossman and Brussaard, op. cit., 148–70, at 153–62; C. P. Rodgers, 'Land management agreements and agricultural practice: towards an integrated legal framework for conservation law', in Howarth and Rodgers, op. cit., 139–64; Lennon and Mackay, op. cit. at G1.1–2.4; Gregory, op. cit., 25–40; Reid, op. cit., 141–95; and M. Whitby (ed.), *Incentives for Countryside Management: The Case for Environmentally Sensitive Areas* (CAB International, Wallingford, 1994).

[55] MAFF News Release 237/95.

[56] Ibid. The six new English ESAs created in 1994 were the Blackdown Hills, the Cotswold Hills, the Shropshire Hills, Dartmoor, Essex Coast and Upper Thames Tributaries.

[57] The Nitrate Sensitive Areas Regulations 1994 SI 1994 No.1729. See also the Nitrate Sensitive Areas (Amendment) Regulations 1995 SI 1995 No.1708, which bring the NSAs in the pilot scheme within the scheme implemented by the Nitrate Sensitive Areas Regulations 1994. For further amendment, see now the Nitrate Sensitive Areas (Amendment) (No. 2) Regulations 1995 SI 1995 No. 2095.

[58] OJ 1992, L215/85. The Agri-environment Regulation is itself complemented by other Community legislation, such as the Nitrates Directive (91/676/EEC) OJ 1991, L375/1; and the Habitats Directive (92/43/EEC) OJ 1992, L206/7. With regard to the former, proposals are in hand to designate Nitrate Vulnerable Zones; and the effects of the latter may now be seen in the Conservation (Natural Habitats, etc.) Regulations 1994 SI 1994 No.2716.

the Countryside Access Scheme, directed to promoting public access on set-aside land.[59]

As indicated, both the set-aside obligations and the more detailed constraints under the avowedly environmental schemes may give rise to breaches of the rules of good husbandry, as set out in s.11 of the Agriculture Act 1947. More specifically, the farmer may find it difficult to comply with the rule that he should maintain his arable land 'clean and in a good state of cultivation and fertility and in good condition'. He may also find it difficult to show that he has taken such steps as are necessary to 'secure and maintain crops and livestock free from disease and from infestation by insects and other pests'. For example, under both the Five Year Scheme and the Arable Area Payments Scheme general use of fertilizers and pesticides has been prohibited.[60]

A counter-argument could be put forward that crop rotation, including a fallow, has traditionally been considered good agricultural practice. However, such a claim may be hard to sustain in the current farming climate; and would not, in any event, seem to extend to guaranteed set-aside under the Arable Area Payments Scheme (or permanent fallow under the Five Year Scheme). Another counter-argument might be based upon the requirement in the European Community legislation that the areas entered into set-aside 'must be cared for so as to maintain good cropping conditions'.[61] Nevertheless, the various management obligations directed to such ends may fail to equate with the standard stipulated in the Agriculture Act 1947.

In the event of a breach of the rules of good husbandry, the tenant would not be subject to any state-administered sanctions – although the landlord could claim for dilapidations on the termination of the tenancy.[62] A perhaps more important consideration, however, is that such a breach may permit a landlord to obtain a certificate of bad husbandry, subsequently serving an effective notice to quit under Case C of the 1986 Act. Further, if the tenancy agreement includes an express term that the holding is to be farmed in accordance with the rules of good husbandry, there may

---

[59] The Countryside Access Regulations 1994 SI 1994 No.2349. Under these a tenant need only notify his landlord in writing of his intention to make an application: there is no requirement of formal consent: Regulation 6(5).

[60] See e.g. paras.6–12 of sched. 2 to the Set-aside Regulations 1988 SI 1988 No.1352 as amended by the Set-aside (Amendment) Regulations 1989 SI 1989 No. 1042 (in respect of, *inter alia*, permanent and rotational fallow); paras.6–10, Part I, and paras.12–19, Part II, of sched. 2 to the Arable Area Payments Regulations 1994 SI 1994 No.947; and now paras.18–25, 28–30 and 32 of sched. 2 to the Arable Area Payments Scheme 1995 SI 1995 No.1738.

[61] See e.g. article 3(2) of Commission Regulation (EEC) 2293/92 OJ 1992, L221/19 (replaced with effect from the 1994/5 marketing year by article 3(2) of Commission Regulation (EC) 762/94 OJ 1994, L90/8).

[62] S.71 of the 1986 Act.

also be scope to serve notice to quit under Case D or Case E.[63] As with Case B the tenant's remedy would be restricted to disputing the reasons given in the notice to quit; and, according to the Scottish decision of *Cambusmore Estate Trustees* v. *Little*, the court has no discretion to refuse a certificate if the rules of good husbandry are broken.[64] The same decision also suggests that *prima facie* breach occurs where there is a complete absence of production.

That having been said, statute may intervene to protect the tenant. In deciding whether or not to grant a certificate of bad husbandry for the purposes of Case C, the Agricultural Land Tribunal must disregard any practice adopted by the tenant in accordance with a 'conservation covenant', i.e. a provision in the tenancy agreement (or in any other agreement with the landlord) which indicates that its object is to promote, for example, the conservation of flora or fauna; or the conservation or enhancement of the natural beauty or amenity of the countryside. Further, under Case D and Case E, such a covenant is to be regarded as a term or condition of the tenancy not inconsistent with the tenant's responsibilities to farm in accordance with the rules of good husbandry.[65]

The major limitation to these defences is the prerequisite that either the tenancy agreement or some other agreement with the landlord should contain such a conservation covenant – and it may be conjectured that the vast majority do not. Even if there is a conservation covenant, the extent of the protection which it affords is not entirely free from doubt. While the land-management obligations under, for example, an ESA agreement would appear to have the appropriate objectives as set out in the statute (e.g. the conservation of flora and fauna), it is less obvious that this is so in the case of set-aside under the Arable Area Payments Scheme. By way of contrast, so far as NSAs are concerned specific statutory provision would seem to achieve both certainty and adequate protection for the tenant. The conservation covenant defences have been expressly extended to cover practices adopted by the tenant in compliance with obligations accepted by or imposed upon him under an NSA agreement. Such practices are, accordingly, to be disregarded by the Agricultural Land Tribunal in determining whether or not to grant a certificate of bad husbandry; and

---

[63] Case D is appropriate if the tenant does not comply with a written notice requiring him within a reasonable time to remedy any remediable breach of a term or condition of his tenancy which is not inconsistent with his responsibilities to farm in accordance with the rules of good husbandry. Case E is appropriate if at the date of the notice the landlord's interest has been materially prejudiced by an irremediable breach of such a term. There is some doubt as to which would be applicable: Densham, op. cit., 182. Perhaps Case E would only be applicable in extreme circumstances.

[64] [1991] S.L.T. (Land Ct) 33. See, in particular, Rule 1 of sched. 6 to the Agricultural Holdings (Scotland) Act 1948.

[65] Paras.9(2), 10(1)(d) and 11(2) of Part II of sched. 3 to the 1986 Act.

they do not constitute a breach of the tenancy agreement.[66] Further-more, there may be little scope to argue that there has been a breach of the tenancy agreement in any event, since it has been a statutory requirement that the landlord's written consent is obtained prior to conclusion of a management agreement in an NSA.[67] The position is different in ESAs, where there is no requirement beyond notice to the landlord.[68] So far as Sites of Special Scientific Interest are concerned, landlord-and-tenant implications are addressed only in ministerial guidance. Aspects covered include a requirement that a tenant should provide written assurance that he or she has made appropriate notification to the landlord; and that, wherever possible, the landlord should enter into the principal agreement or a complementary agree-ment.[69] Under the Arable Area Payments Scheme itself there is no requirement of consent or notification – although as from the start of the Five Year Scheme landlord's consent has been a prerequisite for entry into the non-agricultural use and woodland options; and notifi-cation has been a prerequisite for entry into the fallow options.[70] At best, therefore, protection would seem somewhat uneven.

These difficulties were also specifically addressed by the European Com-munity legislation with regard to set-aside under the Five Year Scheme. The preamble to Commission Regulation (EEC)1272/88 recited that 'al-lowance must be made for cases in which the farmer is not himself the owner of the holding, and particularly cases in which the holding is leased to him, by laying down minimum conditions to prevent any speculation when the scheme is put into effect which might result in termination or refusal to renew such farm leases'.[71] However, such minimum condi-tions have not as yet appeared in the United Kingdom legislation govern-ing the Five Year Scheme. Further, no parallel provision is to be found in the European Community or the United Kingdom legislation governing the Arable Area Payments Scheme. As seen, at Community level this may be a reflection of a reluctance to interfere with landlord-and-tenant relationships in Member States, as evidenced in the *Bostock* judgement. None the less, whatever may be the reason, the absence of specific provi-sion is of little comfort to the tenant.

---

[66] Para.75 of sched. 25 to the Water Act 1989; and para.43 of sched. 1 to the Water Consolidation (Consequential Provisions) Act 1991.

[67] S.95(2) of the Water Resources Act 1991; and Regulation 4 of the Nitrate Sensitive Areas Regulations 1994 SI 1994 No.1729.

[68] S.18(6) of the Agriculture Act 1986.

[69] DoE Circular 4/83.

[70] Regulation 6 of the Set-aside Regulations 1988 SI 1988 No.1352, as amended by the Set-aside (Amendment) Regulations 1990 SI 1990 No.1716.

[71] OJ 1988, L121/36.

Rent

For some time there has been awareness that the adoption of alternative land use by agricultural tenants may have rent review implications.[72] In particular, the arbitrator is directed to take into account *all* relevant factors, including (in every case) the terms of the tenancy, the character and situation of the holding, the productive capacity of the holding and its related earning capacity and the current level of rents for comparable lettings.[73] That the words 'all relevant factors' embrace non-agricultural activities would now seem established. In *Enfield L.B.C.* v. *Pott* the court accepted that the farm shop would indeed constitute a relevant factor, although not under the head of 'productive capacity'.[74]

More recently, in *Trustees of J. W. Childers Deceased's Will Trust* v. *Anker* the County Court held, *inter alia*, that on rent review the arbitrator was entitled to have regard to a management agreement which had been entered into with the Nature Conservancy Council.[75] All the terms of the agreement would need to be considered; and it would be for the arbitrator to assess its importance, while keeping his eye on the target of determining the rent by objective relevant factors. The judge also referred to non-farming income produced from such activities as caravan parks, bed and breakfast, Sunday markets and festivals. He stated that in his view this income also fell to be considered, again emphasizing the requirement to take into account 'all relevant factors'. Moreover, he believed that the prudent and willing landlord and the prudent and willing tenant would look to the profit that the holding was reasonably capable of yielding, whether by farming or non-farming activities; and in this he was reinforced by the terms of the 1986 Act, under which farming profit was but one relevant factor. Finally, he did not think the principle in *Pepper* v. *Hart* applicable, since the material legislation was neither ambiguous nor obscure, and did not lead to an absurdity.[76] That said, for completeness he considered whether the statements made in the parliamentary debates by the Ministers concerned were sufficiently clear. In so doing he highlighted the fact that Lord Belstead in the House of Lords and Mr MacGregor in the House of Commons concurred in the view that income from non-farming activities would fall within 'all relevant factors'.[77]

---

[72] E.g. Muir Watt, op. cit., 49; Densham, op. cit., 95–6; and Rodgers, op. cit., 89 and 92.

[73] Para.1(1) of sched. 2 to the 1986 Act. However, see also the matters which the arbitrator must disregard, as set out in paras.2 and 3.

[74] [1990] 34 EG 60.

[75] Unreported, Cambridge County Court, 8 July 1994. The management agreement had been made under the Wildlife and Countryside Act 1981, the National Parks and Countryside Act 1949 and the Countryside Act 1968.

[76] [1993] AC 593.

[77] Hansard (HL) 7 February 1984, vol.447, col.1010; and Hansard (HC) 6 June 1984, vol.61, cols.377–8.

This aspect of the decision has been upheld by the Court of Appeal.[78] Most notably, it was emphasized that the ability to restrict normal agricultural operations and the existence of compensation were indeed relevant factors for the purposes of the statutory rent formula.

If payments under a management agreement are to be taken into account, it would seem that the same principles will apply in the case of Arable Area Payments.[79] Not least, they are calculated to replace income lost through reductions imposed on intervention prices;[80] and in these circumstances the statutory reference to 'all relevant factors' in the 1986 Act may be seen as preserving a degree of flexibility appropriate to the frequent legislative changes emanating from the European Community.

Reform of the Agricultural Holdings Legislation and Conclusion

As indicated, steps have been taken to address these constraints, in large part through reform of the agricultural holdings legislation. A consultation paper was issued on 13 February 1991, followed by detailed proposals on 10 September 1992. Fresh impetus was provided by a joint announcement on 6 October 1993 by the Agriculture Departments of England and Wales;[81] and on 8 December 1993 the Minister could report agreement between the Country Landowners' Association, the National Farmers' Union, the Tenant Farmers' Association and the National Federation of Young Farmers' Clubs.[82] With such agreement in place, the legislation was accorded priority in the parliamentary timetable and the 1995 Act received royal assent on 9 May 1995, coming into force on 1 September 1995.[83]

The vehicle for this change has been the 'farm business tenancy'. In the detailed proposals it was envisaged that a 'Farm Business Tenancy should always include agricultural land, that agriculture must take place on the holding throughout such a tenancy and that any non-agricultural activity must be ancillary to the agricultural activity and carried out by

---

[78] [1995] EGCS 116.

[79] See, generally, RICS Information Paper on Rent Reviews under the Agricultural Holdings Act 1986 following the Reform of the Common Agricultural Policy (1994); and Lennon and Mackay, op. cit., at G4.13.

[80] See e.g. preamble to Council Regulation (EEC) 1765/92 OJ 1992, L181/12.

[81] MAFF News Release 337/93.

[82] MAFF News Release 436/93.

[83] For a comprehensive commentary on the 1995 Act, see D. Evans, *The Agricultural Tenancies Act 1995* (Sweet and Maxwell, London, 1995). See also e.g. A. Sydenham and N. Mainwaring, *Farm Business Tenancies: Agricultural Tenancies Act 1995* (Jordans, Bristol, 1995); J. Moody with C. Jessel, *Agricultural Tenancies Act 1995: A Practical Guide* (Farrer & Co., London, 1995); RICS Guidance Note on the 1995 Agricultural Tenancies Act (1995); C. Jessel, 'Implications of the Agricultural Tenancies Bill', [1995] 04 EG 150–1; W. Barr, 'A farmyard revolution', (1995) 139 Sol. J. 650–2; and S. J. McNulty and D. Evans 'The agricultural revolution', [1995] 30 EG 82–5.

the same person'.[84] Cited examples of non-agricultural use included 'grading, washing and packing of vegetables or fruit grown on the holding', 'farm shops mainly selling produce from the holding' and 'farm woodlands'.[85] However, in order to preserve flexibility, it was felt that there should be no definition of non-agricultural activities; and the definition of 'agriculture' would remain unchanged.

For the purposes of achieving reasonable certainty, the detailed proposals contemplated that a landlord might serve a notice that the farm business tenancy provisions would apply to the agreement, rather than the 1954 Act together with its right of renewal. The notice, however, would raise no more than a rebuttable presumption; and, if in practice the tenancy fell within the 1954 Act, then the notice would have no effect. The December 1993 agreement would appear to have entrenched such provisions, stating that 'A written agreement by the parties that the letting is a Farm Business Tenancy will protect that character throughout the letting.'

The 1995 Act itself requires that, to qualify as a farm business tenancy, the tenancy must, *inter alia*, satisfy 'the business conditions' *and* either 'the agriculture condition' or 'the notice conditions'.[86] The business conditions are, first, 'that all or part of the land comprised in the tenancy is farmed for the purposes of a trade or business' and, secondly, that 'since the beginning of the tenancy, all or part of the land so comprised has been so farmed.'[87] Accordingly, there must be commercial farming on at least part of the land *throughout* the tenancy. In this regard the tenant may resort to the presumption that, if compliance can be demonstrated at a particular date, it will be taken that there has been compliance since the beginning of the tenancy.[88] However, no guidance is provided as to the extent of use required; and arguably *de minimis* use will not qualify.[89] Further, if through comprehensive diversification the business conditions are not satisfied, then the landlord may find that his tenant has attracted the greater protection available under the 1954 Act.

The agriculture condition is that the character of the tenancy is 'primarily

---

[84] Para.3.

[85] There are arguments that such provisions would have permitted no greater scope for diversification than the 1986 Act. Indeed, in both *Short* v. *Greeves* and *Gold* v. *Jacques Amand Ltd* the tenant was protected by the 1986 Act even though the *majority* of the turnover was derived from non-agricultural items; and the definition of agriculture in s.96(1) of the 1986 Act (set out above) already included 'the use of land for woodlands where that use is ancillary to the farming of land for other agricultural purposes'.

[86] S.1(1) of the 1995 Act.

[87] S.1(2) of the 1995 Act (cf. s.1(4) of the 1986 Act).

[88] S.1(7) of the 1995 Act.

[89] In the tenants's favour it may be noted that the business condition makes reference to 'farming' rather than 'agriculture'; and, under s.38(2) of the 1995 Act, references to 'farming' of land are expressed to *include* references to the carrying on in relation to land of any agricultural activities.

or wholly agricultural', having regard to '(a) the terms of the tenancy, (b) the use of the land comprised in the tenancy, (c) the nature of any commercial activities carried on on that land, and (d) any other relevant circumstances'.[90] This wording echoes s.1(2) of the 1986 Act and clearly envisages the possibility of non-agricultural use. Nevertheless, there are significant differences, in particular the requirement that the character of the tenancy is, at least, 'primarily' agricultural. Further, since the agriculture condition must apparently be satisfied not only on grant but also at the time of any subsequent dispute, this would seem to leave less scope for diversification following the commencement of the tenancy. As seen, for example, in *Short* v. *Greeves*, a tenant protected by the 1986 Act *ab initio* would not lose that protection unless agricultural use had been wholly or substantially abandoned. However, both for the purposes of the agriculture condition, and indeed the 1995 Act as a whole, the definition of 'agriculture' remains unchanged.[91] It may also be noted that, in determining whether at any time the tenancy meets the business conditions or the agriculture condition, 'Any use of land in breach of the terms of the tenancy, any commercial activities carried on in breach of those terms, and any cessation of such activities in breach of those terms' fall to be disregarded, except where the landlord or his predecessor in title has given consent or where the landlord has acquiesced in the breach.[92] Accordingly, notwithstanding the freedom of contract which pervades the 1995 Act, landlords may take advantage of user covenants restricting use to more narrowly defined agricultural activities. That having been said, such restrictions may have adverse consequences on any subsequent rent review.

As an alternative to the agriculture condition, the parties may choose to comply with the notice conditions. On or before the 'relevant day', i.e. the earlier of the date of any written agreement (other than an agreement to enter into a tenancy on a future date) or the beginning of the tenancy, each must serve on the other the appropriate written notice, containing, *inter alia*, a statement that the person giving the notice 'intends that the tenancy or proposed tenancy is to be, and remain, a farm business tenancy'. In addition, at the beginning of the tenancy its character must be primarily or wholly agricultural (having regard in this case 'to the terms of the tenancy and other relevant circumstances').[93] If these requirements are satisfied, there should be little difficulty retaining the agreement within the farm business tenancy regime, even in the face of very considerable diversification. As mentioned

[90] S.1(3) of the 1995 Act.

[91] S.38(1) of the 1995 Act – as advocated in the detailed proposals. That having been said, the definition of 'livestock', which forms a component of the definition of 'agriculture', has undergone slight amendment.

[92] S.1(8) of the 1995 Act. Cf. s.1(3) of the 1986 Act.

[93] S.1(4) of the 1995 Act. For the definition of 'relevant day', see s.1(5). The notice must not be included in the written agreement: s.1(6).

previously, there must also be compliance with the business conditions; but these may be met where merely *part* of the land is farmed for the purposes of a trade or business (and has been so farmed since the beginning of the tenancy). However, in this context a point of potential concern to landlords is that, while they may be able to recover possession successfully on termination of the farm business tenancy, diversification may have rendered the holding no longer primarily agricultural in character – and, for that reason, incapable of further letting under the same code.[94]

With regard to compensation on quitting, the 1995 Act (building on both the detailed proposals and the December 1993 agreement) marks a substantial shift to the tenant's benefit. Most notably, compensation is not restricted to improvements which are agricultural in nature. Indeed, a 'tenant's improvement' is defined as meaning

> (a) any physical improvement which is made on the holding by the tenant by his own effort or wholly or partly at his own expense, or (b) any intangible advantage which – (i) is obtained for the holding by the tenant by his own effort or wholly or partly at his own expense, and (ii) becomes attached to the holding . . .[95]

However, as a prerequisite to compensation, the tenant must obtain his landlord's consent in writing to the improvement (or, in the case of planning permissions, his landlord's consent in writing to the making of the planning application).[96] An important feature is that, as a rule, a tenant may go to arbitration under the Arbitration Acts 1950–79 (rather than the 1986 Act) if aggrieved by refusal of consent, by failure to give consent within two months of a written request[97] or by a variation in the terms of the tenancy required as a condition to consent.[98] It is then for the arbitrator to determine whether it is reasonable for the tenant to provide the proposed improvement. That having been said, in this context two factors may be identified which could limit diversification: first, as an exception to the general rule, the 1995 Act does not make such arbitration available in the case of planning permissions; and, secondly, the arbitrator is confined to giving unconditional approval or withholding approval – he cannot give approval subject to any condition or vary any condition required by the landlord. As an alternative, a tenant may seek to diversify

[94] However, at that stage it would be possible for the landlord to grant a 1954 Act tenancy, having first obtained a court order excluding the provisions of ss.24–8.

[95] S.15 of the 1995 Act.

[96] S.17 of the 1995 Act covers the consent requirements for all improvements except planning permissions, these being dealt with separately under s.18.

[97] This provision is reminiscent of the Landlord and Tenant Act 1988.

[98] S.19 of the 1995 Act. Cf., in particular, s.67(3) of the 1986 Act. 'Routine improvements' apart (broadly, matters of tenant-right), notice demanding arbitration must be given before the tenant has provided or begun to provide the improvement.

so far as possible by means of fixtures and buildings, in respect of which he enjoys greater rights of removal than under the 1986 Act.[99]

Not only is the ambit of 'tenant's improvement' broadened to cover non-agricultural items and, moreover, 'intangible advantages', but – in the case of all improvements except planning permissions – the measure of compensation is 'an amount equal to the increase attributable to the improvement in the value of the holding at the termination of the tenancy as land comprised in a tenancy'.[100] With regard to planning permissions, the measure of compensation is 'an amount equal to the increase attributable to the fact that the relevant development is authorised by the planning per-mission in the value of the holding at the termination of the tenancy as land comprised in a tenancy'.[101] Again arbitration is available in the event of dispute; and it is not difficult to imagine circumstances in which dispute may arise. For example, more individual forms of alternative land use, such as 'war-game' enterprises, may have been of central importance to the departing tenant, while arguably adding little to 'the value of the holding at the termination of the tenancy as land comprised in a tenancy'. Further, novel issues may be raised in the assessment of compensation for 'intan-gible advantages'. As a preliminary matter it may prove necessary to ascertain their nature and extent; and the potential complexities of analysis may be illustrated by Chadwick J's consideration of the nature of milk quota in *Faulks* v. *Faulks*.[102] All these compensation provisions apply notwith-standing agreement by the parties to the contrary.[103]

Three further points may be noted. First, the 1995 Act contains no provision entitling a landlord to serve notice to quit based upon the grant of planning permission (such as Case B under the 1986 Act); and, in the light of decisions such as *Fowler*, this should prove a source of some comfort to the tenant occupying a holding with development potential. Secondly, in the case of tenancies for a term of more than two years, any

---

[99] S.8 of the 1995 Act.

[100] S.20(1) of the 1995 Act. Cf. e.g. ss.66(1) and (2) of the 1986 Act.

[101] S.21(1) of the 1995 Act, 'relevant development' being defined in s.21(2). It may be noted that one of the conditions governing eligibility for compensation in the case of planning permissions is that 'on the termination of the tenancy, the specified physical improvement has not been completed or the specified change of use has not been effected': s.18(1)(c). However, if the physical improvement has been completed or the change of use effected, the tenant may seek compensation in accordance with the provisions which govern the other forms of tenant's improvement; and in these circumstances account may still be taken of the fact that the improvement benefits from planning permission: s.20(4).

[102] [1992] 15 EG 82. It may be noted that the European Court of Justice has referred to milk quota as 'an advantage' – see e.g. *R.* v. *MAFF ex parte Bostock* Case 2/92, [1994] ECR I-955, at I-984. See also the decision of the Special Commissioners in the tax case of *Cottle* v. *Coldicott* [1995] Sp.C.40.

[103] S.26 of the 1995 Act. This section, more restrictive than the 1986 Act, runs counter to the general importance attached to freedom of contract under the new regime.

notice to quit must as a rule be in writing and given at least twelve (but less than twenty-four) months before it is to take effect.[104] This would seem to preclude the use of the early resumption clauses found under the 1986 Act. Thirdly, where the statutory procedure for rent review applies, the 1995 Act places on the arbitrator a general requirement to take into account 'all relevant factors', as under the 1986 Act.[105]

There is no doubt that the 1995 Act will provide encouragement for tenants who wish to reduce their reliance on traditional farming practices. Their position under the 1986 Act may not have been so precarious as perhaps sometimes perceived; but there is now added statutory certainty provided by a regime expressly directed to promoting diversification. Moreover, great impetus must have been created by the change in the Inheritance Tax legislation so as to extend 100 per cent agricultural property relief to land let on tenancies commencing on or after 1 September 1995.[106] That having been said, certain difficulties do remain. For example, farm business tenancies are not subject to any minimum term; and there is every indication that, granted freedom of contract, landowners will opt for short-term agreements hardly calculated to promote applications for planning permission and large-scale investment in non-agricultural enterprises.[107] Further, there is evidence to suggest that many tenants will be established farmers seeking to spread the costs of crop production over a broader acreage.[108] Likewise short-term tenancies would seem inappropriate for environmentally orientated schemes. In some cases the legislation does seek to preserve continuity, for example ESA management agreements do bind successors in title or persons deriving title under or through the offeree. However, even this would not seem to cover the position where the offeree is a tenant holding for only a short term and, during the course of the management agreement, that term expires and the land is taken over by a new tenant with a fresh title.[109] Further, as already indicated, there is nothing to prevent landlords inserting restrictive user covenants (although they may suffer correspondingly on rent

[104] S.7 of the 1995 Act.

[105] S.13(2) of the 1995 Act. For the circumstances where the statutory procedure applies, see e.g. Evans, op. cit., at 8–20–1.

[106] S.155 of the Finance Act 1995. The taxpayer must, none the less, comply with the other conditions stipulated in the Inheritance Tax Act 1984, in particular as to length of ownership.

[107] See e.g. the Central Association of Agricultural Valuers' *Annual Tenanted Farm Survey 1994*.

[108] M. Winter, C. Richardson, C. Short and C. Watkins, *Agricultural Land Tenure in England and Wales* (RICS, London, 1990), 20–1.

[109] S.18(7) of the Agriculture Act 1986; and see Lennon and Mackay, op. cit., at G2.3. A recent example is provided by the Countryside Access Regulations 1994 SI 1994 No.2349, the Countryside Access Scheme being restricted to tenants with tenancies of sufficient length to meet its objectives (definition of 'tenant' at Regulation 2(1)).

review); and certain of the provisions governing consent for improvements may be regarded as of questionable benefit to the diversifying tenant.

Finally, the 1995 Act contains no change to the definition of 'agriculture';[110] and, even if this is still thought adequate, there at least must be a good case for amendment of the rules of good husbandry to take account of the various set-aside management obligations. Indeed, the Agricultural Land Tribunal some time ago suggested that good husbandry may not now necessarily be consistent with achieving maximum output.[111] This case for change can only be reinforced by the reality that set-aside is now effectively compulsory on arable land. There would seem to be a certain lack of logic if a tenant who complies with European Community policy and adopts the sole financially viable option thereby places himself in jeopardy.[112] With the European Community institutions reluctant to intervene, it would seem that the impetus must again be derived from the United Kingdom Parliament. Moreover, this would be in line with its earlier amendment of the 1986 Act so as to ensure the proper protection of tenants concluding NSA management agreements.

[110] See argument for such change at Hansard (HC) 6 February 1995, vol.254, col.82.
[111] Densham, op. cit., 153.
[112] The absence of reported decisions on notices to quit served in such circumstances may indicate that landlords too sense this lack of logic.

Index

abuse-of-rights doctrine, 21
Access Tier, 191–2
Access to Mountains (Scotland) Bill 1884, 171
Action Plan for Crayfish Conservation, 58
aesthetic values, 25
AG for New South Wales v. *Sawtell* [1978] 2 NSWLR 200, 18
AG v. *Wilts United Dairies* (1921) 39 TLR 781, 10
Agri-environment Regulation 2078/92, OJ L215/85, 1, 42n40, 112–13, 132, 191n41, 209
  implementation of, 114–15
Agricultural Holdings Act 1908, 200n17
Agricultural Holdings Act 1923, 200n17
Agricultural Holdings Act 1948, 199n14, 200, 201, 202
Agricultural Holdings Act 1984, 200n16
Agricultural Holdings Act 1986, 4, 129, 134n86, 198, 199–214, 215, 216, 217n98, 218, 219, 220
Agricultural Holdings (Amendment) Act 1990, 206n44
Agricultural Land Tribunal, 211, 220
agricultural pollution, 67, 68
agricultural reforms 1992, 1, 5, 42, 111–37, 197
  cross-compliance, 113–14, 115, 116, 118, 123, 130–2, 136
  and sustainability, 111–13
Agricultural Tenancies Act 1995, 5, 197, 199n11, 199, 202, 214–20
agricultural tenure, 4–5, 6, 198–9
  diversification and Agricultural Holdings Act 1986, 199–214
  reform of legislation, 214–20
  and set-aside, 126–9, 134
agriculture, 1, 51, 90
  codes of practice, 2
  definition, 200, 220

  and forestry, 155
  and water, 42, 67, 68
  see also agricultural tenure; set-aside
Agriculture Act 1947, 5, 134, 200n18, 210
Agriculture Act 1986, 191n41, 209, 212n68, 219
agriculture departments, 149
air, rights to, 21, 25
Air Canada v. *Secretary of State* [1981] 3 All ER 336, 21n40
air pollution, 139
Aitchison v. *Thorburn* (1970) 7 SLR 347, 161n3
Allen v. *Secretary of State for the Environment and Reigate and Banstead Borough Council* [1990] JPL 340, 204
Alphacell v. *Woodward* [1972] 2 All ER 475, 41n33
alternative land use, 196–220
  reform of agricultural holdings legislation, 214–20
  tenants protected by 1986 Act, 199–214
amenity, 25, 148
  loss of, 41
amenity protection, distinguished from nature conservation, 89
Anderson v. *Alnwick District Council* (1993) 3 All ER 613, 75n45
Anglers' Conservation Association, 44
angling, 55
animal rights *see* intrinsic rights
Anisminic v. *Foreign Compensation Commission* [1969] 2 AC 147, 10
anthropocentrism, 13, 14, 15
  of common law, 12, 17–20
aquatic ecosystems, 6, 33–64
  Environment Agency, 36–8
  flood defence and drainage, 50–4
  future for sustainable management of, 62–3